The Story of Wamba

The Story of Wamba

 Julian of Toledo's *Historia Wambae regis*

translated with an introduction and notes by
Joaquín Martínez Pizarro

The Catholic University of America Press
Washington, D.C.

The paper used in this publication meets the minimum requirements of American
National Standards for Information Science—Permanence of Paper for Printed
Library Materials, ANSI Z39.48-1984.

∞

LIBRARY OF CONGRESS CATALOGING-IN-PUBLICATION DATA
Julianus, Saint, Bp. of Toledo, d. 690.
[Historia Wambae regis. English]
    The story of Wamba : Julian of Toledo's Historia Wambae regis / translated
with an introduction and notes by Joaquín Martínez Pizarro.— 1st ed.
    p. cm.
    Includes bibliographic references and index.
    ISBN 13: 978-0-8132-1412-2 (cloth : alk. paper)
    ISBN 10: 0-8132-1412-2 (cloth : alk. paper)
    1. Wamba, King of the Visigoths, d. 687 or 8.   2. Spain—History—Gothic
period, 414–711.   3. Julianus, Saint, Bp. of Toledo, d. 690. Historia Wambae
regis.   I. Martínez Pizarro, Joaquín, 1946–   II. Title.
DP96.J75 2005
946´.01—dc22
2004014870

A mi hermana Maria Gracia y a mi amigo Gérard Lewitus

Contents

Illustrations

Acknowledgments

I wish to thank Paul Meyvaert for constant encouragement, Gérard Lewitus and family, in Montpellier, and Héliette Paris, in Paris, for years of summertime hospitality and stimulation, Professor Hagith Sivan, of the University of Kansas, for letting me read in typescript her valuable study on the Jews of Visigothic Spain, since published in the *Révue des études juives*, Georges Castellvi, of the Université de Perpignan, for information on the fortifications at Clausurae/Les Cluses and for the photograph of the site reproduced here.

David McGonagle and Susan Needham of the Catholic University of America Press dealt with my manuscript and with me with exemplary patience and efficiency.

My New York friends Gabriel Pérez, Stacey Olster, Jackie Geller, Cynthia Capriata, Joshua Sherman and Jorge Martin did their best to provide me with a social life while I was writing this book, and I love them for it.

Abbreviations

HWR: *Historia Wambae regis*

> *Ep.: Epistola Pauli perfidi, qui tyrannice rebellionem in Gallias fecit Wambani principis magni*

> *Hist.: Historia excellentissimi Wambae regis de expeditione et victoria, qua revellantem contra se provinciam Galliae celebri triumpho perdomuit*

> *Ins.: Insultatio vilis storici in tyrannidem Galliae*

> *Iud.: Iudicium in tyrannorum perfidiam promulgatum*

CCSL: *Corpus christianorum. Series latina.* Turnhout: Brepols, 1953–

Claude, *Adel, Kirche und Königtum*: Dietrich Claude, *Adel, Kirche und Königtum im Westgotenreich.* Sigmaringen: Thorbecke, 1971

CSEL: *Corpus scriptorum ecclesiasticorum latinorum.* Vienna, 1866–

Díaz y Díaz: Pedro Rafael Díaz y Díaz, "Historia del Rey Wamba (Traducción y Notas)," *Florentia Iliberritana* 1 (1990), 89–114

HG: *Isidori ivnioris episcopi hispalensis historia Gothorvm Wandalorvm Sveborvm ad A. DCXXIV*, ed. Theodor Mommsen. MGH AA 11.2. Berlin: Weidmann, 1894

Levison: *Historia Wambae regis auctore Iuliano episcopo toletano*, ed. Wilhelm Levison. MGH SSRM V. ed. Wilhelm Levison. MGH SSRM, V. *Passiones vitaeque sanctorum aevi Merovingici*, ed. B. Krusch and W. Levison. Leipzig: Hahn, 1910

LV: *Leges Visigothorum,* ed. Karl Zeumer. MGH LNG I.i. Hanover: Hahn, 1902

MGH: *Monumenta Germaniae historica*

> AA: *Auctores antiquissimi*
>
> Epist.: *Epistolae*
>
> LNG: *Leges nationum Germanicarum*
>
> SSRM: *Scriptores rerum Merovingicarum*

Panégyriques: Panégyriques latins, ed. Edouard Galletier. 3 vols. Paris: Les Belles Lettres, 1949–1955

PL: *Patrologia latina,* ed. J. P. Migne. Paris: 1844–1864

Powers: Sister Theresa Joseph Powers, "A Translation of Julian of Toledo's *Historia Wambae regis* with Introduction and Notes." M.A. dissertation, The Catholic University of America. Washington, D.C., 1941

Prosopografía: L. A. García Moreno, *Prosopografía del reino visigodo de Toledo.* Salamanca: Universidad de Salamanca, 1974

Reydellet, *La royauté:* Marc Reydellet, *La royauté dans la littérature latine de Sidoine Apollinaire à Isidore de Seville.* Bibliothèque des écoles françaises d'Athènes et de Rome 243. Rome: École française de Rome, 1981

Settimane: Settimane di studio del centro italiano di studi sull'alto medioevo. Spoleto: Centro italiano di studi sull' alto medioevo, 1954–

Teillet, *Des Goths:* Suzanne Teillet, *Des Goths à la nation gothique. Les origines de l'idée de nation en Occident du Ve au VIIe siècle.* Paris: Les Belles Lettres, 1984

Topographie chrétienne: Paul-Albert Fevrier and Xavier Barral i Altet, *Topographie chrétienne des cités de la Gaule* VII. *Province ecclésiastique de Narbonne (Narbonensis prima).* Paris: De Boccard, 1989

Vives: *Concilios visigóticos e hispano-romanos,* ed. José Vives. Barcelona and Madrid: Consejo superior de investigaciones científicas, 1963

Votive crown of Reccesvind from the Guarrazar treasure.
Photo courtesy of Museo Arqueológico Nacional, Madrid.

Church of San Juan de Baños (661), province of Palencia. *Photo courtesy of Foto Marburg/Art Resource, NY.*

Nîmes: the *castrum arenarum* today. *Photo courtesy of Vanni/Art Resource, NY.*

An interior view of the *castrum arenarum*. *Photo courtesy of Vanni/Art Resource, NY.*

Clausurae/Les Cluses: fortifications overlooking the Via Domitia. *Photo courtesy of Georges Castellvi.*

Itinerary of Wamba's campaign.

Part I

Introductory Essay

Introduction to the Historia Wambae regis

The *Historia Wambae regis* (HWR) of Julian of Toledo is a sequence of four closely related prose texts which can be regarded as a single composition. Elaborate incipits and explicits as well as the authority of the two main branches of the entirely Spanish manuscript tradition (derived from the Soria and Oviedo manuscripts) indicate that the parts stand in the following order:

a. The *Epistola (Ep.)* opens the series and is the only one of its four elements to lack an explicit. It presents itself as a letter of challenge from the usurper Paul to Wamba, Visigothic king of Spain (672–680), daring him to cross the Pyrenees and meet his rival at the fortress of Clausurae in Visigothic Gaul (Gallia), where they will fight for the Eastern kingdom, which Paul claims as his own and which comprises most of Gallia and part of the Tarraconensis.

b. The *Historia* proper *(Hist.)*, by far the longest part of the sequence, is a third-person narrative that opens with Wamba's election to the throne and royal unction at Toledo in 672 and goes on to cover in some detail a rebellion against him that arose the following year in Gallia, led by Hildericus, the count of Nîmes, and later by Wamba's own general, Paul, who brought some leaders of the Tarraconensis into the conspiracy. The *Historia* describes Wamba's victorious campaign against the usurper, which ends with the taking of Nîmes by the Spanish forces, followed by a public trial of the leaders of the rebellion and Wamba's triumphal return to Toledo.

c. The *Insultatio (Ins.)* that follows is a highly rhetorical invective or vituperation addressed by a "humble historian" (most likely the narrator of the *Historia*) to defeated Gallia, personified as the mother or nurse of the insurrection. This oration also contains what can be described as a balance-sheet of the historical relations between Spain and its Gallic enclave, characterized by magnanimity and protection on one hand and by systematic betrayal on the other.

d. The *Iudicium (Iud.)*, which closes the series, takes the form of a third-person narrative of Wamba's campaign by a member of the king's palatine office who took part in the expedition. It goes over the events covered in the *Historia*, adding lists of names of those involved in the rebellion, and ends with an account of the trial of the chief conspirators in the vicinity of Nîmes, which had been mentioned only in passing in the *Historia*.

The singularity of the HWR, which has discouraged literary criticism, could be attributed to our fragmentary knowledge of Visigothic literature but also, more speculatively, to a search for formal originality on the part of the author, a motivation rarely expressed in seventh-century Europe. The *Historia* proper, the actual narrative of the rebellion that begins with the death of Reccesvind and the election of his successor and ends with Wamba's pageant of victory in Toledo, is in itself unprecedented. No other work of secular history in late antiquity and the early middle ages focuses in this way on a single uprising or centers as the *Historia* does on the event itself rather than its royal protagonist. No other work of the period stylizes a military chronicle into this heroic and surprisingly classical mold, to the point that the most commonly suggested model has been the Sallustian monograph.[1] And the sequence as a whole, a series of four generically heterogeneous texts, is even more anomalous.

The two chapters that follow are intended to reduce the apparent singularity of the HWR by providing contexts for Julian's work

---

1. See Fontaine, "Die westgotische lateinische Literatur," 84; Berschin, *Biographie und Epochenstil* II, 200–201; Collins, "Julian of Toledo and the Education of Kings," 12; Brunhölzl, *Geschichte* I, 103.

in political and literary history. Although the first chapter stresses extra-literary features, and in particular the secular and religious government of seventh-century Spain, and the second consists largely of literary analysis and interpretation, the separation of "History" and "Literature" is a purely pragmatic expository device. A rigorous division of these two spheres would be impracticable, especially for a narrative as closely implicated as the HWR in the struggles of the period it describes.

The historical backdrop to Julian's vivid account must be drawn from the materials available for the period, which present very characteristic limitations, but also exceptional strengths. They are essentially prescriptive, consisting mostly of laws and of the acts of church councils; the context they provide for any particular episode is therefore an abstract and idealized one. But they have been preserved in uniquely full and systematic collections which, read historically, with attention to changes, tensions, and internal contradictions in their rulings, may help us to make political sense of Julian's appealing but isolated narrative, both for the events it claims to represent and for the author's aims in undertaking to portray them.

Visigothic secular law goes back to the Code of Euric, composed in the kingdom of Toulouse circa 469–481, though the text of the Code contains references to earlier written legislation of Euric's father, Theoderic I (419–451). Euric's son, Alaric II, published a Breviary of Roman law. Whether or not these legal compilations were used on a personal/national basis, Euric's Code for the Visigoths and Alaric's Breviary for their Roman subjects, remains a controverted subject today.[2] What seems certain is that they were intended to replace all other laws on Visigothic territory. Later, King

---

2. Most recently Harries, "Not the Theodosian Code," 50, argues, "The question . . . of whether Euric's law was expected to be observed by Goths only or by Romans and Goths is largely immaterial. It was a statement of what people living in his dominions were expected to do; . . ."

Leovigild (569–586) published a Revised Code *(Codex revisus)* based on Euric's and Alaric's collections, which included and reformulated laws given since their time, after the loss of Gaul and the creation of the kingdom of Toledo. That Leovigild meant his Revised Code to replace Euric's Code and Alaric's Breviary is made evident by the fact that the former survives only in fragments and the latter, copied all over Western Europe in the early middle ages as a source for Roman law, can be found in Spain only in one manuscript of the period, and that a palimpsest. That is more than was granted to Leovigild's own Revised Code, no copy of which is extant. His laws, and those of his predecessors, are incorporated as *antiquae* in the next great revision of the Visigothic law, the Book of Judgments *(Liber iudiciorum)* published by Reccesvind in 654.[3] In it new laws, from Reccesvind's father Chindasvind on, are attributed by name to their givers, and this practice is continued in the last comprehensive revision, published by Ervig in 681.

Despite the cumulative nature of these collections, which preserve earlier legislation only in revised form, and selectively, the Book of Judgments presents a fairly transparent record of innovations and shifting political imperatives. Conciliar acts were collected on a very different principle, set next to each other with their differences and contradictions unreduced, and they call therefore for another approach. The Spanish church had already held councils in Roman times, long before the arrival of the Visigoths. The *Collectio hispana*, first assembled circa 633 in Seville and extant in its later *Iuliana* (681) and *Vulgata* (694) versions, preserves, with many other ecclesiastical documents, acts of the Spanish councils from that of Iliberris (300–306) to Toledo XII and XVII, in addition to acts of councils held in the Eastern empire, Gaul, and Africa.[4] For

---

3. But note a possible missing link, Chindasvind's lost compilation of 643–644 argued for in King, "King Chindasvind and the First Territorial Law-Code." King assumes that until that year Alaric's *Breviary* and Leovigild's *Revised Code* would have been used as national/ethnic codes.

4. See Martínez Díez, *La colección canónica hispana* I. *Estudio*, 201–255.

the present study, however, the acts of the general or national councils of Toledo, from Toledo III (589), in which King Reccared announced the conversion of the Goths to Catholicism and the rejection of their traditional Arianism, to Toledo XII (681) and XIII (683), summoned by Wamba's successor Ervig, are of particular importance.

With Toledo III and the conversion, the very meaning of councils changes. Brought together by kings who, now orthodox, claim the prerogative of summoning the bishops of their realm, these assemblies will function throughout the seventh century as the highest instance of ecclesiastical administration and legislation, but also as a forum for dialogue and collaboration between the church and the crown in a kingdom no longer riven by confessional differences.[5] In 653, at Toledo VIII, King Reccesvind, in an attempt to increase the power of the crown over the gathered bishops, introduced three changes in the protocol of the councils, inspired by elements already present in Toledo III, which are clearly reflected from then on in conciliar acts. In the first place, at the opening of a council a letter from the king *(tomus)* is read to the assembly, setting an agenda for their deliberations, a list of issues on which the ruler requires the counsel, the support, or even merely the assent of the church. The sessions of the council, which follow, usually last several days and are largely concerned with subjects of exclusively ecclesiastical interest, not covered by the *tomus.* The bishops' decisions on all matters are listed in the acts as numbered canons. Secondly, courtiers from the palatine office are to attend the meetings of the council and sign the acts at the end, after the bishops and abbots have done so. Finally, a "law in confirmation of the council" *(lex in confirmatione concilii)* is passed by the king, incorporating all or some of the decisions of the council into the laws of the kingdom. A

---

5. The Jews, as the only remaining non-Catholic group, were from then on exposed to increasing discrimination by the law, and bore the brunt of this interpenetration of church and state.

sharp turn in church-state relations after Reccesvind and Wamba
became manifest at Toledo XII, when Ervig, soon to publish his
own recension of the Book of Judgments, preserved the conciliar
format introduced by Reccesvind, but asked the council in his *tomus*
to correct his laws or write new laws themselves.[6]

In secular legislation, the king is presented as the only source of
the law, the giver and creator of every ruling, as indicated by the
constant use of the first person plural of majesty ("our glory," "our
reign," "our peace").[7] His role in summoning the general councils
gave him also great influence over the deliberations of the assembled clergy, an influence that he put to use on the matters submitted in the *tomus*. But the very need for a law in confirmation of the
council indicates that, to the very end of the Visigothic kingdom,
conciliar acts were understood to proceed from an independent
spiritual instance that might cooperate with the crown and overlap
with it in many of its measures, but that was in no way to be identified or confused with the secular authority.

6. Toledo XII, *tomus* (Vives, 383): "De ceteris autem causis atque negotiis
quae novella conpetant institutionem firmari, evidentium sententiarum titulis
exaranda conscribite . . ."

7. On this aspect of the laws, see King, *Law and Society*, chapter 2, "The
King and the Law."

I. History

1. Chindasvind—Reccesvind—Wamba

The narrative of Visigothic history is derived largely from non-narrative sources, most of them law codes or the acts of church councils. The abstract and normative character of Spanish history before 711 can be traced to this circumstance, which makes it sound very different from the history of Gaul or Italy in the same period.[1] The chief narrative account, Isidore of Seville's *Historia Gothorum* (HG) which covers—however thinly—events from the first clash of the Goths with the Roman empire in the Balkans in the middle of the third century to the reign of Suinthila (621–631) and his recovery of the last imperial territories in southeast Spain, has played a decisive role in shaping the story of the Visigoths as we know it today. If we think of it in terms of individual kings and their achievements, this is because Isidore, filled with admiration for Leovigild's consolidation of the kingship (569–586) and of his hold on the territory of the peninsula, as well as for Suinthila's re-conquest, cast the previous history of the Visigoths retrospectively as directed and defined by royal policy.[2] And yet there is considerable evidence that before Leovigild Visigothic kings had at best a very imperfect control of the kingdom of Toulouse and later of

1. Collins, "Julian of Toledo and the Education of Kings," 5, sums up the problem as follows: ". . . the bulk of this evidence is normative rather than descriptive. It is concerned with what its author felt ought to be true about this society, and has only limited applicability to the study of more concrete realities."

2. Cf. Reydellet, *La royauté*, 526.

Toledo, and that kingship was an unstable and embattled institu-
tion, defined and redefined in conflicting ways by the ruler, the
Gothic nobility, and the clergy, and destined to remain a subject of
contention until the fall of the kingdom to the Arabs.

Isidore's outline has also determined what historians regard as
the milestones or turning points of Visigothic history. If the retreat
from Gaul into Spain is the result of Frankish initiative and aggres-
sion (i.e. Alaric defeated by Clovis at Vouillé in 507),[3] Leovigild's
construction of a powerful monarchy,[4] and his son Reccared's decision to have the Goths give up their Arianism and convert to the
Catholicism of the Hispano-Roman majority (at the Third Council
of Toledo in 589),[5] are royal policies that must be interpreted and
evaluated in any modern account of sixth-century Spain. One way
to do so would be to say that these measures address two overlap-
ping divisions in the population of the realm—that between Romans and Goths and that between Catholics and Arians[6]—and that
in attempting to erase them the Gothic rulers were acting to acquire
the loyalty and support of their largely Roman and Catholic population in view of possible conflicts with Catholic powers, and
chiefly with their Frankish neighbors and the Byzantine empire. The
fate of the Ostrogoths in Italy had been taken as a lesson, at a point
when the Eastern empire still held possessions in Baetica and the

3. HG 36 (ed. Mommsen, 281–282): "Adversus quem Fluduicus (i.e. Clovis)
Francorum princeps Galliae regnum affectans . . . bellum movit fusisque
Gothorum copiis ipsum postremum regem (i.e. Alaric) apud Pictavis supera-
tum interfecit."

4. HG 49 (ed. Mommsen, 287): "Levvigildus . . . ampliare regnum bello et
augere opes statuit. studio quippe exercitus concordante favore victoriarum
multa praeclare sortitus est."

5. HG 52–53 (ed. Mommsen, 289): ". . . in ipsis enim regni sui exordiis
catholicam fidem adeptus totius Gothicae gentis populos inoliti erroris labe de-
tersa ad cultum rectae fidei revocat."

6. The overlap is not perfect, as there is evidence of Catholic Goths from
well before the conversion of 589—for instance the chronicler John of Biclaro
(cf. *Prosopografía*, no. 616) and Bishop Masona of Mérida (ibid., no. 435).

southern Cartaginensis. The religious mutation of 589 was in this sense an enormous success, as the dichotomy of Arian and Catholic disappears from Spanish history. There is, in any case, no usurpation, rebellion, or internal division in the succeeding years that can be attributed to religious disunity. The differences between Romans and Goths are another matter. Leovigild before the conversion had done much to bridge them, reformulating Arian dogma to make it more acceptable to Catholics[7] and cancelling the laws that forbade marriages between Romans and Goths.[8] In spite of a growing consensus in contemporary scholarship that by the mid-seventh century the ethnic difference was resolved, so that one could say that Romans and Goths had now become Spaniards, a single nation under a Gothic and Catholic ruler,[9] it can be argued that the evidence is not univocal and suggests at best an unfinished and imperfect fusion.

The *Historia Wambae regis* of Julian of Toledo, which is the only other narrative source for secular history composed in Visigothic Spain, covers events of 672 and 673, the accession of King Wamba and his crushing of a rebellion against him in Visigothic Gaul and the Tarraconensis. The historical context needed to understand these events includes the reigns of Wamba's predecessors Chindasvind (642–653) and Reccesvind (649–672) and the remainder of Wamba's own rule, which ended when he was deposed in 680. In addition to the abundant legislation created by these rulers—the first territorial rather than national code of the kingdom, according to received opinion[10]—and the acts of the church councils held in

7. See Stroheker, "Leowigild," 172–182, and Collins, "Leovigild and the Conversion."

8. LV III, 1, 1 (ed. Zeumer, 122): "... hac in perpetuum valitura lege sancimus: ut tam Gotus Romanam, quam etiam Gotam Romanus si coniugem habere voluerit, premissa petitione dignissimam, facultas eis nubendi subiaceat ..."; see also Zeumer, "Geschichte (III)," 573–576.

9. Teillet, *Des Goths*, 552–555; Claude, "Gentile und territoriale Staatsideen"; Collins, *Early Medieval Spain*, 126–127.

10. Received opinion has taken a beating in recent years; it is handled very

their time (Toledo VII and Toledo VIII), there is a narrative source for the reigns of Chindasvind and Reccesvind: it is the probably Burgundian chronicle of Fredegar, written circa 659, which supplements its record of late Merovingian history with substantial accounts of Spanish and Byzantine affairs.[11] Fredegar introduces Chindasvind and his rise to royal authority with the general consideration that "the Gothic nation has little patience when it is not bearing a heavy yoke."[12] By "Gothic nation" we should understand the Gothic nobility, and by "patience" their endurance of kings. Indeed, although animosity and constant tension between royal power and the nobility run through the entire course of Visigothic history and can be counted among its elements of *longue durée*, they are particularly critical under these three rulers because their reigns, i.e. the period from 642 to 680, constitute an apparently uninterrupted stretch of royal supremacy, the longest and most stable in the history of the kingdom of Toledo, which comes to an end with the deposition of Wamba. It is often said that the Visigoths had an elective monarchy limited to the Gothic nobility, and this formula is in fact preserved in Toledo V, canon 3, and Toledo VI, canon 17.[13] Although there is no competing statement instituting hereditary monarchy, every Visigothic king who had a son attempted to create a dynasty, and sometimes with success, even when this meant rais-

---

critically in Collins's synthesis *Early Medieval Spain,* esp. 28–29. The case against it is argued trenchantly in Liebeschuetz, "Citizen Status and the Law."

11. Cf. *Chronicon* III, 83, 87, and IV, 6, 8, 33, 73, 82 (ed. Krusch; 116–117, 125, 133, 157–158, 162–163). On Spain in Fredegar, see the comments of Teillet, *Des Goths,* 575–584.

12. *Chronicon* IV, 82 (ed. Krusch; 162–163): "Gotorum gens inpaciens est, quando super se fortem iogum non habuerit."

13. Cf. Toledo V, 3 (Vives, 228): "Ut quisquis talia meditatus fuerit, quem nec electio omnium provehit nec Gothicae gentis nobilitas ad hunc honoris apicem trahit, sit a consortio catolicorum privatus et divino anathemate condemnatus." The condition is repeated in Toledo VI, 17 (Vives, 245): ". . . nullus . . . nisi genere Gothus et moribus dignus provehatur ad apicem regni . . ." On elective versus hereditary kingship, see Orlandis, "La iglesia visigoda y los problemas de la sucesión al trono."

ing a child to the throne. But the success was rarely lasting, and sooner or later the noted Gothic impatience made itself felt. The elective principle may therefore be understood as an aristocratic project in permanent conflict with the dynastic practice of the rulers of Spain. In so far as the councils endorse and preserve the elective formula, they speak for the nobility and represent its interests. The success of Chindasvind, Reccesvind, and Wamba in maintaining royal control over the conspiring nobility and the clergy can be measured indirectly by their ability to go for many years without summoning a national council of the church. There is none for the last eighteen years of Chindasvind and none for the entire reign of Wamba. In this way the kings spared themselves having to listen to any open criticism of their policies, as well as any further expression of the elective ideal.[14] The few councils of single ecclesiastical provinces that took place limited their deliberations strictly to church business. It is not surprising therefore that Fredegar perceived the political culture of Spain as different from that of Frankish Gaul. Though no king of the Franks reigned unopposed and rebellions and conspiracies of the nobility were unceasing, dynastic legitimacy had great political power north of the Pyrenees, as is evident from the efforts of warring factions to seize members of the royal family, no matter how junior, in order to present them as their leaders, or from the stories of illegitimate royal descent produced by pretenders to the throne.[15] In Spain there was no comparable sense of the claims of lineage, an absence of which Chindasvind must have been acutely conscious in 642, at the beginning of his reign.

As a member of the Gothic nobility, he had, when he came to

14. Wamba, of course, had been properly elected and would not have had to fear such criticism. Nevertheless, no national councils were summoned in his time.

15. See the useful summary in Fouracre and Gerberding, *Late Merovingian France*, 21–23, which relates several incidents of this type. On the pretender Gundovald and his origins in particular, see Goffart, "Byzantine policy in the West," esp. 96–102, and Wood, "The secret histories," 263–266.

power at the age of eighty or very close to it, spent a long life plotting against the kings of Spain. The throne was occupied at the time by Tulga, the young son of Chintila (636–639) who, though himself elected, had shown the predictable desire to found a royal line. Fredegar reports that Tulga's few years in power were plagued by political disorder, but he is unclear as to the manner of his deposition: on the one hand he writes that there was an assembly of high-ranking Goths at which Chindasvind was elected, on the other that Tulga was ousted and forced to accept holy orders.[16] Knowing well the risks he faced, the new king took immediate measures to neutralize them: he had those who might aspire to the throne killed and gave their widows and daughters in marriage to his supporters, who came into much property this way. Some two hundred of the highest-ranking Goths and five hundred of middle rank were eliminated by these means, and many others had to go into exile.[17] Toledo VII, the only national council to meet in Chindasvind's time (646)—and it met with a record low attendance of twenty-nine bishops—shows the king at a moment of uncontested power and the church in an attitude of unqualified submission, passing resolutions intended to support the royal policies and give them religious validation.[18] This becomes particularly conspicuous

16. *Chronicon* IV, 82 (ed. Krusch; 163): "Tandem unus ex primatis nomine Chyntasindus, collictis plurimis senatorebus Gotorum citerumque populum, regnum Spaniae sublimatur. Tulganem degradatum et ad onos clerecati tunsorare fecit."

17. *Chronicon* IV, 82 (ed. Krusch; 163): "Cumque omnem regnum Spaniae suae dicione firmassit, cognetus morbum Gotorum, quem de regebus degradandum habebant, unde sepius cum ipsis in consilio fuerat, quoscumque ex eis uius viciae prumtum contra regibus, qui a regno expulsi fuerant, cognoverat fuesse noxius, totus sigillatem iubit interfici aliusque exilio condemnare; eorumque uxoris et filias suis fedelebus cum facultatebus tradit. Fertur, de primatis Gotorum hoc vicio repremendo ducentis fuisse interfectis; de mediogrebus quingentis interfecere iussit." See Claude, *Adel, Kirche und Königtum*, 115–119, and Diesner, "Politik und Ideologie."

18. See Ziegler, *Church and State*, 101–105.

in canon 1, which excommunicates those exiles and fugitives who conspire against Spain from abroad—clearly Chindasvind's surviving aristocratic victims—and ends by begging the king never to raise that excommunication by himself, without consulting the bishops.[19]

The king's policy of confiscation from the nobility, so radical that after his death it was denounced by the church at the eighth council of Toledo summoned by Reccesvind in 653,[20] served primarily to strengthen Chindasvind's position by allowing him to buy the allegiance of powerful leaders of the nobility with grants of properties and estates. The pattern, characteristic of the protofeudal logic of the Visigothic state, would enable the ruler to draw on the private armies of Gothic magnates in all military emergencies.[21] Though little is known about military activity in the reign of Chindasvind, there is evidence that he, like almost all the kings of Toledo, had to respond to Basque incursions in the western Pyrenees soon after taking power.[22] The efficacy of Chindasvind's political strategies is proved by the fact that in 649, four years before his death, he was able to raise his son Reccesvind to co-rulership with himself, lastingly and with no aristocratic resistance. This measure, which must have been made necessary by the king's advanced age, and which contrasts with many similar but unsuccessful attempts by earlier rulers, may have owed some of its success to the fact that

19. Cf. Vives, 252: "Contestamur autem, clementissimos principes et per ineffabilem divini nominis sacramentum obtestantes unanimiter obsecramus, ne quandoquidem absque iusta ubi necesse fuerit inploratione sacerdotali excommunicationis huius sententiam a perfidis clericis vel laicis ad externas partes se transferentibus vel consensum praebentibus quaquumque temeritate suspendant . . ."

20. Cf. *Decretum iudicii universalis editum in nomine principis* attached to Toledo VIII (Vives, 289–293).

21. Cf. Pérez Sánchez, *El ejército,* 137. On protofeudalism, see Diesner, "König Wamba," and García Moreno, *Historia de España visigoda,* 332–337.

22. The funerary inscription for Oppila (see *Prosopografía,* no. 108) confirms military activity against the Basques late in 642.

Reccesvind was no longer a child and to the four years of shared power which allowed the nobility and the church to become used to Chindasvind's successor.

Better documented than such economic and political realities is, given the literary nature of much of the extant evidence, the progress that Visigothic theology and legal philosophy had made towards a redefinition of royal power and its prerogatives. Although Isidore of Seville's *Sententiae*, written under Sisebut (612–621), teaches that bad kings, like all rulers, are sent by God, in this case in response to the wickedness of the people *("pro malitia plebium")*, and that it is thus sinful to rebel against them, as against all rulers,[23] it also represents a wholly new formulation of kingship as service, as care of the appointed head *(caput)* of the Christian *regnum* for its members or extremities.[24] Any sense of an intrinsic sacredness residing in the person of the king, any royal charisma, is set aside: the word *"rex"* is derived from *"recte,"* because to be king is to do one's job well.[25] The legislation inherited by Chindasvind, to which he added considerably, systematically avoids the term *"maiestas,"* with its suggestion of an allegiance based on deference or reverence, and draws a distinction between treason against the country and the people and treason against the king.[26]

23. *Sententiae* III, 48, 11 (ed. Cazier; 299): "Irascente enim Deo, talem rectorem populi suscipiunt, qualem pro peccato merentur." On the decisive influence of Gregory the Great on this aspect of Isidore's political philosophy, see Reydellet, *La royauté*, 578–584.

24. Cf. Reydellet, *La royauté*, 572: "C'est l'essence même de la royauté qui est transformée. Le roi est absorbé dans la communion des baptisés. Il perd son mystère; nous assistons à la liquidation définitive de toute transcendance politique, de tout charisme de chef, tels que les avait connu l'Antiquité."

25. *Etymologiae* IX, 3 (ed. Lindsay): "Recte igitur faciendo regis nomen tenetur, peccando amittitur. Vnde et apud veteres tale erat proverbium: 'Rex eris, si recte facias: si non facias, non eris.'"

26. This is argued in Lear, "Contractual Allegiance" and "The Public Law of the Visigothic Code." Chindasvind himself, in his law against the exiles (LV II, 1, 8), refers to their crime as being "contra gentem Gotorum vel patriam" (ed. Zeumer, 54).

To a ruler such as Chindasvind, many of these ideas may have been acceptable because they remained largely within the orbit of theory and, aside from furnishing certain familiar formulas of official and ceremonial language, could have little impact on the actual exercise of power. Other challenges, more directly threatening to the ideological basis of his authority, needed to be countered. To do so, he drew on the Late Roman and Byzantine imagery of imperial majesty, which had been put to use by Visigothic rulers since Leovigild.[27] Formulated in court ceremonies, coinage, and encomiastic poetry, this staging of royal sacredness could help to remystify the powers that law and political philosophy had reduced to duties and responsibilities.[28] Fine instances of this *imitatio imperii* under Chindasvind are Bishop Eugenius (II) of Toledo's letter of dedication and verse preface to a corrected text of Dracontius's *Hexaemeron* that the king had requested. The letter addresses the ruler as "noble and glorious lord Chindasvind, highest prince and greatest of kings."[29] The verse preface, an *envoi* directed to the personified poem, envisions the text approaching the royal presence, which is framed hieratically by the threshold of the *aula:* "O you little book who will see the face of the king / at whose command you deserved to be freed of filth / and to receive a clean garment after

27. On Leovigild's sense of *maiestas,* cf. Isidore, *Historia Gothorum* 51 (ed. Mommsen, 288): "primusque inter suos regali veste opertus solio resedit: nam ante eum et habitus et consessus communis ut populo, ita et regibus erat." See also Reydellet, *La royauté,* 530–534, and Stroheker, "Leowigild," esp. 142–145, in particular p. 143: "Während die fränkischen Merowinger bis zum Ende ihrer Herrschaft in den äußeren Wahrzeichen der königlichen Macht die germanische Herkunft ihres Königtums festhielten, änderte sich nun bei den Westgoten gerade das äußeren Bild des Königtums völlig. Daß Leowigild hierbei das byzantinische Kaisertum vor Augen hatte, ist unverkennbar."

28. On Byzantine influence in these various aspects of court culture, see Stroheker, "Das spanische Westgotenreich und Byzanz," and Hillgarth, "Historiography."

29. Cf. Eugenius, *Dracontiana* (ed. Vollmer, 27): "Inclito glorioso rerum domino Chindasuinto, principi summo et maximo regum, Eugenius vestrorum fidelium servulus."

long neglect / so that you might begin to approach the threshold of the king's hall / and to gaze on the throne, dazzling with radiant gold . . ."[30]

A court life of growing importance hovers behind this conventional imagery. Chindasvind, who had decimated the old nobility, needed a service class to support him in the administrative and ceremonial functions of government. To that end, he created a court nobility, which soon acquired powers and attributions not shared by the rest of the Gothic aristocracy.[31] He allowed slaves and freedmen of the state the right to testify in a court of justice, otherwise denied to those of their station, and made them able to serve in the palatine office.[32] In his one council, Toledo VII, Toledo begins to be called *"urbs regia"*[33] and bishops living near the city are required to spend one month a year in residence there "in honor of the king

30. Ibid.: "Principis insignem faciem visure libelle, / cuius ad imperium meruisti sorde carere / et capere nitidam longo post tempore pallam, / coeperis ut limen aulae regalis adire / atque auro rutilo radiantem cernere sedem . . ." On the Hellenistic philosophical lineage of this staging of rulership, see Straub, *Zum Herrscherideal*, 120.

31. On the rise of this court nobility (referred to in contemporary texts as "seniores," "primates," or "maiores palatii" or as members of the "officium palatinum"), see Claude, *Adel, Kirche und Königtum*, 118–119. In case of treason "contra gentem et patriam," for instance, a king moved to clemency required only the approval of the clergy and of these members of his court: LV VI,1,7 (ed. Zeumer, 256): ". . . cum adsensu sacerdotum maiorumque palatii licentiam miserandi libenter habebit." Resistance to royal power was more likely to come from a more numerous *Geburtsadel*, which Claude, *Adel, Kirche und Königtum*, 120, calls an "autonomous" nobility.

32. See Claude, *Adel, Kirche und Königtum*, 123–124. Chindasvind describes these crown slaves in the law by which he denies the right to testify to all others of their status; cf. LV II,4,4 (ed. Zeumer; 97): ". . . excepto servi nostri . . . ut non inmerito palatinis officiis liberaliter honorentur, id est stabulariorum, gillonariorum, argentariorum, coquorumque prepositi, vel si qui preter his superiori ordine vel gradu procedunt; . . ."

33. According to Teillet, *Des Goths*, 539–540, this starts with Reccesvind, but see Toledo VII, 6 (Vives, 256), entitled "De convicinis episcopis in urbe regia commorantis."

and out of respect for the royal seat."[34] Clearly, the Visigothic capital was becoming a ceremonial stage for the new kingship, and the influence of Constantinople proved very powerful.[35]

The career of Eugenius II of Toledo throws light on certain aspects of Chindasvind's rule, not least the king's own claims as to the source and nature of royal authority. Until 646, Eugenius had been archdeacon and factotum to the aged Braulio of Zaragoza, metropolitan of the Tarraconensis. When he was summoned to Toledo by the king to succeed Eugenius I, who had died that year, Braulio addressed a pathetic letter to Chindasvind, begging him to let him keep his assistant: "Even though I am surrounded by grave troubles, there was one consolation in my life: the sight of your servant and my archdeacon Eugenius . . . But now, at your command, a part of my soul is taken away, and I do not know what I shall do at my age. I am deprived of the light of my eyes, lacking in vigor, destitute of knowledge; therefore I address my prayers to you that you not separate him from me, so that you may not be parted from God's kingdom and your seed may inherit your realm."[36] Chindasvind's reply, or possibly that of his chancery, is preserved:

34. Toledo VII, 6 (Vives, 256): "pro reverentia principis et regiae sedis honore."

35. Cf. Ildefonsus of Toledo, *De viris illustribus,* praefatio (ed. Codoñer, 112): ". . . in sede illa gloriosa Toletanae urbis—quam non ex hominum immensu conuentu gloriosam dico, cum hanc etiam gloriosorum inlustret praesentia principum, sed ex hoc quod coram timentibus Deum iniquis atque iustis habetur locus terribilis omnique ueneratione sublimis . . ." Ildefonsus knew Toledo in the days of Reccesvind, and possibly earlier. On the development of Toledo under the Visigoths, see Ewig, "Résidence et capitale," 31–36, and Adams, "Toledo's Visigothic Metamorphosis."

36. Braulio, *Epistolario,* letter 31 (ed. Riesco Terrero, 132): "Erat mihi utcumque huius uite solamen, etsi in multis necessitatibus constituto, serui uestri Eugenii mei arcediaconi uisio . . . Nunc uero iussioni glorie uestre aufertur a m<e> pars anime mee et quid in hac etate iam agam nescio. Lumine corporis cicutio, uirtute bacillo, scientia destituor, ideoque preces dirigo ut non separes eum a me, sic non separeris a regno dei et semen tuum regnum possideat tuum."

though written in a more turgid Latin than Braulio's, it is remarkable both for the tone in which it answers his request and for the
political ideas it voices. It begins wittily, by turning formulaic
praise of the bishop's epistolary style into a reason for refusing him
Eugenius's assistance: "We have received the petition, adorned with
the most blooming words of your eloquence and equipped with all
verbal harmonies, that your holiness took care to address to our
clemency. In it, the skillful arrangement of your words allows us to
understand that the archdeacon Eugenius is not kept next to you
because you are burdened by intellectual deficiency or reduced by
poverty of knowledge."[37] The letter makes use of a not easily controvertible argument: the king's choice of Eugenius is inspired directly by God: "For Almighty God, whose command is obeyed by
all things, gives inspiration where He wishes so that a man may fulfill His good will and come forth to please his creator by offering a
sacrifice. For the extraordinary kindness of the Lord knows beforehand those whom he has destined for higher things. . . . Therefore,
most blessed man, since you should not think that I will do anything other than what pleases God, it is necessary that according to
our command you should let me have this archdeacon to be a priest
of our church."[38] The king presents himself as an interpreter of the
divine will; his comments are not to be understood as merely hu-

37. Ibid., letter 32 (ed. Riesco Terrero, 134): "Suggessionem eloquentie
uestre uerbis florentissimis adornatam cunctisque eufoniis uerborum succintam, quam ad nostram clementiam tua curauit sanctitas transmittendam, suscepimus. In qua per lucubrationem tuorum uerborum studium nobis datur intelligi nulla uos intellectus necessitate conpressos, nullaque indigentia sapientie
exiguos aput uos Eugenium arcediaconum retineri."
38. Ibid. "Nam Deus omnipotens, cuius nutu universa deseruiunt, ubi uult
ispirat donec suam bonam uolumtatem impleat, ut ad immolandum sacrificium
suo creatori placiturus accedat. Nam preminens Domini pietas hos iam
presciuit quos etiam in melius predestinare desiderat. (. . .) Ergo, beatissime uir,
quia aliut quam quod Deo est placitum non credas me posse facturum, necesse
est ut iuxta nostra<m> adortationem hunc Eugenium arcediaconem nostre
cedas eclesie sacerdotem."

man directives determined by moral and political considerations; they originate in God's own plans for mankind, and should never be disputed.[39] An effort to resacralize the kingship and place it in some way beyond human criticism is evident in this correspondence. A letter sent by Eugenius to Braulio from Toledo and his new dignity discloses realities of church-state relations rarely mentioned elsewhere and comes closer to conveying a personal voice than most productions of Visigothic literature. Though learned, Eugenius was inexperienced in matters of church government; he was now confronted for the first time with the need to make decisions on difficult and sensitive questions. He submits a few of these issues to his old teacher and superior, humbly soliciting his opinion. "Two matters have come up in your church which much oppress my soul, and my mind does not know what remedy to bring to them if your advice does not provide one." The first case is especially instructive: "We have heard of a brother who, not having been ordained as a priest, nevertheless performs the office of one and, that you should know the reason more clearly, I will explain it here in detail. This brother was highly disliked by my lord Eugenius (i.e. Eugenius I). He, asked by the king to ordain [the brother] to the priesthood, was unable to refuse the king's command and thought of this stratagem: he led him to the altar, did not impose his hand, and while the clerics sang the *In excelso*, he pronounced a curse instead of a blessing, as he himself made known later to appropriate persons who were most dear to him, making them swear to be silent about it for as long as he was alive."[40] As might be ex-

---

39. On this episode see Claude, *Adel, Kirche und Königtum*, 126–127, and Diesner, "Politik und Ideologie," 18–19 and 26–27. For Ildefonsus of Toledo, only one generation later, Eugenius had been made bishop "by royal imposition" ("principali uiolentia": cf. *De viris illustribus* XIII [ed. Codoñer, 132]).

40. Braulio, *Epistolario*, letter 35 (ed. Riesco Terrero, 140): "Dua res obhorte sunt in aeclesia tua, unde nimium contabescit anima mea et quit remedii adhibeam, nisi consilium uestrum prebuerit, penitus scientia nostra non abet.

"De quodam fratre repperimus qui non ac<c>epto presbiterii gradu pres-

pected, the newly appointed bishop does not know what to do with this person, in particular whether he should allow him to go on performing the duties of a priest. What emerges here is not only the intimacy and mutual trust between Braulio and Eugenius, unaltered even if frustrated by royal fiat, but also the sense of Chindasvind's despotic interference in ecclesiastical government, the acceptability among churchmen of quite scandalous devices to oppose royal initiatives, and the need to keep such measures secret, the private knowledge of those appropriate and very dear persons who can be trusted.

Eugenius's later epitaph for Chindasvind has been read as an outburst of loathing for the old king, a personal reaction that could at long last be expressed, just as blunt criticisms of his policies were voiced immediately after his death at Toledo VIII. This interpretation ignores the first nine lines of the poem, written in the most conventional penitential tone, in which Chindasvind himself urges all listeners to weep and pray for him: in light of these, the self-incrimination that follows can be understood as a dramatic gesture of humility, a public confession such as any dying Christian burdened by his sins could be expected to make.[41] Visigothic poetry offered little place for outbursts of unmediated feeling; emotions had to be modulated through literary and religious stereotypes.

---

biteri peragit officium. Et, ut causam certius agnoscatis, omnia sing[u]lariter innotesco. Fuit idem ipse frater molestissimus domino meo Eugenio. Rogatus a rege ut eum presbiterum ordinaret, quia iussioni principis resistere non preualuit, hoc genus factionis inuenit. Duxit eum ad altarium, manum non inposuit et, cantantibus clericis *In excelso*, pro benedictione maledictionem effudit, sicut ipse hoc personis idoneis et sibi carissimis postmodum publicabit, coniurans ut hoc quamdiu uiueret, reticerent."

41. This reading of the poem is supported by Fredegar's account of the king's last days: *Chronicon* IV, 82 (ed. Krusch; 163): "Chyntasindus paenetentiam agens, aelemosynam multa de rebus propries faciens, plenus senectute, fertur nonagenarius, moretur." In view of the complaints made at Toledo VIII about his taking over of crown property, the remark about giving alms "de rebus propries" is remarkable.

Knowing what we do about the careers of Chindasvind, Eugenius, and Braulio, however, it is impossible to read certain parts of the epitaph without thinking that Eugenius derived much satisfaction from what the penitential formula allowed him to say: "There was no guilty act that I did not long to commit, / I was myself the greatest and the foremost in vices. / I am now turned to ashes who once bore regal scepters, / he whom royal purple covered now lies under the dirt. / The purple-dyed garments of kingship are no use to me now, / nor green gems, nor the shining crown. / Silver does not help, nor lustrous gold, / the palace couches do not please, nor do treasures satisfy."[42] The garments, insignia, and luxuries that had framed Chindasvind's Byzantine-modeled authority become here objects of a *contemptus* directed primarily at the king's person, at his moral identity.

In 649, four years before his death, Chindasvind had raised his son Reccesvind to the throne, anticipating by this shared rule the choice of a successor. A letter of Braulio of Zaragoza to the king is extant in which the aged bishop in his own name and in those of a Bishop Eutropius and a certain Celsus who was probably a military administrator in the Tarraconensis,[43] begs Chindasvind to do precisely that. Perhaps remembering the disagreement over Eugenius, Braulio begins by claiming some divine empowerment himself: "He who holds the hearts of monarchs in his hand, as our faith main-

---

42. Eugenius, *Carmina* 25, 15–22 (ed. Vollmer, 251): "nulla fuit culpa, quam non conmittere vellem, / maximus in vitiis et prior ipse fui. / en cinis hic redii sceptra qui regia gessi: / purpura quem texit, iam modo terra premit. / non mihi nunc prosunt biblattea tegmina regni, / non gemmae virides, non diadema nitens. / non iuvat argentum, non fulgens adiuvat aurum, / aulica fulcra nocent nec mihi gaza placet." Collins, *Early Medieval Spain*, 126, stresses the sincerity of Eugenius's dislike of the king, as do Claude, *Adel, Kirche, und Königtum*, 132 ("ein bitteres Schmägedicht"), and Diesner, "Politik und Ideologie," 34 ("von einer wirklichen Abneigung des Bischofs getragen"). Saitta, *L'antisemitismo*, 63–64, cannot explain the disloyalty of the poem ("quello sleale epitaffio") otherwise than as a manifestation of senility on the poet's part.

43. *Prosopografía*, nos. 646 and 32.

tains, also rules everything. It is not, then, without his inspiration that we desire to make a request of your clemency."[44] Alluding generally to the dangers the country has survived and the many lasting threats to the security of the realm, Braulio implores the king that "since we can think of nothing more advantageous to your peace or to our fortunes, in your lifetime and while you are in good health your servant Lord Reccesvind [should become]our lord and king, as one for whose years it is fitting to make war and endure the exertion of battles, with the assistance of divine grace."[45] Spanish theologians had made little use of the Old Testament stylization of monarchy that was to become popular later. Braulio, however, ends by sounding an early note in this direction, implicitly comparing father and son, as co-rulers of Spain, to David and Solomon.[46] It is difficult to tell whether the letter represents Braulio's own sentiments about the succession or mere compliance with the king's wish to be asked to do what was his intention in any case.[47] The

44. *Epistolario*, letter 37 (ed. Riesco Terrero, 148): "Qui corda regum in manu sua tenet, ut fides nostra habeat, ipse et omnia regit. Unde non est sine illius inspiramine quod clementie uestre cupimus suggerere."

45. Ibid. ". . . quia conpendiosius nicil nec quieti uestre nec casibus nostris prospicimus, in uita tua et te bene ualente seruum tuum dominum Recesuindum dominum nobis et rege deposcimus, ut cuius etatis est et belligerare et bellorum sudorem sufferre, ausiliante superna gratia . . ."

46. Ibid. "Unde celorum regem et sedium omnium rectorem supplici prece deposcimus, qui et Moysi Ihesum succesorem et in David trono eius constituit Salomonem, ut clementer insinuet uestri<s> animis ea que suggerimus . . ."

47. There is no consensus as to the sincerity of the letter: Reydellet, *La royauté*, 552–553, sees Braulio as writing in the tradition of Isidore, who had no preference for the elective principle. Collins, *Early Medieval Spain*, 115, believes the letter to be dictated by a perceived need for political stability. On the other hand Claude, *Adel, Kirche und Königtum*, 132, noting the antagonism expressed by the bishops at Toledo VIII, doubts that Braulio would have wanted to support Chindasvind's dynastic projects. "Demnach dürfte das Schreiben vom König 'angeregt,' wenn nicht erzwungen worden sein." Diesner, "Politik und Ideologie," 31, who speaks of "einem vom König wohl selbst gewünschten Brief," comes to similar conclusions. Orlandis, *España Visigótica*, 167, explains the letter as

eighth council of Toledo, held in 653, the first year of Reccesvind's sole rule, shows such a violent dislike of Chindasvind on the part of the gathered bishops as to make it appear unlikely that the letter was wholly sincere.

The old king died on September 30, 653, and the council summoned by his heir met on December 16 of that year. Before the council, and very probably before Chindasvind's death, when Reccesvind was already the effective ruler of Spain, a rebellion in the northeast challenged the new monarch's authority. We know of it from a preface addressed by Braulio's successor, Taio of Zaragoza, to Quiricus, bishop of Barcelona.[48] Under Chindasvind, Taio had been sent to Rome to find and bring back manuscripts of the works of Gregory the Great that were not available in Spain. Taio's own *Sententiae* were derived entirely from Gregory, and in his preface to his work, he reports that he had composed it during the siege of Zaragoza by "a pestilential and demented man [named] Froia, who, bent on usurpation, gathering to himself the wicked supporters of his crime, and deploying a campaign of deceit against the orthodox and God-worshiping Prince Reccesvind, [rose] by arrogant exertion to bring war to this Christian country. The fierce people of the Basques, emerging from the Pyrenees for the sake of this evil, [swarmed] about and [brought] ruin to Iberia by various forms of destruction."[49] The episode, which ended with the delivery of

based on the popularity of Reccesvind: "Parece, pues, probable que la propuesta partiera de la espontánea iniciativa de los firmantes del escrito, bien dispuestos hacia Recesvinto y sinceramente preocupados por peligros que se intuían para un futuro próximo . . ."

48. *Prosopografía*, nos. 592 and 584.

49. Taio, *Sententiae*, praefatio 2 (PL 80, col. 727): ". . . quidam homo pestilens atque insani capitis Froja tyrannidem sumens, assumptis sceleris sui perversis fautoribus, adversus orthodoxum magnumque Dei cultorem Recesuinthum principem fraudulenta praetendens molimina, superbo adnisu Christianam debellaturus aggreditur patriam. Hujus itaque sceleris causa gens effera Vasconum Pyrenaeis montibus promota, diversis vastationibus Hiberiae patriam populando crassatur."

Zaragoza and a victory for Reccesvind, has the appearance of a dress rehearsal for the rebellion of Paul against King Wamba in 673 that is the subject of the *Historia Wambae regis,* even if in the earlier instance Reccesvind's triumph was enhanced by the ignominious death of his opponent.[50]

Froia was most probably one of the *"refugi vel perfidi"* against whom father and son had legislated so harshly, and his attempt to take power, reminding the new king of the constant danger represented by the exiled nobility, may have persuaded him to seek the support of the church by summoning a council. Reccesvind must have called for Toledo VIII directly on his father's death, possibly even before it. Canon 10 of the council, with its reference to "the treasonable disorders of rustic peoples" as a circumstance that should not influence royal elections, appears to point directly to Froia's manipulation of the Basques.[51] With four years of rule behind him, Reccesvind knew well that, much as he needed the backing of the church for the policies he intended to announce at the council, he was also to expect a measure of criticism and open reluctance from bishops who had not met in seven years and had often resented his father's interference in church business. Clearly, he intended to negotiate, and the new format for national councils used for the first time in Toledo VIII had been designed to allow both sides to voice their arguments, though on the whole—given Reccesvind's position of strength—it proved advantageous for the king. It would be a mistake to read the acts of this council, as of

50. Ibid. (PL 80, col. 728): "Misso igitur coelitus propugnatore fortissimo, hunc auxilio omnipotentiae suae sublevat: illum vero tyrannicae superstitionis auctorem repentino casu condemnat: isti tribuens palmam victoriae copiosam, illo vero inferens atrocissimae mortis ignominiam."

51. Toledo VIII, 10 (Vives, 283): "Abhinc ergo deinceps ita erunt in regni gloriam perficiendi rectores, ut aut in urbe regia aut in loco ubi princeps decesserit cum pontificum maiorumque palatii omnimodo eligantur adsensu, non forinsecus aut conspiratione paucorum aut rusticarum plebium seditioso tumultu; . . ."

many others held in Visigothic Spain, in terms of church-state opposition. The bishops did not represent a sufficiently distinct interest by themselves, and when they opposed or confronted royal initiatives they can be understood to have been speaking for the
nobility as well.[52]

The council met in Toledo—which from now on is systematically called *"urbs regia"* in the acts of church councils—at the church
of Saint Peter and Saint Paul, whereas the established meeting-
place before had been the church of Saint Leocadia the Martyr. We
know little about Visigothic Toledo, but there is a strong likelihood
that this church imitates or "quotes" the church of the Holy Apostles in Constantinople, built by Constantine and rebuilt by Justinian.[53] The acts refer to it as an *"ecclesia praetoriensis,"* which would indicate that, like its original, it was designed as a palatine church,
built in the royal quarter of the city in the vicinity of the palace,
and that it was reserved for important ceremonies in the staging of
kingship. Visigothic rulers had retained the prerogative of summoning church councils, and this aspect of royal power was further
emphasized at Toledo VIII when Reccesvind opened the deliberations by presenting the bishops with a *tomus* or agenda in the form
of an opening speech, listing the subjects to be discussed. The
canons of the council include matters of purely ecclesiastical concern that are not anticipated in the royal *tomus:* unchaste bishops
(canon 4), persons forced to take holy orders who now wish to renounce them (canon 7), ignorant priests (canon 8). But canon 10,
which addresses the very sensitive political issues of royal succession—reaffirming the principle that the king must be elected—

52. The nobility as a whole, that is, and not just the palace nobility. The
point is made well by Reydellet, *La royauté,* 524 note 68: "Il ne s'agit pas na-
turellement d'un conflit entre l'Église et l'État au sens moderne du terme. Plus
exactement, il faudrait parler d'un conflit latent entre la royauté et une aristo-
cratie laïque et ecclésiastique."

53. On the Church of the Holy Apostles and its influence on medieval
Western Europe, see Beckwith, *Early Christian and Byzantine Art,* 104.

and of the difference between the king's personal possessions and crown property, does so without any prompting or encouragement from Reccesvind. In the *tomus* itself, the king introduces another novelty in conciliar procedure: members of the palatine office—aristocratic laymen—are present and will participate in the deliberations and sign the council acts. He mentions an ancient custom or *mos primorum* by virtue of which they are entitled to do so, but there can be little doubt that this had not been done before and that the courtiers are there to represent the royal interest.

The most important instruction in the *tomus* is discussed at length in canon 2 and proves extremely revealing.[54] It concerns the ecclesiastical penalties that had been decreed against conspirators and traitors in Toledo VII canon 1. At that earlier council, with Chindasvind at the height of his power and in no mood for negotiation with the rebellious, the bishops had imposed life-long and almost irrevocable excommunication, strengthened by solemn oaths and by anathemas against whoever tried to lift it. Reccesvind, however, who was making a new start, needed some leeway in his dealings with the nobility and with the exiled rebels of his father's time, so he requested that the bishops review the matter and inquire whether for the sake of mercy it might not be possible to undo this harsh sentence without incurring the charge of perjury. The response of the council is inordinately long, with repertories of scriptural and patristic quotations on the issue of mercy *(pietas, misericordia)* versus the keeping of oaths. It can be read as a theological analysis of the value of compassion, and in this sense proves directly relevant to the ideology of royal clemency *(clementia principis)* that would be frequently invoked from now on in discussions of policy.[55] But the function of these concepts at Toledo VIII and

54. On Toledo VII canon 1, see above note 19. The deliberations behind Toledo VIII canon 2 are discussed in terms of consensus, governance, and conflict resolution in Stocking, *Bishops, Councils, and Consensus*, 1–4.

55. On the classical background of these theories, see Adam, *Clementia*

elsewhere can be grasped only if, in addition to the philosophical and theological ancestry of the arguments, we also take account of what they allow the ruler to do. Reccesvind is asking the bishops to untie what his father had made them bind, and if the bishops take many pages rationalizing before they agree, it is only to dramatize the fact that this is no easy thing and that their decisions cannot be lightly altered to suit the political requirements of the moment.[56]

The procedure of royal succession and the distinction between the king's personal property and that of the crown are both outlined briefly in canon 10, without naming Chindasvind or making any specific reference to the circumstances of his rule. It is said very clearly, nonetheless, that the monarch must be elected and, as if to establish some common ground with the lay nobles present at the council, that the right of election is limited to the high clergy and the palatine nobility, no longer to the bishops and the nobility in general, as had been decided at Toledo IV.[57] This canon is part of the acts signed by all those who attended the council. But a lengthy law project submitted to the king that drew the consequences of canon 10 has survived as an appendix to the acts, together with the law that Reccesvind finally promulgated in response to these docu-

---

principis, esp. 88–107 on the influence of Seneca. Cf. also Reydellet, *La royauté*, 546 and 585.

56. Ziegler, *Church and State*, 112, sees Toledo VIII as marking a dramatic change in the attitude of the high clergy to the crown: "In this council the Church sided with the palatines against royal tyranny." The bishops' willingness to let mercy rule in the treatment of exiles and fugitives shows only that "the council was presumably in nowise loath to change the policies in vogue under the harsh old king" (p. 106). However, they had subscribed to those policies seven years earlier and, as Ziegler himself writes (ibid.), they yielded only "after an interminable theological disquisition on the binding power of oaths."

57. Cf. Toledo IV, canon 75 (Vives, 218): "nemo meditetur interitus regum, sed defuncto in pace principe primatus totius gentis cum sacerdotibus successorem regni concilio communi constituant . . ." and Toledo VIII canon 10 (Vives, 283): ". . . [rectores] cum pontificum maiorumque palatii omnimodo eligantur adsensu."

ments. The proposal paints an extremely frank picture of the policy of expropriation practiced by a king who had ruled in "times of harsh domination" *("temporibus durae dominationis")* with "strong authority" *("potestas gravis")* and ends by spelling out what must be done with whatever "King Chindasvind of glorious memory appropriated to himself from the day that he obtained the kingship."[58] In presenting his *tomus* to the council, Reccesvind had described the king's role in the commonwealth in terms of the relation of the head to the extremities,[59] and as if in response to this simile the bishops compare the effects of royal extortion to those of a belly that will not feed the limbs: "... so that alone the royal belly was full, and all the limbs of the people, emptied, languished from starvation."[60] Particularly significant, both politically and theologically, is a formulation of the nature of royal authority presented here that takes to its logical conclusion the Isidorian understanding of kingship as an office: the power, it is said, by virtue of which the king can take over property, is not based on his person but on the law, so the property thus confiscated should not become personal. "The king is made such by the law, not by his person, for he does not hold his place through his mediocrity but by the honor of high station ..." For its time, this is the most radical and also the most coherent statement of a legalistic, Roman conception of office that refuses all belief in the personal sacredness of rulers.[61]

It is not surprising, then, that Reccesvind never confirmed the

58. Toledo VIII, Decretum iudicii universalis (Vives, 292): "... quae a gloriosae memoriae Chindasvinto rege a die quod in regno dinoscitur conscendisse reppertus, quodlibet modo extiterit augmentasse ..."

59. Toledo VIII, tomus (Vives, 261): "Unde quia regendorum membrorum causa salus est capitis, et felicitas populorum non nisi mansuetudo est principum, votive decrevi vobis coram positis et votorum meorum deliberationem sanctionem patula reserare et studiorum acta sincera exhibitione deferre."

60. Toledo VIII, Decretum iudicii universalis (Vives, 292): "... sicque solo principali ventre subpleto cuncta totius gentis membra vacuata languescerent ex defectu ..."

61. Toledo VIII, Decretum iudicii universalis (*La colección canónica hispana* 5

decisions of the council by a law, as was generally done, and that in legislation aimed exclusively at this proposal of the bishops, which begins auspiciously with a reference to "the immoderate greed of princes" *("immoderatior aviditas principum")* he proceeds to gut their statement on the succession as well as on royal property.[62] Though he outlaws rebellion and the use of armed force in the selection of a ruler, he makes no mention of election, which had been absent from his own accession to power. The matter of property and confiscations he handles entirely in general, without once bringing up his father's name, and passes a law intended to apply to property acquired by kings from as far back as the reign of Suinthila (621–631), which defines as crown property whatever the king has not bequeathed in his will rather than, as the bishops wanted, whatever he had not brought to the throne as personal possessions.[63]

Reccesvind, presumably, had learned his lesson and called for no national council in the remaining nineteen years of his reign. He did allow three provincial synods, Toledo IX and X and Mérida, which handled internal church policy almost exclusively. Because it met in the *urbs regia*, Toledo IX in 655 was attended by four members of the palatine office in addition to the bishops of the Cartaginensis. Toledo X in 656 contains one brief canon (canon 2) establishing

[ed. Martínez Díez and Rodriguez; 452]): "Regem etenim iura faciunt, non persona, quia nec constat sui mediocritate sed sublimitate honore, . . ." The passage is discussed in Beumann, "Zur Entwicklung transpersonaler Staatsvorstellungen," esp. 215–223.

62. Cf. Toledo VIII, Lex edita in eodem concilio (Vives, 293–296). Ziegler, *Church and State,* 109, describes the king's law as follows: "Superficial reading of this [edict] would seem to indicate that Receswinth was quite in agreement with the none too softly worded memorial of the council to him; deeper examination reveals him as interpreting things differently and arranging matters entirely according to his own interests."

63. Toledo VIII, Lex edita in eodem concilio (Vives, 295): ". . . quaequmque forsitan princeps inordinata sive reliquit seu reliquerit, quoniam pro regni apice probantur adquisita fuisse, ad successorem tantundem regni decernimus pertinere . . ."

punishments for members of the clergy who violated their oath of fidelity to the ruler, so inducements to commit this offence may have been in the air.[64] The council of Mérida in 666, for the Lusitanian province, contains an interesting provision (canon 3) for prayers and masses to be said whenever the king goes out to battle, evidence that the military emergencies in view of which Braulio had asked Chindasvind to raise his son to the throne had not disappeared, even if we no longer know what they involved.[65] All in all, Reccesvind's ability to rule for nineteen years without summoning a national council shows an extraordinary degree of assurance for a Visigothic king, a quality clearly inherited by his successor Wamba, who in his years in power allowed one provincial synod (Toledo XI) only, so that the bishops of Spain and their lay supervisors or allies in the palace went from 653 to 681 without coming together in Toledo. Councils before and after the Chindasvind-Reccesvind-Wamba period show a very different state of mind on the part of rulers, especially in the numerous dispositions that attempt to guarantee the safety and well-being of the king's family and close personal associates after the king's death, dispositions that were often struck down by the following council as soon as a new king came to power.[66]

Although it appears increasingly unlikely that the code promul-

64. Toledo X is unusual: held with metropolitans of other sees in attendance (Seville for Baetica and Braga for Gallaecia) but with a very low total number of bishops present—seventeen, plus five episcopal representatives—it is not introduced by a *tomus* or visited by members of the palatine office. Magnin, *L'Église wisigothique*, 49, and Schwöbel, *Synode und König*, 24–25, list it as a provincial synod while Orlandis, *La vida en España*, 103, and Stocking, *Bishops, Councils, and Consensus*, 15 note 53, count it as national.

65. Cf. Mérida, canon 3 (Vives, 327–328). Such masses to be said throughout Lusitania for the king's prosperity in arms should not be confused with the *Ordo quando rex cum exercitu ad prelium egreditur* preserved in the Visigothic *Liber Ordinum* and published in Férotin, *Le Liber Ordinum*, cols. 149–153, which could only be performed at Toledo, in the palatine church, and with the participation of the ruler.

66. Chintila and Ervig prompted many such rulings. See for the former

gated by Reccesvind soon after Toledo VIII constituted the first territorial legislation of Spain, intended to apply equally to all the king's subjects whatever their ethnic origin,[67] it is certain that the king meant it to supersede all previous law codes and to be used exclusively throughout the country.[68] In the new code, Reccesvind contributes to the debate with the nobility and the clergy as to the king's prerogatives and the source of royal authority. According to one of his laws, the king legislates in obedience to commands from heaven, and his laws apply to him as much as to his subjects.[69] The

---

Toledo V, canon 2 ("De custodia salutis regum et defensione prolis praesentium principum" [Vives, 227–228]); canon 6 ("Ut regum fideles a successoribus regni a rerum iure non fraudentur pro servitutis mercede" [Vives, 229]); Toledo VI, canon 13 ("De honore primatum palatii" [Vives, 241]); canon 14 ("De remuneratione conlata fidelibus regi" [Vives, 242]); canon 16 ("De incolomitate et adhibenda dilectione regiae prolis" [Vives, 248–249]); and especially canon 18 ("De custodia vitae principum et defensione praecedentium regum a sequentibus adhibenda" [Vives, 245–246]). For Ervig, see Toledo XIII, canon 4 ("De munitione prolis regiae" [Vives, 419–421]); canon 5 ("Ne defuncto principe relictam eius coniugem aut in coniugio sibi quisque aut in adulterio audeat copulare" [Vives, 421–422]). Cf. also for Egica, Ervig's successor, Toledo XVI, canon 8 ("De munimine prolis regiae" [Vives, 505–507]).

67. See above note 10. An argument has been made that the code was actually compiled and promulgated under Chindasvind, cf. King, "King Chindasvind and the First Territorial Law-code." Chindasvind passed at least as many laws as his son. A letter by Braulio of Zaragoza addressed to "our glorious lord King Reccesvind" apologizes for lateness in the revision of a codex entrusted to him (*Epistolario*, letter 38 [ed. Riesco Terrero, 150]: "Mendositas etenim codicis, quem ad emendandum accepi, omnes uires suas contra caligines meas armauit . . .") and it has long been suspected that the codex contained the new legislation. Since Braulio died in 651, halfway through Reccesvind's corulership, the code could easily be the work of the old king.

68. Cf. LV II, 1, 10 "De remotis alienarum gentium legibus" (ed. Zeumer, 58). Although the reference to "alien peoples" is baffling, the text leaves no doubt as to exclusive use in Spain and abrogation of the Roman law: "Adeo, cum sufficiat ad iustitie plenitudinem et prescrutatio rationum et conpetentium ordo verborum, que codicis huius series agnoscitur continere, nolumus sive Romanis legibus seu alienis institutionibus amodo amplius convexari."

69. Cf. LV II, 1, 2 (ed. Zeumer, 46): "Gratanter ergo iussa celestia amplectentes, damus modestas simul nobis et subditis leges, . . ."

two, however, are not subject to the law in the same way: subjects are compelled by necessity to respect the law, the king by his will.[70] The conceit of the head and the extremities as a figure for the ruler and his subjects, touched on lightly by Reccesvind when presenting his *tomus* at Toledo VIII, is now elaborately developed, with special consideration of the role of illness in the dynamics between the two: "Rightly did God, the creator of things, in designing the form of the human body, place the head above and command that all the nerves of the extremities should derive from it; and hence he decided that it should be called 'head' *('caput')* from 'to originate in' *('a capiendis initiis')*,[71] placing in it the light of the eyes, so that they might see any approaching dangers, and also setting there the power of understanding, so that through it the will might control and foresight might direct the subordinate and connected members. This is why expert physicians are especially careful that medicine should be administered to the head before the extremities."[72] The consequence is that the king's business has priority over that of anyone else.

Rivalry between the king and the nobility remained at this point a critical fault-line of Visigothic society. The question is whether the use of a territorial code, whether or not it is the first of

70. Ibid.: ". . . quatenus subiectos ad reverentiam legis inpellat necessitas, principis voluntas." I adopt the emendation "principes" for "principis" proposed in King, *Law and Society*, 44.

71. Zeumer, 47 note 2, points to the origin of this etymology in Isidore, *Etymologiae* XI, 1, 25: "Prima pars corporis caput, datum illi hoc nomen eo, quod sensus omnes et nervi inde initium capiant."

72. LV II, 1, 4 (ed. Zeumer, 47): "Bene Deus, conditor rerum, disponens humani corporis formam, in sublimem caput erexit adque ex illo cunctas membrorum fibras exoriri decrevit; unde hoc etiam a capiendis initiis caput vocari precensuit, formans in illo et fulgorem luminum, ex quo prospici possent quecumque noxia concurrissent, constituens in eo et intelligendi vigorem, per quem conexa et subdita membra vel dispositio regeret vel providentia ordinaret. Hinc est et peritorum medicorum precipua cura, ut ante capiti quam membris incipiat disponi medella."

its kind to be applied, can be taken as an indication that already in the time of Reccesvind the divide between Roman and Goth can be considered a thing of the past. Are there sufficient grounds for believing that by the mid-seventh century the term *"Gothus"* has changed meaning and should be translated as 'Spaniard,' that the *Gothi* now were both the ethnic Goths and the Hispano-Romans, and that the phrase *"exercitus Gothorum"* in the HWR refers simply to a Spanish national army?[73] With unity of worship, intermarriage possible from the end of the previous century, and perhaps soon thereafter a single legal standard for the entire population of Spain, Reccesvind's subjects had made progress towards a blending of ethnicities and cultures, and the small numbers of the Goths would have favored this development.[74] The subject is hard to discuss because it is generally agreed that by the seventh century names are no longer a reliable guide to nationality. Although it has been suggested that around this time Hispano-Romans started to take Gothic names out of a snobbish identification with the Gothic elite, there are in fact, given the paucity of ethnic identifications in texts of the period, more certified instances of the opposite development.[75] Approaching names quantitatively, it is noticeable that at Toledo

73. Cf. Teillet, *Des Goths,* 554: "En realité, *Gothi* et *Romani* représentent indifférement les *populi* de la *gens Gothorum,* plus tard designés sous le nom de *Hispani* aussi bien que de *Gothi.*" Ibid., 516: "Même si son titre officiel est celui d'*exercitus Gothorum,* comme il apparait dans un canon du VIIe concile de Tolède . . . il est évident qu'il comporte, outre des *Gothi* et sans doute en grand nombre, des *Romani;* . . ." See, however, Hillgarth, review of *Des Goths,* esp. 581.

74. Numbers for the Gothic population of Spain are highly conjectural. A recent figure given for the late fifth and sixth centuries on the basis of archeological data is 130,000: see Ripoll López, "The Arrival of the Visigoths in Hispania," esp. 161–162.

75. See d'Abadal i de Vinyals, "A propos du legs visigothique," esp. 557 and 573. Whereas we know that John of Biclaro, Fructuosus of Braga, and Renovatus of Mérida (on whom see *Prosopografía,* no. 438) were Goths, we have no equally certain illustrations of d'Abadal's hypothetical fashion for Gothic names among the Hispano-Romans.

VIII members of the *officium palatinum* bear almost exclusively Gothic names while over half of the 52 bishops gathered there bear Latin names, not surprising given that most Goths would have been Catholics of fairly recent date. The pattern suggests a strong connection between names and ethnicity in 653: Gothic names, in any case, were still closely tied to Gothic ethnicity. If so, the fact that sixty years after the conversion not only most positions at court but also half of the episcopal sees were occupied by Goths is evidence that under Chindasvind and Reccesvind Gothic origins still conferred a disproportionate social advantage.[76] To the very end of the century there are indications that the political significance of ethnic difference may have survived intermarriage and a territorial law-code. A text of the importance of Ervig's military law, issued in 681, proclaims its validity for any subject of the king "whether he is a Goth or a Roman,"[77] And the *lex in confirmatione* of Toledo XVI, held in 693 under Egica, decrees that the king's *spatarius* or sword-bearer Theudemund shall no longer perform the office of *numerarius* or officer of the treasury in Mérida, adding that he has done so for a year *"contra generis vel ordinis sui usum,"* where it would seem that *"genus"* refers to ethnic origin and that the king is assuming that a Goth should not perform this civil-service job.[78] It

76. Thompson, *Goths in Spain*, 210–217, argues on similar grounds, and because the great majority of military commanders bore Gothic names, that a reform of the administration under Chindasvind and Reccesvind which largely militarized the government of Spain and replaced the old Roman civil authorities with military ones involved a systematic disenfranchisement of the Roman upper class. But see also King, *Law and Society*, 19 note 3, who finds little or no evidence of this reform.

77. LV IX, 2, 9 (ed. Zeumer, 377): "et ideo id decreto speciali decernimus, ut, quisquis ille est, sive sit dux sive comes atque gardingus, seu sit Gotus sive Romanus, necnon ingenuus quisque vel etiam manumissus . . . quisquis horum est in exercitum progressurus, decimam partem servorum suorum secum in expeditione bellica ducturus accedat; . . ." Teillet, *Des Goths*, 557, notes the phrase but does not attempt to explain it.

78. Cf. Toledo XVI, Lex edita in confirmatione concilii (Vives, 517–518), and the comments of Thompson, *Goths in Spain*, 213–214.

might thus be premature to conclude that by the 670s there was no longer a politically relevant ethnic divide in the kingdom of Toledo.[79]

The absence of sources for the reign of Reccesvind after Toledo VIII need not be taken as an indication that these years were uneventful. The reference in the acts of Mérida in 666 to military expeditions led by the king is likely to allude to campaigns more recent than the one against Froia in 653. The strongest probability is that Reccesvind would have had to confront the usual incursions of Basques in the northwest. On the other hand, this was for Spain a period of peace with its immediate neighbors, and especially with the Franks, who were kept busy by their own internal conflicts. The decades of international stability that began with the rule of Chindasvind enabled the monarchy to strengthen its hold upon the country and to foster a class of court-based administrators who could be trusted to back the reigning monarch against pretenders to the throne and aspirants to the succession. It is the power of this class in 672 that made possible the apparently unopposed election of Wamba.

If there are few written sources, two of the most impressive monuments of Visigothic art can be placed with certainty in the reign of Reccesvind and in direct relation to the king himself. The church of San Juan de Baños, south of Palencia and some forty-five miles northeast of the probable site of Gérticos, the royal villa where Reccesvind died, was commissioned and dedicated by the ruler in honor of Saint John the Baptist. A dedication in hexame-

79. It is unlikely that the distinction would have become irrelevant, since it involved important social and political advantages for a small fraction of the population. Its survival would be bound less with the desire of members of this group to continue to live as Goths, which seems implausible after the conversion, than with the wish to limit these advantages to themselves. See the comments of Giorgio Ausenda in the round-table discussion "Current Issues," 501–503, which suggest as much on the basis of contemporary ethnographic models.

ters is set into one of the inner walls, on a slab of white marble held in place by four finely decorated stone corbels. It reads: "O forerunner of the Lord, martyr John the Baptist, keep this dwelling built as an eternal gift, which I myself, the devout King Reccesvind, lover of your name, dedicated to you in my own right,[80] in the third year after my tenth as noble companion in kingship.[81] In the era six hundred and ninety-nine."[82]

As a country church, San Juan de Baños would have been simpler and smaller than the churches and palaces in Toledo, none of which have survived. The boldness of its original plan (in so far as it can be made out after many alterations) and the refinement of its sober decoration of crosses and geometric patterns on walls, thresholds, and windows can be connected to Byzantine and other Eastern Mediterranean models, although the church remains highly distinctive.[83] Its sophistication allows us to envision Reccesvind's country residence in the vicinity less as the hunting lodge of a Germanic ruler than as a senatorial retreat of the late empire, the scene of seasonal *villeggiature* for the king and selected courtiers.

The second monument that can be attached to Reccesvind is the votive crown that bears his name, found as part of the treasure of Guarrazar in 1859 near Toledo. It is one of several extant crowns

---

80. This literal translation of "proprio de iure" agrees with de Palol, *La basílica*, 69: "por derecho propio." The translation of Navascués, *La dedicación*, "de lo mío propio" brings up a different possibility related to what by then must have been the vexed issue of the king's property. Fontaine, *L'art préroman* I, 175, proposes "consacré en toute proprieté."

81. The phrase refers to Reccesvind's association to the kingship by his father in 649.

82. Cf. *Inscripciones cristianas* 314 (ed. Vives, 106): "+ Precursor D̄n̄i, martir Babtista Iohannes, / posside constructam in eterno munere sede, / quam devotus ego rex Reccesuinthus, amator / nominis ipse tui, proprio de iure dicaui / tertii post d̄ēc̄m regni comes inclitus anno, / sexcentum decies era nonagesima nobem." The Spanish era date (which adds 38 years) translates into 661.

83. On San Juan de Baños, see Fontaine, *L'art préroman* I, 173–195, and de Palol, *La basílica*.

of this type and the most impressive of them all, if not the oldest (one had been offered by Suinthila some twenty years earlier). Votive crowns are meant to be suspended in churches in honor of specific martyrs, as an allusion to the crown of martyrdom.[84] The prototype and the idea are Byzantine. Reccesvind's crown, which is richly decorated with openwork and with inset jewels, has the letters of the sentence "King Reccesvind offers" hanging individually from golden chains; a Latin cross is suspended below it. The decoration of the crown itself involves the same friezes of intersecting circles found on the walls of San Juan de Baños. Together, church and votive crown suggest that the sumptuous Byzantine staging of majesty was not a verbal screen intended to hide the reality of a barbarian court, but that Visigothic poets and court writers were to some degree inspired by reality when they referred to dazzling gems, golden thrones, and a sacred palace.[85]

The election of Wamba at Gérticos on the very day of Reccesvind's death by the unanimous acclamation of the clergy and the court nobility present there is an unmistakable statement of continuity, the more important because the new king was not related to his predecessor and no claim is made that he had been designated for the throne by the dying Reccesvind.[86] Wamba's very presence at the royal deathbed identifies him as a member of the inner circle of advisors and assistants of the king, expected therefore to rule on similar principles and in the interest of the same group. He is very likely identical with the *vir inluster* of that name mentioned in one of the decrees attached to Toledo X, who appeared before that council on Reccesvind's orders to present to the bishops the testament of Martin of Braga concerning his monastery of Dumio, a document presumably preserved in the royal library or

84. The blessing recited at the dedication of the crowns is preserved in the Visigothic liturgy; cf. Férotin, *Le Liber Ordinum*, cols. 165–166.

85. On Reccesvind's crown, see Fontaine, *L'art préroman* I, 242–246.

86. Cf. Collins, "Julian of Toledo and the Education of Kings," 15–16.

archive.[87] Not being a relative of the royal house, which had ignored the elective principle for the previous thirty years, he was in
the paradoxical position of having to stress the legitimacy of his
own election to be accepted as the lawful successor. This is one
reason why Julian of Toledo's account of Wamba's election in the
HWR, written in support of the king and almost certainly within
the first three years of his rule, stresses compliance with every
point of the elective procedure: acclamation, acceptance after a ritual refusal, a delay of the ceremony of unction, and finally the rites
of accession in Toledo. Wamba's tearful refusal of power is the less
to be taken as an actual rejection of the throne in that it conforms
in every respect, as Julian describes it, to a well-documented gesture of late imperial accessions.[88] The delay imposed by the new
king on the public ceremonies at Toledo was a further note of elective legitimacy, intended as it was to allow the assent of those elec-
tors living furthest from Gérticos and Toledo to reach the *urbs regia*.[89] The ceremony by which the ruler-elect became king of Spain
appears to have involved the rite of unction and the swearing of re-
ciprocal oaths on the part of the ruler and his subjects. A coronation that Julian would have taken for granted and thus left unre-
ported should not be assumed. Isidore of Seville's statement that

87. Cf. Toledo X, Item aliud decretum (Vives, 322): "Adeo mentis inten-
tionem orisque simul studia deducentes agnitione audiendi negotii delantum
est ad nos in conventu sancti concilii ex directo gloriosi domini nostri Rece-
suincti regis per inlustrem virum Ubanbanen testamentum gloriosae memoriae
sancti Martini ecclesiae Bracarensis episcopi, qui et Dumiense monasterium vi-
sus est construxisse, ut reserato eo quid illic memoratus beatissimus vir de-
crevisset nostrae cognitioni pateret: . . ." and *Prosopografía*, nos. 162 and 407. The
evidence for libraries and archives in Toledo under Reccesvind is discussed in
Collins, "Literacy and the laity," 114–116.

88. See Béranger, "Le refus du pouvoir," and Wallace-Hadrill, "Civilis princeps," esp. 36–37.

89. Chindasvind and Ervig made similar delays: see for Ervig the *Laterculum*
47 (ed. Mommsen, 468) and in general Sánchez-Albornoz, "La 'ordinatio principis,'" 13–14, note 43.

Reccared *"regno est coronatus"* need only imply a conventional phraseology of kingship and not the actual use of crowns.[90] Julian's description of Wamba's unction is the earliest account extant of royal anointing in Western Europe, though it remains uncertain whether Wamba was the first Visigoth to be thus made king, especially in light of the references to kings as the Lord's anointed in the famous 75th canon of Toledo IV, the acts of which are attributed to Isidore.[91] On the other hand, it is also quite possible that the ceremony was used for the first time—since it was familiar from Scripture—to enhance the legitimacy of Wamba, who would soon have to confront quite predictable challenges to his authority in Gallia and the Tarraconensis.[92]

2. From Toledo to Nîmes and Back

No other event in the history of Spain in the seventh century has been narrated in as much detail as the rebellion of Paul against

90. Cf. Isidore, *Historia Gothorum* 52 (ed. Mommsen, 288): "Levvigildo defuncto filius eius Recaredus regno est coronatus . . ." Sánchez-Albornoz, "La 'ordinatio principis,'" 6–9, argues for the use of crowns by Visigothic rulers. Reydellet, *La royauté*, 536–539, favors "une interprétation purement symbolique" of Isidore's phrase.

91. Cf. Toledo IV, canon 75 (Vives, 217): "Illi ut notum est inmemores salutis suae propria manu se ipsos interimunt, in semetipsos suosque reges proprias convertendo vires et dum Dominus dicat: 'Nolite tangere Christos meos': et David: 'Quis, inquit, extendet manum suam in Christum Domini et innocens erit?'" See also Isidore, *Etymologiae* VII, 2, 2 (ed. Lindsay): "Christus namque a chrismate est appellatus, hoc est unctus. Praeceptum enim fuerat Iudaeis ut sacrum conficerent unguentum, quo perungui possent hi qui vocabantur ad sacerdotium vel ad regnum: et sicut nunc regibus indumentum purpurae insigne est regiae dignitatis, sic illis unctio sacri unguenti nomen ac potestatem regiam conferebant; et inde Christi dicti a chrismate, quod est unctio." For Sánchez-Albornoz, "La 'ordinatio principis,'" 12–15, the evidence points to an early practice of unction, which might go back to Reccared.

92. See Müller, "Die Anfänge der Königssalbung," esp. 333–339. Reydellet, *La royauté*, 566–568, esp. note 238, concludes that the evidence for unction before Wamba is not compelling. Teillet, *Des Goths*, 589 and 600–601, simply assumes that the rite was used for the first time at Wamba's accession.

King Wamba. Julian of Toledo's work is a *unicum* in Visigothic historiography, and this has caused the events which it reports to take up a disproportionate amount of space in modern accounts of the period.[93] Rather than political importance, Paul's attempted usurpation has typical value, and in his treatment of it Julian seizes on the familiarity of such uprisings, which were already equipped with a range of literary themes and *topoi*, and uses the well-known narrative of rebellion and defeat to enhance the legitimacy of the new ruler. The late Western Empire has been described as "a nursery of pretenders to the throne,"[94] and the phrase applies from as early as the third century. The kingdom of Toledo took up the characteristic features of late imperial usurpations: an open challenge to the ruler in office, the weakened position of the *princeps*, who was no longer the leader of his armies, the attempt on both sides to create standards of legitimacy, and the eventual defeat of most pretenders.[95] Rebellions such as those of the *dux* Argemund against Reccared and Froia against Reccesvind, though reported with extreme brevity, display the exemplary traits that became attached to such incidents as soon as the pretender was defeated, and in particular the narrator's emphasis on the public spectacle of the pretender's humiliation and/or death.[96] Aware as Julian is of the inher-

---

93. See for example Orlandis, *España Visigótica*, 254–263, and Pérez Sánchez, *El ejército*, 146–155.

94. Goffart, "Rome, Constantinople, and the Barbarians," 18.

95. On the challenge, see Flaig, "Für eine Konzeptualisierung der Usurpation," 19: "In meiner Theorie des Prinzipats bezeichnet der Begriff Usurpation die offene Herausforderung des amtierenden Monarchen." The definition serves to explain the importance of the *Epistola* for the HWR as a whole, even though its composition and reception are left unmentioned in the *Historia*. On the hollowness of all criteria of legitimacy, which could always be claimed by the opponent, ibid., 18: "Ein Verfahren kann nur dann Legitimität stiften, wenn die betreffende Gruppe das Verfahren monopolisiert, wenn also alle anderen Gruppen es fraglos unterlassen, dieses Verfahren ebenfalls anzuwenden." The ruler's loss of authority over his armies is discussed in Martin, "Zum Selbstverständnis," 127. On defeat, see Elbern, *Usurpationen*, 117–125.

96. Cf. John of Biclaro, *Chronica*, anno viii Mavrici imperatoris 3 (ed.

ited stereotypes for his subject, however, he does not sacrifice the facts of the case to a rigid paradigm of illegitimate ambition, defeat, and punishment, but manages to do justice to many distinctive and singular features of the conflict he describes.

The transition to a new ruler would have been a critical and dangerous moment in terms of political stability, especially when it took place under the exceptional circumstance of a royal election. Wamba is said to have refused the kingship originally on account of the many impending disasters ("tot ruinis imminentibus") (Hist. 2), which suggests that some of the disorders with which he was threatened predated the death of Reccesvind, or in any case were clearly foreseeable at the time of his passing. Julian's narrative has Wamba facing three sources of unrest almost immediately after his accession,[97] the Basques, the Galli, and certain factions in the Tarraconensis, though they are reduced to two once Paul associates the rebellion he had started in the Tarraconensis to the originally independent uprising led in Gallia by Hildericus of Nîmes. It is significant that the Historia opens its narrative of the campaign almost in medias res, with Wamba already in Cantabria fighting against the Basques, who were a chronic focus of unrest for Visigothic kings from Leovigild to Reccesvind and therefore agents of the kind of "disaster" that Wamba could have predicted before his election.[98] As a challenge to his authority, these northern tribes were wholly different in kind to the forces set in motion by usurpers and con-

Mommsen, 219–220): "ipse autem Argimundus, qui regnum assumere cupiebat, primum verberibus interrogatus, deinde turpiter decalvatus, post haec dextra amputata exemplum omnibus in Toletana urbe asino sedens pompizando dedit et docuit famulos non esse superbos." On Froia's "atrocissimae mortis ignominiam" in Taio's account, see above note 50.

97. Cf. Hist. 29: "Hispaniam rediit sedemque sui solii sexto postquam inde commigraverat mense repetiit." The campaign occupied the second half of his first year in power.

98. On Basques and Visigoths, see Vigil and Barbero, "Sobre los orígenes sociales de la Reconquista," esp. 301–330, and Besga Marroquín, Consideraciones sobre la situación política de los pueblos del norte.

spiring nobles: they did not aspire to replace Wamba, but rejected his claims over their territory and persisted in raiding into the lands subject to him. In addition, they regularly offered support to successive pretenders: they had served Froia against Reccesvind and were later approached successfully by Paul.

Julian introduces the uprising in Gallia first (*Hist.* 5), announcing in this way that its suppression will be at the center of his work. Wamba dispatches the *dux* Paul to crush the rebels, presumably from Toledo, and Paul, deciding to use the situation and the forces in his command to his own advantage, creates a twin rebellion in the Tarraconensis (*Hist.* 7); on arrival in Gallia, he brings both movements together under his own direction (*Hist.* 8). A parallelism between the two stages of the uprising is created by matching figures of exemplary loyal prelates, Aregius of Nîmes and Argebadus of Narbonne, who choose to defy the usurpers Hildericus and Paul respectively. Paul has been characterized as a bad choice for the job on the part of Wamba because a thirteenth-century source makes him a Byzantine, and as such unlikely to be loyal to a Visigothic ruler.[99] But aside from the fact that the late source has very weak authority at best,[100] it is highly probable that Paul was a Goth. His status of *dux* and, chiefly, Julian's total silence on a non-Gothic extraction when kingship had long been reserved explicitly to the Gothic nobility make this a near certainty: such an obvious objection to the pretender would hardly have been left unstated. His name, interestingly, is one of the few Latin ones frequent among members of the palatine office: it occurs three times among their signatures in council acts.[101] On the other hand, the words of Paul to his men during the defense of Nîmes (*Hist.* 16), denying

---

99. Cf. Diesner, "König Wamba," 9.

100. The evidence is set out in *Prosopografía* no. 111, note 1.

101. Toledo VIII and IX, "Paulus comes notariorum" (Vives, 289 and 307), Toledo XVI, "Paulus comes ss" (Vives, 521). *Prosopografía* no. 110 takes the first two as one person.

"that famous bravery of the Goths" (*"Gothorum illa famosissima virtus"*) to the present enemy, words which would be curious coming from a Goth, may perhaps be explained by the fact that he is speaking to the Galli and their allies, and therefore doing what he can to distance himself from the rulers of Spain.

The Basques, first to be dealt with, are actually brought in last in the telling, and Wamba is fighting them or on the point of doing so when he receives the news of Paul's treason (*Hist.* 9). In this way Julian indicates that this intermittent struggle of the kings of Spain in the north is not the main subject of his narrative: it works as a setting from which the action can take off and gives increased value to Wamba's readiness to move directly to a new front for which he and his army had not prepared. The king is already there, which means that his solemn departure from the *urbs regia* at the head of an army has not been shown. The ceremony at the church of Saint Peter and Saint Paul for the king's departure on a military expedition must nevertheless have taken place: a golden cross containing a relic of the holy cross, handed in the course of this liturgy to the king for use as a *signum* or standard in battle, is raised by Wamba as he exhorts his troops[102] to join him in an immediate attack on the usurper and his forces.[103]

In every respect, the portrayal of Wamba so far has been minimal, and this should probably be read as an endorsement of the legalistic view that identifies rulership with the acquired function rather than the person of the king, the *honos sublimitatis* and not the personal *mediocritas.* Wamba has not been quoted so far, or only very

102. Although he is supposed to be speaking to the *primates palatii*, who cannot make up their minds, he addresses them as *"iubenes,"* which turns his words into an allocution to the troops.

103. Cf. Férotin, *Le Liber Ordinum*, col. 152: "Post hec non statim absoluitur, sed mox accedit diaconus ad altare, et leuat crucem auream, in qua lignum beate Crucis inclusum est, que cum rege semper in exercitu properat, et adducit eam ad episcopum. Tunc episcopus, lotis manibus, tradit eam regi, et rex sacerdoti, qui eam ante se portaturus est." See also McCormick, *Eternal Victory*, 308.

briefly in indirect speech. At this point (*Hist.* 9), he speaks for the first time in *oratio recta,* and at much greater length than anywhere else in the HWR. His speech, a tissue of martial and heroic commonplaces, succeeds in persuading the armies to follow him east in order to face the rebels directly without first returning home to renew their equipment and provisions. Wamba makes no strategic points, but national slurs play a large role in his reasoning: the enemy are characterized as either Galli or Franks, and their traditional inferiority to the Goths on the battlefield is stated repeatedly. This aspect of the royal oration can be used—and has been—to support an interpretation of the HWR as a vehicle for Gothic or Spanish nationalist ideology.[104] But it is also possible to understand the length and importance of the speech in terms of the realities of government in the early 670s, and this is precisely one of the moments when the HWR moves beyond the literary commonplaces of usurpation and its defeat to allow a glimpse of the political issues at stake at the beginning of Wamba's government. The *primates palatii* are in doubt as to whether the army should face the new insurrection without delay, or whether the troops should be dismissed to restore their strength and then reconvene for a new offensive. Why is it so important that the king's eloquence should block this second option and move the army to stay in the north and strike immediately? At the time, the Visigothic army was already made up very largely of contingents contributed by the nobility, and this dependence of the crown on the private forces of the Gothic magnates allowed the latter to wrest concessions from the king and weaken the hold of the monarchy on political authority. Had Wamba's army scattered and the various troops returned to their home territories, the king would have had to negotiate with the nobility to get them to return.[105] We do not know whether it had been difficult to assemble this army originally, but there is a clear difference between a

104. This is mainly Teillet's argument: see *Des Goths,* 621–636, but cf. also Claude, "Gentile und territoriale Staatsideen."

105. The point is made by Pérez Sánchez, *El ejército,* 147.

campaign against the Basques, an alien and marginal people against whom the Goths had traditionally fought, and the aristocratic conspiracies of Gallia and the Tarraconensis, led largely or even exclusively by fellow Goths. Given a chance to reconsider, the patrons of many of the warrior-bands gathered around Wamba might have decided to throw in their lots with the usurper, or set a higher price on their loyalty to the crown. By keeping the army in place, however he really achieved this, Wamba is depriving the nobility of its chief bargaining instrument, a policy which he went on to confirm and make permanent by his law of that same year, issued soon after the rebellion had been put down, which imposes draconian penalties on the nobility and even the clergy who fail to fulfill their military obligations.[106] The devastating impact of this law is reflected—probably with much exaggeration—in the acts of Toledo XII, held under King Ervig in January 681, soon after Wamba had been deposed. The new ruler, exaggerating freely, denounces the sweeping measures of his predecessor that have deprived almost half the population of the right to testify in court, and the bishops decree that this right be restored to those who have lost it, on presentation of evidence of their former good standing.[107] In 673 or 674, however, as Julian composed the HWR, the king's refusal to let the army dis-

106. The inclusion of the clergy is clearly spelled out: LV IX, 2, 8 (ed. Zeumer, 371): ". . . seu sit episcopus sive etiam in quocumque ecclesiastico ordine constitutus, seu sit dux aut comes, thiufadus aut vicarius, gardingus vel quelibet persona, qui aut ex ipso sit commissu, ubi adversitas ipsa occurrerit, aut ex altero, qui in vicinitate adiungitur, vel quicumque in easdem provincias vel territoria superveniens infra centum milia positus . . ." as is the fact that the penalties apply to them too: ibid.: "Si quisquam ex sacerdotibus vel clericis fuerit et non habuerit, unde damna rerum terre nostre ab inimicis inlata de propriis rebus satisfaciat, iuxta electionem principis districtiore mancipetur exilio. Hec sola sententia in episcopis, presbiteris et diaconibus observanda est. In clericis vero non habentibus honorem iuxta subteriorem de laicis ordinem constitutum omnis sententia adinplenda est . . ." On the singularity of this suspension of clerical immunity, cf. Ziegler, *Church and State*, 113.

107. Cf. Toledo XII, tomus (Vives, 383): ". . . cuius severitatis institutio dum per totos Spaniae fines ordinate decurrit dimidiam fere partem populi

band could be read as a powerful assertion of royal authority, a manifestation of the same self-assurance that allowed Wamba to rule for eight more years without seeking the support or the endorsement of the assembled bishops of Spain.

In his *Epistola,* Paul had styled himself "anointed king of the east" *("unctus rex orientalis"),* creating thus a new name for the region he aspired to rule for the time being. That no other provinces joined the rebellion and that the retaking of Barcelona and Gerona in the Tarraconensis is made to seem almost effortless may be attributed to the intense regional particularism of early medieval Spain. The mutual distrust and suspicion between the *Spani* in Paul's army and their temporary allies in Gallia will come to the fore later on (*Hist.* 18). Fighting in the HWR takes place almost exclusively in Gallia and consists very largely of siege warfare. Julian presents Gallia as a territory hostile to Spain and to the Goths. The view of Gallia as not part of Spain was well-established and can be found as early as Toledo III (589), for example, with its opening reference to the bishops "of all Spain and Gallia"[108] and in Toledo IV (633), which repeats that phrase and also calls Sisenand "king of Spain and Gallia."[109] Wamba himself, in his military law, proclaims his legislation to be in force "within the borders of Spain, Gallia, Gallaecia and in all those provinces which are under the authority of our government."[110] Though its borders with the Frankish kingdoms appear to have been effective in blocking commercial and cul-

---

ignobilitati perpetuae subiugavit; ita ut quia in quibusdam villulis vel territoriis sive vicis peste huius infamationis habitatores ipsorum locorum sunt degeneres redditi, quia testificandi nullam habent licentiam, . . ." and ibid., canon 7 (Vives, 394–395): ". . . ut hii qui [per] supradictum legem testificandi dignitatem perdiderunt, recepto testimonio pristinae dignitatis causas exequi possint debitae actionis, qualiter nobilitatis solitae titulum reportantes et quae de praeteritis legitime testificare voluerint licentiae obtineant votum et a iudicibus nullis prohibitionibus arceantur, . . ."

108. "totius Spaniae vel Galliae" (Vives, 107).

109. "rex Spaniae atque Galliae" (Vives, 186).

110. LV IX, 2, 8 (ed. Zeumer, 372): ". . . infra fines Spanie, Gallie, Gallecie vel in cunctis provinciis, que ad ditionem nostri regiminis pertinent, . . ."

tural exchanges,[111] Gallia was felt by Visigothic ideologists such as Julian to have housed too many Jews and foreigners and to be therefore seething with disloyalty to the mother country.[112] The southern border of Gallia along the Pyrenees was defended by forts *(clausurae)* built in the mountain passes that protected the Tarraconensis from possible incursions of the Franks. These fortifications were staffed by *limitanei,* troops settled and given land in the region to ensure a constant military presence.[113] They had been occupied by the rebels, and Wamba was forced to divide his army so as to attack several of them simultaneously as he made his way into Gallia.

Certain incoherences in Julian's account of the movements of Wamba's troops across the Pyrenees confirm that he was not an eyewitness and had little familiarity with the region, or none: after taking Gerona, the king divides his army into three sections, one of which is said to enter Gallia by way of Vich *(Vicus Ausetanorum),* which is actually southwest of Gerona, an unlikely route; another section seizes the fortress of Clausurae only after taking Collioure *(Caucoliberis),* which would involve an equally implausible backward movement.[114] Julian must have worked from a detailed factual re-

111. See James, "Septimania and its Frontier."

112. The acts of the provincial synod of Narbonne (589) forbid work on Sunday (canon 4, [Vives, 147]) to "omnis homo tam ingenuus quam servus, ghotus, romanus, syrus, graecus vel iudaeus" and announce that the presence of sorcerers "in quuiuscumque domo gothi, romani, syri, graeci vel iudaei" will be punished severely (canon 14 [Vives, 149]). The formula, or an equivalent, does not occur anywhere else in Spanish conciliar documents.

113. Vigil and Barbero, "Sobre los orígenes sociales de la Reconquista," 314–320, connect these fortifications with the Byzantine system of strongholds built under Justinian to defend borders, mountain passes, and roads. The Visigoths would have raised theirs in imitation of similar Byzantine structures they might have seen in the south of Spain protecting the imperial territories before 624. However, it seems at least equally likely that they would have used Roman fortifications already in place, such as the ones at Clausurae (today Les Cluses, near the Col du Perthus), which overlook the Via Domitia and have been dated to the fourth century.

114. See Pérez Sánchez, *El ejército,* 152. These errors go unnoticed in Miranda Calvo, "San Julián, cronista de guerra."

port provided by Wamba's generals or by the king himself: he is fully aware of the distribution of the *clausurae* across the mountains,
which makes it necessary to split the troops (*Hist.* 10); he knows
that Narbonne and Maguelone can be besieged by sea as well as by
land (*Hist.* 12 and 13), has possibly heard about a church of Saint
Mary in Narbonne (*Hist.* 12) and of the presence in that city of
relics of the martyr Felix (*Hist.* 26); he knows that Nîmes, now a
stronghold rather than a city, defends the northeastern limit of
Gallia, beyond which Paul and his forces may not retreat, and that
the Roman circus there has been turned into a further bastion
within the city walls (*Hist.* 18). On the basis of this information,
much of which he could have found in the *Iudicium,* Julian fashions
a narrative of the recovery of Gallia that deliberately lacks all sus-
pense, as the victory of the rightful, divinely approved ruler must
be a foregone conclusion.[115] As the army moves north, the narrative
describes the gradual cornering of the rebels, which ends in the *castrum arenarum:* those not captured when the various cities south of
Nîmes fall to Wamba's forces escape to bring the news of defeat to
the final refuge of rebellion. The account is also wholly epicized,
with elements familiar from heroic and panegyric poetry, especially
the motifs tied to siege warfare: teichoscopies, defiant speeches and
insults from the battlements, the unexpected arrival of reinforcements at the critical moment and its contrasting impact on either
side of the walls. All of these are sufficiently well-known as poetic
commonplaces to indicate that a critical reading is necessary, but
also plausible enough that they cannot be discounted out of hand.
Other aspects of Julian's narrative, particularly what he tells about
the disintegration from within of the alliance crafted by Paul, correspond too closely to the exemplary treatment of the Fall of

---

115. García Moreno, *Romanismo y Germanismo,* 360: "Combinando el ataque
por tierra a un bloqueo marítimo, Wamba, prácticamente en un paseo militar,
lograría apoderarse con cierta facilidad de Narbona, Béziers, Agde y Maguel-
onne."

Usurpers found in ancient and late antique historiography and encomia to be entirely credible, even though they too remain within the bounds of possibility.

The real tensions of Visigothic political life emerge once again where the issues of punishment and royal clemency are touched on. The king's obligation to punish, formulated by Isidore of Seville in the maxim that "he does not rule who does not chastise,"[116] was already upheld by Wamba when he had some rapists among his troops circumcised. The king justified this eccentric measure by invoking the scriptural example of Eli, who failed to punish his abusive sons and was destroyed, with the comment that "the fair judgement of God will condemn me if, seeing the wickedness of the people, I do not punish it" (*Hist.* 10). The king's obligation to display clemency, however, had been established by Reccesvind in the *tomus* to Toledo VIII and by the ostentatiously troubled acquiescence of the bishops in canon 2 of that same council, authorizing the king to pardon the "fugitives and traitors" who had been dealt with so harshly by his father.[117] This argument for royal clemency appears to echo in the famous letter addressed by Fructuosus of Braga to Reccesvind requesting the king's pardon for conspirators sentenced in the reign of Chintila (i.e. up to thirteen years earlier): Fructuosus says plainly that the king must pardon others if he expects to be pardoned himself. His further point that no previous oath, however solemn, may be allowed to stand in the way of mercy has obvious and direct application to any perceived conflict between clemency and the letter of the law, especially given the phrasing of Reccesvind's own legal code according to which the king's compliance with the law, unlike that of his subjects, is only voluntary.[118] Although the debate on these issues remains throughout on

---

116. *Etymologiae* IX, iii, 4 (ed. Lindsay): "Non autem regit, qui non corrigit."
117. See note 54 above.
118. *Epistolae Wisigothicae* 19 (ed. Gundlach, 688): "Frustra iuramentum causa impietatis obtenditur, quod pro certo contrarium Christi sermonibus adpro-

the most abstract and theoretical moral plane, it is clear that political considerations of the sort that would particularly concern a
king at the beginning of his reign might be the ones to tip the
scales in favor of mercy. While there is life there is hope, and it is
possible to negotiate; the extreme instability of power and political
alliances in late Visigothic Spain would have made it ill-advised for
a ruler to let his hands be tied by the sentences of his predecessors,
and the injunction to have "entrails of mercy" provided an easy
and respectable way out of this bind.

For all that, the representation of these matters in the HWR is
conflicted and contradictory, suggesting that in the king's confrontation with the rebellious nobility a final settlement had not
been reached even at the time of writing. Paul before his capture is
already presented as a fitting subject for royal compassion, having
renounced the arbitrary cruelty of usurpers and touched the depths
of humiliation at the hands of his own followers and allies (*Hist.*
20). Although he and his associates expect to be executed and left
unburied (*Hist.* 21), they send out Bishop Argebadus of Narbonne,
who had not compromised himself by joining the rebellion, or had
done so only at the last moment and under pressure. Crouching in
the dust before the horse of the triumphant Wamba, Argebadus
begs for clemency, and in doing so introduces a new factor into
what so far has been a dispute between king and nobility: that of
the deference due to a prelate even in such circumstances. Wamba's
response is complex: he grants the rebels their lives, but reacts with
anger when Argebadus goes on to request that they not be punished
at all. There is no indication in this scene that Julian is accusing the
king of insufficient compassion, or of deficient reverence for men
of God.

After he is dragged out of the *castrum arenarum* with his accomplices (*Hist.* 24), Paul is subjected to a series of public humiliations

---

batur: nulla fides est, que bonorum operum et misericordiae caret affectu." For
Reccesvind's understanding of royal compliance with the law, see above note 70.

and then, on the third day after his capture, judged in front of Wamba's army and sentenced to death (*Hist.* 27). The *Iudicium*, based on an original composed in Nîmes contemporaneously with the events, or shortly thereafter, gives a fuller version of the sentence: capital punishment was to be commuted only with blinding, if the king's compassion so dictated, and the property of the rebel leaders was to be confiscated and taken over by the ruler. Blinding as a "merciful" alternative to death reflects the legislation on treason that was in force in Wamba's time.[119] Julian, on the other hand, though he had used the *Iudicium* and almost certainly created the revised version of it that is appended to the *Historia* and the *Insultatio,* says nothing about confiscation of property, and states that the sentence of death was changed to decalvation "as is required" (*"ut praecipitur"* [*Hist.* 27]), the present tense of which might appear to imply a recent alteration in the law that would date the *Historia* to the reign of Ervig.[120] This punishment, however—whatever *"decalvatio"* may mean—had been used in Visigothic Spain long before Wamba and in almost identical circumstances, when under Reccared the *dux* Argemund "desiring to commit usurpation" was seized, whipped, decalvated, had his right hand cut off, and was paraded all over Toledo riding an ass.[121] With a few changes (e.g. camels for

119. LV II,1,8 (Reccesvind) (ed. Zeumer, 55): "Quod si fortasse pietatis intuitu a principe fuerit illi vita concessa, non aliter quam effossis oculis relinquatur ad vitam . . ." On the punishment of blinding in early medieval Europe, see Bührer-Thierry, "'Just Anger' or 'Vengeful Anger'?"

120. This is the conclusion drawn by García López, "La cronología."

121. See above note 96. For the very similar execution of the usurper John in Aquileia under Galla Placidia in 426, cf. Procopius III, 3, 9. Late imperial models appear to have been as persistent in public rituals as in literature and the arts. A strikingly similar treatment for defeated usurpers was preserved in the Maghreb until very recent times. On August 20, 1909, the *Rogui* or pretender Abou Hamara, who had led insurrectionary forces for the previous eight years, was brought into Fez in chains, inside an iron cage placed on the back of a camel. He was executed twenty days later. See Weisgerber, *Au seuil du Maroc moderne,* 180–198, with a remarkable photograph between pages 196 and 197 of the pretender entering Fez. I am indebted to Michel Thévenot for this information.

asses), this must be what happened to Paul, as the HWR was obviously intended to circulate in Toledo, and the public there would have witnessed and remembered the ignominious parade of the pretender and his cohorts in Wamba's triumphal procession (*Hist.* 30).[122]

Whether *decalvatio* involved actual scalping or only a shameful and brutal shaving of the head remains a question.[123] Spanish authors certainly used *"decalvare"* to mean the latter, as when Isidore in his *Allegoriae* 130, 81 writes that Delilah *"Samson verticem decalvavit,"*[124] interpreting Judges 16.19, according to which she shaved seven locks from his head *("et rasit septem crines eius")*. The practice of actual scalping can be found as close to Spain as Vandal North Africa, where Victor of Vita, in his *Historia persecutionis vandalicae* describes in some detail the method used.[125] But he adds that those who suffered this punishment went blind, or died of the pain, and he does not use the words *"decalvare"* or *"decalvatio."* The Spanish texts never imply that decalvation could endanger life; the writers most often seem to be assuming that the subjects of this penalty will live to experience the disgrace of such treatment. There are grounds, therefore, for thinking that the punishment imposed on Paul and his followers was a fairly violent and dishonorable shaving or plucking of the head, and not a scalping. Even more ambiguous than his statement that they all rode into Toledo *"decalvatis capitibus"* is Julian's

122. Cf. McCormick, *Eternal Victory,* 313–314.

123. See the comprehensive but inconclusive discussion in Lear, "The Public Law of the Visigothic Code," 159–161 (Appendix B). The controversy between Hoyoux, *"Reges criniti"*; Kaufmann, "Über das Scheren"; and Cameron, "How did the Merovingian Kings wear their Hair?" concerns Frankish evidence only, and the verbs *"tundere"* and *"tondere,"* although it raises many of the same points as *"decalvatio."*

124. PL 83, col. 112.

125. *Historia* II, 2, 4 (ed. Halm, 15): ". . . palis minoribus dentatis iectis in capite crinibusque in eisdem colligatis, ac vehementius stringentes, simul cum capillis omnem pelliculam capitis auferebant. Nonnulli, dum fieret, statim oculos amiserunt, alii ipso dolore defuncti."

description of Paul in this pageant of disgrace as *"picea ex coreis lau-rea coronatus,"* which has been interpreted to mean that he was wear-ing a black crown made of leather straps.[126] I would propose in-stead that *"picea"* means 'of pitch,' as that substance had been used from antiquity to punish slaves,[127] and that this sarcastic inversion of the usual meaning of such wreaths, which serve as the reward of victory, signifies simply that the usurper's head was smeared with pitch or tar. The leather straps, which make little sense as elements of a burlesque crown, are possibly bits of torn skin left by the bru-tal handling of Paul's scalp. If so, *"ex coreis"* should be read as close-ly connected in sense to *"excoriare,"* the verb most frequently used in legal sources for 'to flay.'

In all of this, it is remarkable that Julian omits any mention not only of the confiscated property of the rebels, but also of their loss of status, which meant among other things that they could no longer testify in court. Property and rights might now serve as in-struments of royal pressure, and in the *tomus* and canon 1 of Toledo XIII (683) Ervig and his bishops returned them to the rebels of ten years before, not without some general considerations about mercy and the *pietatis viscera*.[128]

Julian's understanding of the rebellion remains Toledan and provincial. The Franks, as an *"externa gens"* (*Hist.* 7), are mentioned only to bring out how entirely the Galli depend on other nations to do their fighting for them and, later, when they are disgracefully

126. Powers, 47: "crowned with a black garland of leather thongs"; Díaz y Díaz, 107: "coronado con una banda de cuero negra."

127. See for instance, in Plautus, *Captivi*, 597 (ed. Lindsay; 260), in a dia-logue between two enslaved gentlemen, the curse "Pix atra agitet apud carnu-ficem, tuoque capiti inluceat." In medieval Latin, the connection between pitch and punishment was sufficiently familiar that Du Cange (*Glossarium*, s.v.) cross-references "pix" and "latro."

128. Characteristic are the opening words of Canon 1 (Vives, 415): "Prae-conabile signum est illis semper negotiis interesse, quae et a pietate incipiunt et per pietatis viscera temperantur. 'Pietas enim, ut ait Apostolus, ad omnia utilis est.'"

chased back into their territories (*Hist.* 27), to enhance the magnitude of Wamba's victory. Aside from the name of their leader (*Hist.* 27: *"unum e ducibus Franciae nomine Lupum"*) there is no indication of the fact that these are not actually Franks or subjects of the Merovingians—who at this time were briefly unified under Childeric II—but Gallo-Roman Aquitainians with a very real overlordship over the Basques, and that their leader, the *dux* Lupus, had taken on the authority of a ruler over the entire region.[129] As for the Basques, these *"feroces gentes"* (*Hist.* 9) who had already given so much trouble to the rulers of Spain were certainly more familiar, but Julian was unable to determine clearly to what degree they were acting independently or in collaboration with the rebels in Gallia.

3. Julian and Wamba: Two Careers

A praise-filled narrative such as the HWR makes sense only soon after the events and Julian, a native of Toledo educated at the cathedral school of the *urbs regia* by Eugenius II, must have written his account of Wamba's victory in 674 or 675, while he was still a deacon or a very recently ordained priest, consecrated at the canonical age of thirty.[130] It is likely that this early work brought him the king's favor and that he garnered merits and praise at court and in the higher ecclesiastical circles of Toledo until early in 680, when on the death of Bishop Quiricus, who had anointed Wamba, he succeeded him as bishop of Toledo and metropolitan of the Cartaginensis, an appointment which lay entirely in the ruler's hands.

On the night of October 14 of that year, a Sunday, the king was taken ill and, while unconscious, received the sacrament of penance (*ordo poenitentia*), which could not be repeated and which conferred on the penitent a public status incompatible with any worldly occu-

---

129. Cf. Rouche, *L'Aquitaine*, 99: "C'est donc un ensemble politique nouveau qui vient de surgir, totalement separé des Francs."

130. Cf. *Prosopografía* no. 251 and Hillgarth, *Opera* I, viii–xiii.

pation.[131] When, later that same night, Wamba recovered consciousness, he could no longer be king and was replaced on the throne by Ervig.[132] The speed with which this all happened is remarkable and suspicious, since Ervig appears to have taken power already on October 15. Then in January 681 the twelfth council of Toledo met in the church of Saint Peter and Saint Paul, the first national council to be summoned since 653. Among the very first measures adopted by the assembled bishops was the approval of Ervig's kingship, after a cursory and not very clear account of the circumstances that had rendered his predecessor unable to rule. This discussion was followed by the revocation of laws, policies, and ecclesiastical initiatives of Wamba, who was charged with abuse of power, coercion, and frivolity with a bluntness not heard previously in the diplomatic and cautious language of the councils. Toledo XII was presided by Julian, who had anointed Ervig one week after his election.[133] The facts are extremely suggestive and have been interpreted in various ways, from a sort of ritual accident by the more exculpatory scholars, to a palace coup in which Bishop

131. Because it could not be repeated, penance was postponed as much as possible and often administered to those in danger of death. Although it involved a tonsure and the wearing of monastic garments, it did not turn penitents into members of the clergy: see Toledo VI, canons 7–8 (Vives, 238–239), and Wolf, *Conquerors and Chroniclers*, 161 note 11.

132. Cf. *Laterculus* 46–47 (ed. Mommsen, 468): "accepit quoque paenitentiam praedictus princeps die dominico exeunte, hora noctis prima, quod fuit pridie id. Oct; luna XV, aera DCCXVIII. suscepit autem succedente die, II feria, gloriosus domnus noster Eruuigius regni sceptra . . ."

133. *Laterculus* 47 (ed. Mommsen, 468): ". . . dilata unctionis sollemnitate usque in superveniente die dominico, quod fuit XII k. Nov., luna XXII, aera qua supra." According to the acts of Toledo XII, generally attributed to Julian, Wamba requested that his successor be anointed by the bishop of Toledo: (Vives, 386–387): ". . . aliam quoque informationem iam dicti viri in nomine honorabilis et sanctissimi fratris nostri Iuliani Toletanae sedis episcopi, ubi sub omni diligentiae ordine iam dictum dominum nostrum Herbigium in regno unguere deberet et sub omne diligentia unctionis ipsius celebritas fieret; . . ."

Julian played a leading and sinister part.[134] The incident was fraught with consequences for the late Visigothic kingdom, and in order to grasp its logic, it may be useful to survey what is known about the careers of Julian and Wamba, and how the personal aims and ambitions of these two men, the king and the bishop, may have impinged upon each other.

Wamba was at least two decades older than Julian if, as is almost certain, he was already working for Reccesvind at Toledo X in 656. That council, although a provincial synod of the Cartaginensis, was held in the presence of metropolitans and bishops of other provinces.[135] After general deliberations and the signing of the council acts, the bishops discussed two matters of church discipline, the second relating to the will of Richimer, the most recent bishop of Dumio, which contained large bequests to the poor of his see and was being impugned by the clergy of Dumio.[136] The

134. Murphy, "Julian of Toledo," 15, admits no more than "a suspicion of foul play in the matter of Wamba's dethronement," while Hillgarth, *Opera* I, xiii, will grant only that Julian played "a passive role in the conspiracy against Wamba." Wengen, "Julianus von Toledo," 20, saw no contradiction between Julian's earlier role as propagandist for the king in the HWR and his full participation in the plot to depose him: "Wir sind vielmehr gezwungen, aus seinen frühern guten Einvernehmen mit Wamba und den schnellen Anschluss an den Usurpator auf seine Charakterlosigkeit zu schliessen, die sich da, wo sie etwas gewinnen kann, in massloser Schmeichelei äussert, da hingegen, wo die Sache verloren scheint, sich durch schnellen Anschluss an das Neue zu retten sucht." The most strongly worded accusation is that of Teillet, "Un coup d'état au VIIe siècle," esp. 106–112, who, among other charges, makes Julian responsible for the thorough—even if transparent—coverup of the conspiracy in the council acts: "D'ailleurs, qui aurait pu composer ce chef-d'oeuvre d'hypocrisie que représentent le *tomus* d'Ervige, et ces deux premiers canons, sinon Julien, tout à la fois théologien, spécialiste de droit canon, et habile rhéteur?"

135. See above notes 64 and 87.

136. The presence at the council of Fructuosus of Braga, metropolitan of Gallaecia, is accounted for by the fact that the affairs of Dumio were to be investigated. The clergy of Dumio were successful in setting aside the will of their late bishop, cf. *Prosopografía* no. 407 and García Gallo, "El testamento de San Martín de Dumio."

testament of Martin of Braga, the earliest and most admired figure of that church, was of importance as a precedent and as a term of comparison, and the courtier chosen to bring it before the council can hardly have been an inexperienced youth. Wamba is the more credible when, sixteen years later, at Gérticos, he pleads not to be made king because he is already "worn out by age" (*"senio confectus"* [*Hist.* 2]). His relatively advanced age and lack of an heir, suggested strongly by the absence of any reference to a wife or family, are likely to have contributed to his unanimous acclamation at Reccesvind's deathbed.[137]

Concerning Wamba's election and the character of his reign, one of the decisive factors remains unknown, and that is the strength of the court nobility and the palatine office, that chose him to rule, relative to that of the nobility of birth, whose power-base lay far from Toledo. That opposition to the new king could come to a head in a distant province is illustrated by Hildericus of Nîmes and his revolt in eastern Gallia. Paul's failure to persuade more than a few leaders in the Tarraconensis to join his own conspiracy later on reveals the fragmentation of the nobility of Spain that made it possible for an aggressive ruler to keep the upper hand.[138] But the relative weight, stability, and composition of the factions on which Wamba's power rested remain undetermined.

What is known about Julian's beginnings is both interesting and important, though it calls for a measure of speculation. If it was in the seventeenth year of Reccesvind's reign that he took holy orders, being made deacon and later priest, he must have been born

137. The often unreliable ninth-century *Crónica de Alfonso III* makes Egica, Ervig's son-in-law and successor, a nephew of Wamba: cf. textus Rotensis 3 (ed. Gil Fernandez, 118): "[Ervigius] filiam quoque sua nomine Ciscilonem magno viro Egicani consubrino Bambani regi in coniugio dedit." Ibid. 4: "Quumque [Egica] regnum conscendit, abungulus eius Bamba rex ei precepit ut coniugem dimitteret."

138. On the territorial/regional basis of this phenomenon, see García Moreno, *Romanismo y Germanismo*, 359–360.

circa 642, as the prescribed age for ordination as a deacon was twenty-five.[139] This calculation agrees well with the fact, also certified by Felix of Toledo's *vita* of his predecessor, that Julian was taught by Eugenius II, bishop of Toledo from 646 to 657.[140] Clearly, Julian was educated for and by the church from an early age. Felix writes that while still very young he became the close friend of a fellow student, the deacon Gudila—most probably a Goth—and that the two had planned to live as monks, if necessary by running away, but that their project came to nothing when they had to take up positions in the secular clergy, and that Gudila died in 679 or 680. The story is not totally convincing: it displays well-known motifs of hagiography and monastic biography such as the spiritual friendship of two young men and their decision to renounce the more worldly forms of the religious life in favor of the strenuous path of contemplation, void of secular rewards.[141] The incident serves to confirm the purity and disinterestedness of Julian's aims, a function not dissimilar to what the initial refusal of the throne does for Wamba, and that is precisely why it calls for some skepticism.[142] One more fact is known about the rising course of Julian's

139. Felix, *Vita* 4 (PL 96, cols. 446–447): ". . . a decimo septimo ferme anno Reccesuinthi principis, necnon et per omne Wambonis imperii tempus usque ad tertium regni gloriosissimi Egicanis regis annum, in levitici, presbyterii ac pontificatus honore consistens, celebre nomen obtinuit."

140. Cf. *Vita* 1 (PL 96, col. 445): "Julianus discipulus Eugenii secundi, . . ." and *Prosopografía* no. 248.

141. *Vita* 2–3 (PL 96, col. 445): ". . . quique divino afflante Spiritu theoreticae, id est, contemplativae quietis, delectati sunt perfrui bono, et monasticae institutionis constringi repagulo. Sed quia aliter in superni numinis fuit judicio, eorum est nihilominus frustrata devotio." Cf. Braulio, *Vita S. Emiliani* 12 (ed. Vásquez de Parga, 18): "Durum illi primum uideri ac grave, refugere ac reniti et quasi de caelo traduci ad mundum, de quiete iam paene nancta ad officia laboriosa, uitamque contemplatiuam transferri in actiuam; tandem coactus est inuitus obedire quapropter in ecclesia Vergegio presbiterii est functus officio."

142. Among the signatures at Toledo XI (675) (Vives, 367–369) are those of a "Gudila ecclesiae Toletanae arcediaconus" and two abbots of the name of Julian, one "Iulianus indignus abbas" and a "Iulianus ecclesiae monasterii sancti

fortunes in the Toledo of Wamba and Bishop Quiricus: the young priest established at this time a relation with Count Ervig, who would succeed Wamba in 680, and dedicated to him what appears to have been an early compilation from Scripture, a "Book of Divine Judgements" that has not survived.[143] After Ervig became king, Julian wrote other books for him, notably the *De comprobatione sextae aetatis.* It is noteworthy that the new ruler whom Julian anointed in October 680 was an old acquaintance and former patron of his.[144]

Far more significant in its implications is the testimony of the Mozarabic chronicle of 754 that Julian was of Jewish stock, although the son of Christian parents.[145] The fact in itself is entirely credible, especially given that the author of the chronicle expresses throughout the greatest admiration for Julian and seems well informed about his life. The silence of Felix's *vita* in this regard is also comprehensible: the late 690s, when he wrote, were years of intense anti-Judaic agitation in Spain, and Felix would not have mentioned anything that might compromise the reputation and standing of

Michaelis abba." Wengen, "Julianus von Toledo," 10, argues that neither one of these last two can be our Julian, as his ecclesiastical titles, listed in Felix, *Vita* 4 (see above note 139), include no monastic dignities. Teillet, "Un coup d'état," 106, asserts that "en 675, [Julien] a tenu une place de premier plan au concile précédent, où il n'était encore que simple prêtre," but with no evidence.

143. Felix, *Vita* 10 (PL 96, col. 450): "Item libellum de divinis judiciis, ex sacris voluminibus collectum, in cujus principio est epistola ad dominum Ervigium, comitatus sui tempori pro eodem libello directa."

144. The *Ars grammatica* attributed to Julian (ed. Maestre Yenes), today believed to be the work of one of his students, contains the following references to Wamba's successor: p. 24, "puta, si interroges me: 'cuius equus?' respondeo tibi per genitiuum casum: 'Domni Eruuigi Regis.'" Ibid., p. 40: "Item quare dicitur [pronomen] minus quam finitum? Eo quod de cognita et absente persona loquor, ut puta si dicam: 'scis Domnum Eruuigium? Ipse est Princeps Hispaniae.'"

145. *Crónica mozárabe* 38 (ed. López Pereira, 56): "In cuius tempore iam Iulianus episcopus, ex traduce Iudaeorum ut flores rosarum de inter uepres spinarum productus, omnibus mundi partibus in doctrina Xpi manet preclarus, qui etiam a parentibus Xpianis progenitus splendide in omne prudentia Toleto manet edoctus, ubi et postmodum in episcopio extitit decoratus."

his subject.[146] Since Julian participated passionately in anti-Jewish polemics, particularly in the HWR, it is necessary to consider what effect his origin could have had on his career, and to what degree it might have shaped his ideological stance.

A mapping out of Julian's rise in the church and of his development as a writer and theologian against the history of the Jewish community in seventh-century Spain, highly desirable though it would be, offers insurmountable difficulties. The legal and religious status of the Jews is richly documented in law codes and council acts, but it does not translate easily into historical reality: the prescriptive and abstract character of Visigothic sources is especially pronounced on this subject. Legal and ecclesiastical texts warn repeatedly against neglecting to apply the existing legislation,[147] new penalties are decreed not only against Jews who disobey but against Christians who help them defy the law.[148] To what extent, then, was the escalating harshness of laws regarding the Jews a reality of life? Does the fact that Chindasvind and Wamba did not concern themselves with the Jews and passed no laws relating to them mean that the Jewish community had an easier time during their reigns? Inhuman statutes from before these rulers remained in force and might still have been applied . . . or not.[149]

146. Cf. Murphy, "Julian of Toledo," 5, and Hillgarth, *Opera* I, viii note 2.

147. Cf. Toledo VIII, canon 12 (Vives, 285): ". . . nicil aliud pro his ex nostra sententia definitur, quam ut decreta concilii Toletani, quod divae memoriae Sisenandi regis adgregatum est tempore, a nobis ac posteris omnimoda suppleantur intentione: . . ." and LV XII,2,3 (Reccesvind) (ed. Zeumer, 413–414): "Quapropter eternam legem iubemus et sacrarum scripturarum iussu decernimus tam nostrarum legum edicta, quam precessorum nostrorum regum legali serie sententias promulgatas, que contra eorum perfidiam et personas data consistunt, eterna consecratione inviolata persistere et perenni custodia observata manere."

148. Cf. LV XII,2,15 (Reccesvind) (ed. Zeumer, 423–424): the title reads "De interdicto omnibus christianis, ne quisque Iudeum quacumque factione adque favore vindicare vel tuere pertemtet."

149. The legal position of the Jews during their reigns is described in Saitta, *L'antisemitismo*, 61–64 and 70–74.

Equally disorienting is the fact that the laws concerned two quite different communities: one of recent converts to Christianity, perhaps not excessively zealous and hence suspected of crypto-Judaism, and another of recalcitrant Jews, who were nevertheless forbidden to practice the observances of their religion. The law forbidding Jews to testify in court against Christians, for example, applies in fact to recent converts too; only second-generation Christians could testify.[150] A further note of unreality derives from the fact that the available evidence is exclusively non-Jewish: responses or reactions of the Jews themselves have not survived, or even the names or identities of their community leaders; the *placitum* of the Jews included among the Visigothic laws was composed for them by their Christian overlords. Especially baffling, given the Jewish tradition of commemoration, is the utter silence of Spanish Jews after 711 on the subject of their ancestors under the Visigoths and the oppression and persecution they had endured. As a named and prominent Spaniard of Jewish origin, Julian of Toledo is a rare exception in this period. Two not incompatible ways of accounting for the extreme elusiveness of the Visigothic Jews are the possibility that many of the Spanish Jews after 711 were recent immigrants with no ties to the previous community of their faith, and on the other hand the likelihood of massive conversions to Christianity before that date (and laws and councils do constantly address themselves to baptized Jews).[151]

On first impression, Julian's development seems easy to grasp, from vicious anti-Jewish invective under Wamba (*Hist.* 5; *Ins.* 1–2) to an escalation of oppressive laws and canons under Ervig and Egica,

150. Cf. LV XII,2,10 (Reccesvind) (ed. Zeumer, 416–417): "Merito ergo testificari proibiti sunt Iudei, seu baptizati, sive non extiterint baptizati. De stirpe autem illorum progeniti si morum provitate et fidei plenitudine habeantur idonei, permittitur illis inter christianos veredica quidem testificandi licentia, sed non aliter, nisi sacerdotem, regem vel iudicem mores illorum et fidem omnimodis conprobantes."

151. See Sivan, "The Invisible Jews of Visigothic Spain."

during the decade when he is bishop of Toledo and primate of Spain. It is tempting on this basis to view Julian's anti-Judaism as preemptive and defensive, and to explain much of his career in terms of warding off potential blows aimed at his fairly recent Christianity.[152] As the son of converts, he would have been sharply aware from early on of rulings that affected his parents: Toledo IV canon 62, for instance, which outlawed all contacts between converted and unconverted Jews or, even more offensive, Toledo IX canon 17, which required all converts to spend both Christian and Jewish holidays under episcopal supervision. But Julian's concern with Jewish theological speculation in such works as *De comprobatione* and the *Antikeimena* seems deeper and more personal than might be expected from a man who stood two generations away from the religion of his family. He dedicated one of his last works, the widely read and copied *Prognosticon*, to Bishop Idalius of Barcelona, whom he had met at Toledo XV (688), and sent it to him with a Jewish messenger who was received by Idalius with some displeasure.[153] Julian had chosen the Jew to carry the book to his fellow prelate, which suggests that—at least in his maturity—anti-Judaism was

152. Cf. Saitta, *L'antisemitismo*, 76: "Di discendenza giudaica, ma di genitori cristiani, avvertì per tutta la vita il fastidio di un origine che riteneva un peso, ma che tuttavia non gli aveva vietato di percorrere le tappe più prestigiose della carriera ecclesiastica e di divenire il vescovo più potente di Spagna.

"Proprio per volere fare scordare questa sua origine vissuta quasi come una colpa, si sforzò, pervenendo talora a punte di fanatismo quasi ossessivo, di dimostrare la sincerità della propria fede e il proprio zelo antigiudaico . . ."

153. Idalius, *Epistola ad Iulianum* (ed. Hillgarth, 4): "Adveniens namque quidam iudaeus, nomine Restitutus, quasi brutum, ut ita dixerim, animal, materiam lumini congruentem deportans . . ." The "materiam lumini congruentem" is in this case the manuscript of Julian's work. Idalius's insult has a deeper meaning than merely to call his colleague's messenger an ass: as a Jew, and thus the bearer of an ancient and true revelation, the man is like a beast of burden, unable to grasp the value of what it carries. It is remarkable that the Jew bears what seems to be quite unmistakably a baptismal name: Restitutus is the one who has been restored to God and to the true faith. This would be another indication that baptized Jews were, in many ways, still Jews in the Spain of the 680s.

not a personal sentiment but a matter of policy, probably guided by the ambition of converting as many Jews as possible.

Julian would not have needed to maintain a public attitude of anti-Judaic zeal with no basis at all in private conviction. That the HWR had been commissioned by Wamba, or that it formed the first step in the ladder of advancement, is highly probable, but Julian's literary talent, his theological learning, and his exceptional familiarity with classical authors would always have enabled him to thrive in the church of Toledo, where these qualities were prized, and the king's favor could be earned by never standing in the way of his decisions and by formulating the intellectual support and doctrinal justification for them that was expected of the higher clergy. That Julian then or later was sharply conscious of what could be said for and against the keeping of appearances in religion, and particularly where his own situation was concerned, is suggested by *Antikeimena* 2, 60, where the question is how, if Paul tells us in Galatians 5.2 Christ will be of no advantage to the circumcised, it is possible to explain that the Apostle himself, according to Acts 16.3, had let his disciple Timothy submit to circumcision. Julian's answer, based on the strategic notion that scandal (i.e. controversy) is to be avoided within the church, and on the historical consideration that the early Christians were too close to their Jewish origins to dispense comfortably with such a fundamental rite, quotes Augustine to the effect that Paul had honored the ancient custom in Timothy, "who was born of a Jewish mother and a Greek father . . . from prudent counsel and not false dissimulation."[154]

154. PL 96, col. 693: "Utraque prudenti salubrique consilio in principio nascentis Ecclesiae acta sunt, ut et carnalis circumcisio in Christo impleta, praedicante Apostolo, jam cessare deberet, et tamen in primis illis Christianis, qui ex circumcisione crediderant, contra diuturnam consuetudinem non statim carnis circumcisio prohiberetur, ne ex hoc scandalum Ecclesiae nasceretur, sed paulatim persuadendo ad intellectum perfectum duceretur. Sic enim de ejusmodi quaestione in libris contra Faustum beatus disputat Augustinus. Ait enim [Lib. XIX, cap. 17]: 'Primos illos Christianos, qui ex Judaeis crediderant, qui

The years of Julian's professional and literary debut cover the entirety of Wamba's reign. We know less about the king than about the future bishop, but the style and tendency of Wamba's government emerge with clarity from the surviving documents: he is a complex figure and in no way a mere third edition of Chindasvind and Reccesvind, another wilful and authoritarian ruler. For one thing, imitation of Byzantine forms is less conspicuous; Wamba made only moderate use of the imperial epithets beloved of Reccesvind, *"serenissimus,""sacratissimus,"* and the like.[155] More significantly, he passed few though important laws, although it could be said that Reccesvind had preempted him as a legislator. His coinage does display some imperial characteristics: the cruciform scepter, a cross mounted on three or four steps, and the invocations "IN CHRISTI NOMINE" and "IN DEI NOMINE," analogous to Justinian's "IN NOMINE DOMINI DEI NOSTRI JESU CHRISTI."[156] On the other hand, he appears to have had a strong sense of the symbolic importance of the *urbs regia* as center of his kingdom. The Mozarabic chronicle commemorates his restoration of Toledo in 675 and preserves the verse inscription placed at his command over the gates of the city: "With God's help the noble King Wamba raised this city, / extending the celebrated honor of his people" and, on the defensive turrets over the gates, an invocation to the martyrs: "You, holy saints of the Lord, whose presence shines here, / protect this city and people with your accustomed favor."[157]

---

secundum legis veteris praecepta nati erant atque instituti, jusserunt eos apostoli patrium ritum traditionemque servare, et eos quibus hoc opus erat, ut congruerent illorum tarditati moribusque, monuerunt. Inde est quod Timotheum Judaea mater et Graeco patre natum, propter illos ad quos talis cum eo venerat, etiam circumcidit Apostolus (Act. XVI, 1 seq.), atque ipse inter eos morem hujusmodi custodivit, non simulatione fallaci, sed consilio prudenti.'"

155. On *Titulatur,* see Ewig, "Zum christlichen Königsgedanken," 27–28.

156. Cf. Miles, *The Coinage of the Visigoths,* 367–374, and Ewig, "Zum christlichen Königsgedanken," 25–26.

157. *Crónica Mozárabe* 35 (ed. López Pereira, 54): "Erexit factore Deo rex

Many unanswerable questions surround Wamba's deposition in 680, chiefly because no information has survived about the nature and evolution of his power-base in Toledo and how and why it turned against the king so that he could finally be ousted by a bloodless palace coup, without any kind of armed insurrection. At Toledo XII and XIII, the bishops, making a common front with the nobility, provide remedies for the disastrous effects of the military law with no mention of the fact that, for the first time, the clergy had been made to share these obligations. When, years later, Ervig passed a military law of his own (LV IX,2,9), he made the duties and the penalties harsher and more precise, introducing as his only mitigation of Wamba's law a total and silent exception of the clergy. Wamba's two other laws, given in 675, are aimed exclusively at the ecclesiastical establishment: one forbids bishops from seizing or appropriating donations made by private benefactors to churches in their dioceses (LV IV,5,6); the other forbids freedmen of the church, who still owe service to their masters, from marrying free women, whose children would then be numbered among those under the *patrocinium* of the church. If such marriages take place, the children born of them are to become fiscal slaves in the king's service.[158] The evident aim of this ruling is to limit the spread of the church's sphere of patronage, which had been allowed until then to expand at the expense of the state. Toledo XIII canon 6 strikes back by forbidding all slaves and freedmen except those of the state from occupying positions in the palatine office, thus limiting the king's ability, acquired under Chindasvind, to recruit servants loyal only to himself, and avoiding the danger that former servants and freedmen of the nobility and the church might turn against their masters once they came under the protection of the crown.[159] The

---

inclitus urbem / Uuamba sue celebrem protendens gentis honorem." Ibid.: "Vos, sancti domini, quorum hic presentia fulget, / Hanc urbem et plebem solito salvate fabore."

158. See Claude, "Freedmen in the Visigothic Kingdom," 172–173.

159. (Vives, 422): "Multos enim ex servis vel libertis pluri[m]um ex regio

policy changes of the early 680s give us some idea of how Wamba had used his power and, possibly, of why it was taken from him.

This brings us to the night of October 14, 680, the final transaction between Wamba and Julian, after which the king disappears from the stage of history and the bishop enters upon the most succesful period of his career, as primate of Spain, presiding over national councils—from which kings now withdraw after having presented their *tomus*—and authoring prestigious theological works and compilations. The account in the late ninth-century *Chronicle of Alfonso III*, not renowned for credibility, owes its popularity to the melodramatic, highly colored story it provides:

> In the time of King Chindasvind a man of the name of Ardabast came from Greece. The aforesaid man was chased by the emperor from his native country and, crossing the sea, came to Spain. The above-mentioned King Chindasvind received him splendidly and gave him a cousin of his to marry, and from this union a son was born named Ervig. This Ervig, who had been raised in the palace and promoted to the rank of *comes*, possessed by ambition, plotted cunningly against the king. He gave him to drink an herb the name of which is 'spartus,' and immediately the king's memory was lost. When the bishop of the city and the palace nobles—who were loyal to the king and to whom the working of the potion was unknown—saw the king lying there without any memory, moved by pity and so that the king would not pass away without the sacrament [i.e. of penance], they at once administered to him the rite of confession and penance. When the king awoke from the potion and

---

iussu novimus ad palatinum officium fuisse pertractos, qui tamen affectare cupientes sublimitatem honoris quam illis subtrahebat natio offuscatae originis, dum aequales dominis per susceptum palatium officium facti sunt, in necem dominorum suorum vehementius crassaverunt, et quod nefas est dicere, etiam hii qui a dominis suis libertatis beneficio potiuntur ipsi quoque dominis suis regio iussu tortores existunt." The reference to "regio iussu" at the end is remarkably direct.

understood what had happened, he went to a monastery and remained there as a man of God for as long as he lived. He was king
for eight years and one month and lived in the monastery for seven
years and three months.[160]

The story compels disbelief, not only because of its extremely
novelistic character, with a half-Byzantine villain[161] and mysterious
potion of forgetfulness,[162] but because it gets some of the facts
demonstrably wrong. In particular, the statement that Wamba lived
for over seven years as a monk after his deposition is in conflict
with the acts of Toledo XIII, which in 683 already refer to him as
"divae memoriae."[163] The author of the *Chronicle*, in fact, has Wamba
surviving Ervig and—presumably from his monastery—influenc-

160. Textus Rotensis 2 (ed. Gil Fernandez, 116): "Tempore namque Cinda-
suindi regis ex Grecia uir aduenit nomine Ardauasti, qui prefatus uir ab imperatore a patria sua est expulsus mareque transiectu[s] Spania est aduectus. Quem
iam supra factus Cindasuindus rex magnifice suscepit et ei in coniungio con-
subrinam suam dedit, ex qua coniunctionem natus est filius nomine Eruigius.
Quumque prefatus Eruigius palatio esset nutritus et honore comitis sublimatus,
superuia elatus callide aduersus regem est excogitatus. Erban cui nomen est
spartus illi dedit potandam; statimque ei memoria est ablata. Quumque episcopus ciuitatis seu et obtimates palatii qui regis fideles erant, cui penitus causa po-
tionis lateuat, uidissent regem iacentem et memoriam nullam abentem, causa
pietatis commoti, ne rex sine ordine migraret, statimque ei confessionis ordinem seu et penitentie dederunt. Quumque rex a potione surrexit et factum
persensit, ad monasterium perrexit ibique quamdiu uixit in religione permansit.
Fuit in regno annis viii, m.i, et in monasterio uixit annis vii, m. iii."
161. On Visigothic anti-Byzantinism, which dates back to Athanagild and
the imperial occupation of southeastern Spain in 552 and which is expressed in
part through deliberate imitation, see Stroheker, "Westgotenreich und Byzanz."
The unusual name of Ervig's father points to one of the great Alan families in
imperial service.
162. This would not be the first pharmacological mishap to affect a Visigothic ruler: cf. Isidore, *Historia Gothorum* 58 (ed. Mommsen, 291–292), on the
death of Sisebut: "hunc alii proprio morbo, alii immoderato medicamenti
haustu, alii ueneno asserunt interfectum."
163. Tomus (Vives, 412): ". . . divae memoriae praecessoris nostri Wambae
regis temporibus . . ."

ing Egica, Ervig's successor and Wamba's nephew, against Ervig's remaining family.[164] Characteristic of this version is that it blames Ervig, whose accession it denounces as a usurpation,[165] and very pointedly exculpates Julian and the palatine office, adopting their story that they had acted entirely out of compassion and loyalty.

Contemporary and more believable sources provide a report that is narratively less full, presents contradictions or at the very least implausibilities, and appears to compromise Julian and the court nobility: these are the acts of Toledo XII, which met some three months after the events, and the *Laterculus regum Wisigothorum*, usually dated to 710.[166] Both coincide in saying that the king received the sacrament of penance, and the assumption is that since the sacrament conferred the status of penitent on all recipients it was impossible for them to go back to their worldly occupations. As to the circumstances in which the sacrament was administered, the *Laterculus* says nothing at all and the acts, using what appears to be deliberately vague and obscure language, declare in canon 1, immediately after the creed that initiates all conciliar deliberations, that Wamba "was constrained by a chance event of irrevocable necessity" *("inevitabilis necessitudinis teneretur eventu")* and so adopted the ecclesiastical habit and tonsure. According to the acts, a document

---

164. See above note 137.

165. Textus Rotensis (ed. Gil Fernandez, 118): "Post Bambanem Eruigius regnum obtinuit que tirannide sumsit."

166. The similarity of the two following phrases, one used to describe Wamba in *Hist.* 2 and the other for Ervig in Toledo XII canon 1 (Vives, 387) suggests that Julian himself was responsible for the council acts: ". . . Wamba princeps, quem digne principari Dominus voluit, quem sacerdotalis unctio declaravit, quem totius gentis et patriae communio elegit, quem populorum amabilitas exquisivit, qui ante regni fastigium multorum revelationibus celeberrime praedicitur regnaturus." / ". . . hunc solum serenissimum Ervigium principem obsequendum . . . quem et divinum iudicium in regno praeelegit et decessor princeps successurum sibi instituit, et quod superest quem totius populi amabilitas exquisivit." Teillet, "Un coup d'état," 106 note 39, has brought out the significance of these parallel passages.

was signed by the members of the palatine office who were present certifying that the king had received the sacrament. In addition to this letter, which had already been examined by the bishops for authenticity, there were two written communications from Wamba himself, one designating Ervig to be his successor and another, addressed to Julian, instructing him to anoint Ervig. The acts testify that these letters of Wamba too had been checked and authenticated.

If this narrative is true, in the space of one night the fateful sacrament, whose consequences were known to all, was administered, and Wamba proceeded almost immediately to make arrangements for the succession, including the drafting or at least signing of several documents which made it unnecessary for him to appear in public again.[167] The smoking gun, however, is found in canon 2, which follows this account and unfolds an elaborate justification of the irrevocable character of penance received unsolicited and in a state of unconsciousness. The subject had never been discussed before at this length in the Visigothic councils,[168] and its relevance to the specific historical moment is not left implicit: at the end of the canon the bishops issue a decree that "those who, in whatever way, received penance will never again wear the military belt."[169] The military belt, or *cingulum*, was the emblem of military obligation and stood for a ruler's chief function, which Wamba had brilliantly

167. There was perhaps a good practical reason for this: Ziegler, *Church and State*, 116, and Teillet, "Un coup d'état," 103, believe these documents were forged.

168. The larger question of the obligation to honor the sacraments one had received, whether willingly or not, had come up as early as Toledo IV (633), where the council had resolved that those Jews who had been forced to convert to Christianity under Sisebut should remain faithful to the religion that had been imposed on them. Canon 57 (Vives, 211) decrees that they must do so "quia iam constat eos sacramentis divinis adsociatos et chrismate unctos esse et corporis Domini et sanguinis extitisse participes . . ."

169. (Vives, 389): ". . . sed hos qui qualibet sorte poenitentiam susceperint ne ulterius ad militare cinculum redeant religamus."

fulfilled. The connections between canons 1 and 2 could not be more pointed. It is remarkable that no reference is made to a law of Chindasvind, presumably in force, against "those men and women who betray the tonsure and the habit of religion" and which concerns, evidently, the consequences of penance (LV III,5,3). It contains a very clear exception to its strictures which would have made Wamba's penance invalid: "We make those persons immune from the present sentence who enter the order of penance or tonsure when in such violent illness that they neither know that they have received it nor remember asking for it."[170]

A second smoking gun, though less obvious, is Toledo XII canon 6, by which the bishop of the *urbs regia* is empowered to nominate bishops for the other ecclesiastical provinces of Spain. Even then, appointment to these bishoprics remained primarily in the king's hands, and the only ones to lose power by this decree were Julian's fellow metropolitans. This innovation, therefore, might not deserve to be described as a payment or reward from the state to the church for the legitimacy and support it was giving the new ruler.[171] But Ervig is generally thought to have been a weak king, who in seven years convened two national councils and had them pass canons intended to protect his wife and family after his death; it is unlikely that he would have imposed his choices for the episcopate on the church of Spain. Julian, on the other hand, emerged with considerably augmented powers as the founder of the primacy of Toledo, after giving penance to Wamba, authenticating his sup-

---

170. (Ed. Zeumer, 162): "Illos etiam ab hac sententia inmunes efficimus, qui sic invalescente langore ad penitentie vel tonsure pervenerint ordine, ut id se nec accepisse tunc noverint nec petisse meminerint." This clause would appear to correct the specification in Toledo IV canon 17 (Vives, 244–245) that he cannot be made king who has been tonsured or worn the habit of religion ("nullus sub religionis habitu detonsus"). Zeumer, "Geschichte der westgothischen Gesetzgebung III," 617, argues that this provision of the secular law, though still valid, had no impact on canon law.

171. See Hillgarth, *Opera* I, xiii.

posed letters on the succession, anointing Ervig, and presiding over Toledo XII.[172] It is difficult to find no more than a suspicion of foul play here, or to limit Julian's participation to a passive role.[173] And perhaps the most notable irony of the whole affair is that the strongest evidence against Julian comes from his own hand, since he composed, or in any case edited and approved, the acts of the council.

Much must remain conjectural. If a passing—and very brief—unconsciousness of Wamba was involved, this would imply that the coup was carried out on the spur of the moment, by a disaffected clergy and court nobility who profited from a lucky chance, even though given the king's probable age, illness and its manifestations would not have been entirely unforeseen. More improbable is the hypothesis that the king's swoon was induced by a potion or a drug, chiefly on account of the novelistic character of that explanation: once it is given up, the whole idea of a long-standing, carefully planned conspiracy becomes untenable. That the entire episode took place overnight, in the isolation and intimacy of the king's quarters, also argues for a palace intrigue, carried out in Toledo by those close to the ruler and not plotted at a national or even provincial level.

Contradictory and deliberately obscure as these council acts are, they project a narrative of Wamba's fall that can be studied as an alternative to the one in the *Chronicle of Alfonso III*. Two elements of this story correspond to deep-set religious and cultural values of Visigothic Spain. One is the non-negotiable character of penance which, as we have seen, had been the subject of both conciliar and secular legislation. Baptism and penance had been identified as the two sacraments that could not be repeated, and the validity of forced baptism had been emphatically asserted since Toledo IV

172. On the Toledan primacy and its history, see Feige, "Zum Primat der Erzbischöfe von Toledo," esp. 688–691.

173. See note 134 above.

(633).[174] A matching argument about penance remained in force among the clergy, in spite of Chindasvind's exception in favor of unconscious and unwilling penitents. The other element is the legal prestige of *contropatio,* the examination of handwriting, about which Chindasvind, Reccesvind, and later Egica passed comprehensive laws.[175] In the acts of Toledo XII, this practice gives to the authentication of Wamba's last communications the same note of decisive expertise found in the scene in *Iudicium* 6 where Paul and his followers are confronted in court with their signatures on oaths of loyalty to Wamba and with other, treacherous oaths that they had required the people of Gallia to swear. These parallel scenes, though largely implicit and lacking dramatic elaboration, are scripted by the legal culture of seventh-century Spain and cast unexpected light on the functions and meanings of literacy at the time.[176]

By disappearing into a monastery after October 15, 680, and dying at some time in the two years that follow, Wamba brings to an end the story of the relations between the king and his bishop/historian at the court of Toledo. Wamba, of course, is still present in spirit at Toledo XII, and the reactions expressed there to his style of government are, although delayed, a necessary confirmation of what the lack of national councils during his reign had suggested only *e silentio.* Such phrases as "by the unjust decrees of King Wamba" (*"iniustis Wambae principis iussionibus"*) and "the aforesaid prince,

174. On the provisions concerning forced baptism, which was disapproved of in itself, see above note 167. Penance in Visigothic Spain is described in McCarthy, "The Pastoral Practice of the Sacraments of Cleansing."

175. Cf. LV II, 5, 15 (Chindasvind) (ed. Zeumer, 115): "De contropatione manuum, si scriptura vertatur in dubio"; LV II, 5, 16 (Reccesvind) (ibid., 115–116): "De olografis scripturis"; LV II, 5, 17 (Reccesvind) (ibid., 116–117): "De contropatione scripturarum et earum pena solvenda"; LV II, 5, 18 (Egica) (ibid., 117–118): "Ne aliut quis per testem, aliut per scripturam alligare presumat." On these laws and *contropatio* generally see Zeumer, "Zum westgothischen Urkundenwesen," and King, *Law and Society,* 103, note 1, and 110.

176. On the recurrence of *"scriptura"* in Toledo XII canon 1 and its implications, see Teillet, "Un coup d'état," 108 note 47.

acting on a frivolous opinion" *("praedictum principem, consilio levitatis agentem")* in canon 4, which eliminates Wamba's new episcopal sees, are uncommonly bold and confrontational and contrast even with the fairly open language used to criticize Chindasvind at Toledo VIII.

Julian himself was left at the very top of the ecclesiastical hierarchy of Spain, and it is characteristic of his ambition and temperament that he not only reached that place at the summit but made the position itself more powerful than ever before. It is in these years that he wrote his most influential theological works, the *Prognosticon futuri saeculi* and the *De comprobatione sextae aetatis.*[177] Like his teacher Eugenius, he lectured on rhetoric and literature, and the *Ars grammatica* preserved under his name was probably put together by one of his students.[178] An echo of the intemperate and passionate voice that resounds throughout the HWR can still be heard in the *Apologeticum per tribus capitulis,* in which he replied officially to some strictures of Pope Benedict II on formulations Julian had used in a refutation of monotheletism: charging the pope with having read carelessly *("incuriosa lectionis transcursione")* and ending by attributing any further disagreement to hostile and ignorant readers *("si ab ignorantibus aemulis censeatur indocilis"),* the bishop of Toledo appeared to be challenging Rome to a theological battle.[179]

The kingdom Julian and Wamba left behind suffered from a marked weakness and insecurity of the state, a propensity to plots and conspiracies, and unmatched harshness in anti-Jewish legislation. It would be simple-minded to attribute these developments to the clash of two figures with conflicting aims and ambitions. The figures themselves, rather, are representative of a severely shaken

177. Cf. Hillgarth, *Opera* I, xiv–xxi.

178. Cf. ibid., xv.

179. The text was preserved in the acts of Toledo XV (Vives, 453–464), of which it is a part. Cf. Murphy, "Julian of Toledo and the Condemnation of Monotheletism."

system that had thirty years left to go; they express the system, though they cannot be reduced to it. Some elements of the national councils from Toledo XII to Toledo XVII (694) are symptomatic of this final phase. In Toledo XIII (683) the bishops, led by Julian, give back the right to testify, together with all confiscated property, to the followers of Paul (canon 1). They also pass decrees protecting Ervig's descendants and his wife after the king's death. The acts of Toledo XV (688) consist of only two parts in addition to the *tomus* of the new king Egica: first the full text of Julian's reply to the pope in the *Apólogeticum,* then a lengthy consideration and approval of Egica's request to be absolved from the oath that he had sworn to Ervig, his father-in-law, that after his death he would protect his family. The oath is attacked as contrary to the king's obligation to provide equal justice, and annulled. The transaction here should be compared to Reccesvind's appearance at Toledo VIII asking the bishops to release him from the oath that he would maintain the harsh sentences of Toledo VII against traitors and rebels. But whereas Reccesvind only wanted some freedom to negotiate with the nobility, Egica is clearly asking for permission to persecute his predecessor's family, and it is granted.

Untaught by this experience, Egica, at Toledo XVI (693) and XVII (694), has the council pass resolutions protecting his own family (canons 8 and 7 respectively). To put beyond doubt that these decrees are what the king wants, the acts of Toledo XVI, Julian's last council, present them as a compensation for Egica's pious support of further anti-Jewish laws: "our unanimous assembly cannot find anything else with which to repay him."[180] The king must be content with what have generally proved to be useless and easily revoked measures of protection; what the church gets in exchange is considerably more real. Fooled by Egica's apparent vulnerability, Ju-

---

180. (Vives, 506): "Quo circa quoniam pro tot tantisque beneficiis quae multimoda devotio ecclesia Dei vel gentis suae populis prorogare studet, quid aliud illi unanimitas nostra condigne respondeat invenire non praevalet."

lian's immediate successor, Bishop Sisbert of Toledo, led in person a conspiracy against the king. Though perhaps inspired by the assertiveness of Julian, he was arrested, excommunicated, and exiled.[181] When Toledo XVII met in 694, with Egica still in power, it was presided by Felix, Julian's biographer.

181. Cf. *Prosopografía* no. 252.

II. Literature

1. Authorship

The brief *vita* of Julian by Felix, his next-to-immediate successor as bishop of Toledo, lists among his works "likewise a book of history about what happened in Gallia in the time of King Wamba."[1] Unfortunately, this description applies just as well to the entire sequence of four texts as to its second element alone. The *Epistola (Ep.)*, which opens the sequence, is a short letter of challenge sent by the usurper Paul to King Wamba; it is followed by the *Historia* proper *(Hist.)*, the narrative core of the HWR, which begins with the election and accession of Wamba, months before the rebellion broke out. Third comes the *Insultatio (Ins.)*, a highly rhetorical invective addressed to the personified province of Gallia, reviling it for its role in bearing and fostering the original conspiracy, and fourth and last the *Iudicium (Iud.)*, which provides a supplementary account of Paul's uprising and of the open trial of the conspirators held in the vicinity of Nîmes. All four parts can be said to be "about what happened in Gallia in the time of King Wamba," but Felix could easily be talking about the *Hist.* only. The likelihood of this is somewhat strengthened by the fact that the *Hist.* alone has a double incipit, the first part of which refers to Wamba as dead and to Julian as bishop of Toledo and thus, unlike the other headings, must be dated at least eight or ten years after the composition of the *Hist.* in the mid-670s.[2] This incipit would appear to indicate

1. Felix, *Vita* 10 (PL 96, col. 450): "Item librum historiae de eo quod Wambae principis tempore Galliis extitit gestum."
2. Cf. Levison ed., 501 note 1.

that at some point in the early history of the text the *Hist.* circulated by itself, without the *Epistola,* the *Insultatio,* or the *Iudicium,* which
are often listed by scholars as separate works appended to the *Hist.*
Certain features of the *Ep.* and of the *Iud.* suggest that in their original form they may have been genuine documents of the rebellion,
used by Julian of Toledo as sources for the *Hist.,* but not composed
by him. There are indications, however, that even these compositions as they have come down to us were revised by Julian, and that
the sequence of four texts with its connecting headings, with the
single exception of the obviously late first incipit of the *Hist.,* is
very likely Julian's work.

For the *Ep.,* Herwig Wolfram has argued that Paul's adoption of
the title "Flavius," also used by the Visigothic kings in their laws
and official acts, gives the letter a note of authenticity, though he
adds that his calling himself "anointed king" *("rex unctus")* would
seem to betray the hand of Julian by stressing the significance of
unction.[3] More persuasive is Wilhelm Levison's observation that the
letter, with its extreme rhetorical exaggeration and inflated vocabulary (in particular Paul's use of *"opopumpeum grandem"* to refer to himself) is too evidently designed to present the usurper as a boastful
and deluded man to be the work of anyone but Julian.[4] Levison
takes into account features of composition that characterize the *Ep.*
as a whole and seem difficult or impossible to explain away in order
to make the *Ep.* an actual letter of challenge. There would also seem
to be, in the unusual conceit about competing with wild animals, an
echo either of Pliny's panegyric of Trajan or of the short pseudo-
Isidorian *Institutionum Disciplinae,* which quotes Pliny directly and is a
very likely source of inspiration for other passages of the HWR.[5]
These features are too literary and too closely tied to the generic

3. See Wolfram, *Intitulatio* I, 70–71 (and especially p. 71 note 93). "Flavius,"
however, had also become the highest *status nomen* in the late empire, and was
very widely used; cf. Salway, "What's in a Name?" esp. 137–140.

4. Levison ed., 492.

5. On the *Institutionum Disciplinae* see Riché, "L'éducation à l'époque wisi-

models of the *Hist.* for the *Ep.* to be other than Julian's work, or extensively revised by him.

In the same way, there can be little doubt that Julian is the author of the *Insultatio.* The incipit, with its reference to the speaker/author of the piece as a *"vilis storicus,"* identifies him explicitly with the author of the *Hist.* The arraignment of wretched Gallia draws even more strongly than the *Hist.* on the verse and prose panegyrics of late antiquity. Figures of speech of the *Hist.* are completed and elaborated in the *Ins.* For instance, the charge in *Hist.* 5 that Gallia, like an evil mother or nurse, nourished the treasonous limbs it had begotten is matched in *Ins.* 3 by the indignant question why Gallia fostered such disloyalty at all instead of casting it away like a rotting limb. Even the curious trait of quoting anonymous authors is shared with the *Hist.* (e.g. *Ins.* 9: the verses by "a certain wise man"). Unlike the *Ep.*, the *Ins.* could have had no extra-literary function: it is conceived as a rhetorical exercise, as a subjective, emotional complement to the largely factual narrative that precedes it.

There are, on the other hand, powerful reasons to believe that Julian did not write the *Iudicium,* in its original form at least.[6] Although its first chapter is a declamation in the style of the *Ins.*, chapters 2 to 4 repeat the story of Wamba's campaign and victory over the rebels. The account, far more concentrated than that of the *Hist.*, nevertheless adds numerous factual details and particularly names of conspirators not mentioned elsewhere, as required by the judicial perspective that becomes even more pronounced in the final chapters. Certain details suggest that the original document was composed at Nîmes, where the facts of the campaign and the geography of the area would have been more familiar: thus *Hist.* 11 places the capture of Clausurae before the taking of Collioure,

---

gothique," and, more recently, Fontaine, "Quelques observations." The passage from Pliny is given below in note 17.

6. Cf. Levison ed., 491: ". . . a clerico quodam palatino compositum, qui et legis Gothicis saecularis et canonici peritus erat."

which is geographically unlikely and contradicts *Iud.* 3.[7] It seems clear that Julian was not an eyewitness, and these chapters of the *Iud.* may have served as the basis for his reconstruction in the *Hist.*[8] Chapters 5 to 7 provide an important factual supplement to the *Hist.* by giving particulars of the trial of the conspirators, barely mentioned in *Hist.* 27: "and after that he is judged with the others before the whole army." In addition to the accusatory and punitive rhetoric of chapter 1, other details indicate that the original document underwent a literary revision, most likely by Julian. The adjective *"maturatus"* in chapter 1 (*"maturatam perniciem"*) echoes both *Hist.* and *Ins.*,[9] and the phrase "the many lands that lie between us" (*"tot interiacentibus terris"*) in *Iud.* 3, already used in *Ins.* 8, goes back to Orosius (*Historiae* 2, 11, 5: *"tantis spatiis maris terraeque interiacentibus"*), the author most frequently—though anonymously—cited in the HWR, but it is also quoted by Braulio of Zaragoza (*epistola* 21: *"tot interiacentibus terris tantisque interiectis marinis spatiis"*), who had been the teacher of Eugenius II, Julian's own master.[10]

2. The Four-Text Sequence

We must imagine, then, Julian revising one (*Iud.*) and possibly even two texts (*Iud.* and *Ep.*), perhaps from a documentary file he had used to compose the *Historia* proper, and then arranging them with the *Historia* and *Insultatio* to form an unusual series. The *Ep.* opens it with a startling and untraditional flash-forward, taking the

7. Cf. Levison ed., 511 note 4, and Pérez Sánchez, *El ejército*, 152.

8. Teillet, *Des Goths*, 603: ". . . le texte qui a servi de trame au récit de Julien, le *Iudicium* ou Jugement de Paul, rédigé sans doute en Gaule Narbonnaise lors des événements de 673, et qui nous a été conservé." See also García López, "La cronología," 128 note 21.

9. Cf. "tyrannidem celeriter maturatam," *Hist.* 7 (quoting Orosius); "maturatum iter," *Hist.* 15; "nisi maturato sui cordis . . . consilio," *Hist.* 27; "maturate tibi occurrit," *Ins.* 7.

10. Orosius (ed. Arnaud-Lindet, vol. 1, 107); Braulio, *Epistolario* (ed. Riesco Terrero, 108).

rebellion and Wamba's expedition against it as accomplished facts, assuming them and issuing an ornate challenge full of obscure ironies without explaining any of the circumstances that have brought Paul and Wamba to this pass. The brief missive, written in the second person, is followed by the third-person narrative of the *Historia*, the factual, yet formal and epically stylized account of a single uprising. Coming after the *Historia*, the *Insultatio* brings a sharp shift from narrative to rhetorical performance or oration and from third person back to second. There is also an important break with the perspective of the *Historia*, which had focused blame, and therefore attention, on the person of Paul; the *Insultatio*, by contrast, redirects its anger to the personified province of Gallia, where the conspiracy first blossomed, initially without Paul. The sequence closes with the *Iudicium* and a return to narrative, but this time in the first person plural of an anonymous member of Wamba's entourage, and the distinctively official and legalistic language of a public statement, filling in gaps left by the account of the *Historia*. The headings that bind these four texts to each other reflect their discontinuity and ideological oscillation. They share some of the basic vocabulary of the texts: *"perfidia"* and *"perfidus," "tyrannus," "tyrannis,"* and *"tyrannice."* The *Ep.* is the only one of the four to have an incipit and no explicit. The *Hist.* presents itself as "The story of King Wamba, about his expedition and victory . . ." but closes with the explicit "Here ends the story of Paul," which agrees with the sense of many readers that by the end of its narrative the pathetic and doomed usurper has become a more present and real figure than the rightful king. The "humble historian" *("vilis storicus")* arraigning Gallia in the incipit of the *Ins.* gives way to "wretched Gallia" *("vilis provincia Gallia")* in the explicit. The *Iud.* is, once again, directed against the human leaders of the rebellion and thus "pronounced against the treachery of usurpers" *("in tyrannorum perfidia promulgatum")*. It, together with the entire sequence, ends happily or fortunately *("explicit feliciter")*, even though the rebels had persuaded their followers to refer to Wamba as an "ill-omened king" (*"rex infaustus"*).

Unusual and even baffling as its form is, the HWR is not wholly lacking in analogues and potential models, even in the literature of Visigothic Spain, with its relative dearth of narrative compositions. Isidore of Seville's *Historia Gothorum*, the long version of which can be dated to 624 or 625, displays a number of common points. It starts with a second-person address to a personified Spain presented first as a mother and praised extravagantly as such, and then as the bride of the Gothic nation. The actual history then follows, a laconic third-person account of the Gothic people from their mythical origins in Central Europe to the conquest and settlement of Spain and the series of their kings. The scope here is of course much vaster than that of the HWR, but the chief difference lies in Isidore's extreme *brevitas* and his systematic avoidance of dramatic narrative. A brief *Recapitulatio* provides a concise but flattering portrait of the national character of the Goths, which cannot be considered narrative, as it remains static and unhistorical. Finally, two chapters, *Historia Vandalorum* and *Historia Sweborum*, derived directly and almost verbatim from earlier authors, are added to the series.[11]

A different set of analogies to the HWR can be found in a work composed some twenty-five or thirty years after it, the so-called autobiographical writings of Valerius of Bierzo, a hermit domiciled in the wilds of Galicia in the very late Visigothic period.[12] The parts and their order, less uniformly vouched for by

11. An additional trait shared with the HWR is the influence of Orosius, here too the most frequently cited author by far. On his influence in Visigothic Spain see Hillgarth, "The *Historiae* of Orosius in the Early Middle Ages," esp. 166–167.

12. Aherne, *Valerius of Bierzo*, 33–34, can give no certain or even approximate date for them. Collins, "The 'Autobiographical' Works of Valerius of Bierzo," 435, suggests from internal chronology that "these 'autobiographical' works, if we may still so call them, were composed late on in Valerius's career, and this is likely to have been in the period c. 695–700 A.D."

the manuscript tradition than those of Julian's work, are the following: three texts in first-person narrative prose, chapters of an account of Valerius's spiritual trials, visions, and temptations, entitled "Story of My Sufferings" *("Ordo querimoniae")*, "Further Account from My First Conversion" *("Replicatio sermonum a prima conversione")*, and "What Is Left of My Sufferings" *("De superioris querimoniis residuum")*, the last a particularly incoherent and very likely incomplete text. In addition, binding these prose narratives in by no means linear sequence, there are three acrostic poems *(epitamera)*, prayer-like compositions in the first person, the first two of which connect the *Ordo querimoniae* and the *Replicatio* while the last one follows the *Residuum.* All texts have elaborate incipits but no explicits. The names of the prose sections have been shown to derive from judicial practice and represent various formal statements made in the course of a trial.[13] Valerius speaks as if standing before God's tribunal to defend himself and denounce his enemies. Due perhaps to his limited literary skill, the narrative parts sound very much alike and fail to convey a sense of different moments in a trial. Their legal titles recall the *Iudicium,* but the names of the elements of the HWR sequence, *Epistola, Historia, Insultatio,* as well as *Iudicium,* emphasize the different literary genres of these texts and thus the sheer formal variety of the work as a whole.

The analogies between Isidore's *Historia Gothorum,* the HWR, and Valerius's writings are incomplete and inconclusive; it is unlikely that any one of them served as a model for the others. And yet we cannot dismiss them as random similarities: there is too much in common for these shared features to be purely accidental, especially in the Spain of the seventh century. The most plausible explanation for these resemblances would seem to be that they go back to a tradition of prose sequences, perhaps characteristically Visigothic, the aim of which was rhetorical and generic diversity. In

13. As pointed out in Collins, "The 'Autobiographical' Works," 432–434.

these sequences, the order of the texts served to sharpen contrasts and to frame individual sections with formally divergent treatments of the same subject.

3. Sources and Models

a. *Epistola Pauli Perfidi*

It is not possible to tell whether the *Epistola* that opens the HWR is a pure invention, intended to start the sequence *in medias res* and provide a hostile version of the usurper's voice at the time of his prosperity, elated and bombastic, or whether, for all its excess and exaggeration, it is based on a letter actually sent by Paul to Wamba. This second possibility is supported by the presence of a further letter of Paul quoted later in the *Historia* (*Hist.* 11), this one addressed to Amator, bishop of Gerona. From *Iud.* 6 we know that among the many documents presented at the trial of the conspirators were the oaths of fidelity to Paul that had been signed by his followers; these might have been part of a file put together by members of the palatine office bringing together documents of the rebellion to use in the arraignment. Such a collection could have included Paul's letters, and might later have served Julian as a source.

Although very different, the two letters have points in common, including phrasing: "*tu festinas* **ad nos venire**" in the *Ep.* and "*rex cum exercitu* **ad nos venire** disponet" in the letter to Amator, and what seem to be sarcastic references to the heart as seat of the emotions. The *Ep.* asks Wamba whether "[your] heart rises in self-assurance" ("*ascendit* **cor tuum** *ad confortationem*") only to enjoin him in that case "then come down to Clausurae" ("*descende usque ad Clausuras*"), where his rival intends to confront him. In his letter to the bishop, Paul assumes that Amator may be troubled by news of Wamba's imminent arrival and pleads "but do not let your heart be shaken by this" ("*sed* **cor tuum** *ex hoc non conturbetur*"), using a scriptural phrase (2 Kings 6.11: "*Conturbatumque est cor regis Syriae pro hac re*"), perhaps pointedly, as this king of Syria was an enemy of Israel.

Paul's letter also preserves a characteristic feature of letters of challenge in that it appoints a meeting-place for the two armies: "then come down to Clausurae, for there you will find a mighty champion with whom you may legitimately fight."[14] The emphatic *"ibi"* recalls the message sent by Riciarius, king of the Sweves, to Theoderic II of the Visigoths according to Jordanes: "If you grumble against me because I am on the move, I will come to Toulouse where you reside. Wait there, if you can."[15]

The literary sources of the *Epistola* have not been pinned down with certainty, but they matter because—surprisingly for such a short text—they may offer clues to the sources of the HWR as a whole.[16] Whether they do so depends on the curious passage in which Paul describes Wamba, in the conditional, as competing with wild beasts in properly animal abilities: "If you have already traversed the harsh and uninhabitable cliffs of the mountains, if you have already broken deep into the forest by narrow passes, like the lion of mighty breast, if you have already utterly defeated the goats at running, the deer at springing, and the bears and wild pigs in voracity, if you have already disgorged the venom of snakes and vipers . . ." This unusual motif echoes, ironically but quite precisely, Pliny's description, in his panegyric of Trajan, of the emperor's athletic pursuits: "What other relaxation is there for you but to ex-

14. ". . . descende usque ad Clausuras; nam ibi invenies opopumpeum grandem, cum quo possis legitime concertare." The use of "legitime" this early in the sequence to denote a value that matters to Wamba introduces the central theme of the HWR and, whether placed here by Julian or by Paul himself, puts the entire conflict under the sign of legitimacy and its function as a claim in the struggle for power.

15. *Getica* 44 (ed. Mommsen, 116–117): "'si hic murmuras et me venire causaris, Tolosam, ubi tu sedes, veniam; ibi, si vales, resiste.'" Riciarius had tried to move into Visigothic teritory from his traditional seat in Gallaecia and Lusitania, and was eventually defeated and killed.

16. Levison (ed., 492) would not commit himself beyond Orosius: "Ut autem verum scriptores antiquos legisse credendus est, et si praeter Orosium certa vestigia apud eum non indagavi . . ."

plore the forest, chase wild beasts from their dens, climb the highest peaks of mountains, and tread on bristling crags without a helping hand or a guide to your steps, while also visiting the sacred groves and encountering the gods? Once this was the training, these the pleasures of youth, these the exercises by which future leaders were shaped: to compete in swiftness with the fleetest beasts, in strength with the boldest, in cleverness with the most cunning . . ."[17] Little or nothing is quoted verbatim, but the ideas are identical, with the single difference that what in Pliny is honest praise appears in the *Ep.* as deliberate bombast, with the suggestion that the elderly Wamba will possibly boast of such prowess, of which he is wholly incapable.[18] The Pliny passage is quoted exactly, however, in a text of controverted origin, the short treatise on the education of young noblemen known as the *Institutionum Disciplinae* and once attributed to Isidore of Seville,[19] and there the borrowing is preceded immediately by a list of the sports a young hero must practice that is taken from Sallust's account of the youth of Jugurtha, the Numidian usurper and tyrant.[20] Remarkable here is that the only models or sources of inspiration that have been seriously considered so far for the HWR as a whole are the Latin panegyrics of antiquity, in prose and verse—and Pliny's panegyric is the first and oldest in

17. *Traiani panegyricus* 81, 1–2 (ed. Durry, 171): "quae enim remissio tibi nisi lustrare saltus, excutere cubilibus feras, superare immensa montium iuga et horrentibus scopulis gradum inferre nullius manu, nullius vestigio adiutum atque inter haec pia mente adire lucos et occursare numinibus? Olim haec experientia iuuentutis, haec voluptas erat, his artibus futuri duces imbuebantur, certare cum fugacibus feris cursu, cum audacibus robore, cum callidis astu, . . ."

18. The rhyme *edomuisti*/*evomuisti* ("you have tamed" / "you have vomited") is possibly there to mark the intended irony, like the word-play on *ascendit*/*descende* later on, which concerns the swelling of Wamba's spirits, *"cor tuum."*

19. The attribution is found in one of the two manuscripts of the work, the Paris ms.; see Beeson, "Isidore's *Institutionum Disciplinae*," and Fontaine, "Quelques observations."

20. *Bellum Iugurthinum* 6, 1 (ed. Rolfe, 140): ". . . equitare, iaculari, cursu cum aequalibus certare . . ."

the Gallic corpus of *Panegyrici latini*, the chief repository of prose works in that genre—and the historical monographs of Sallust, with their focus on single uprisings and their interest in conspiracy and usurpation.[21] The *Institutionum Disciplinae* counts now as pseudo-Isidorian, but even the most critical and detailed analysis, which places it speculatively in Carolingian or pre-Carolingian Gaul, attributes the text nevertheless to the Visigothic diaspora into the Frankish realms after 711.[22] It is clear then that the *Institutionum Disciplinae*, in its use of Pliny and Sallust side by side, reflects dominant influences in the literary culture of Visigothic Spain, and that modern attempts to place Julian of Toledo's unusual work in a literary and historical tradition have not been off-track. The alternative of Sallust and the panegyrics cannot be solved by looking at the brief *Epistola*, but the elements of the problem have been established from the very opening of the sequence.

If the ironic tone of the *Ep.* remains unclear in the end, it is perhaps because Paul's letter takes on a double task that is hard to perform neatly in one greeting and two sentences. On the one hand, it must characterize the writer as arrogant and delusional (hence the title he gives himself, the far-fetched vocabulary and literary allusions), on the other he must appear to be mocking Wamba while keeping to the traditional formula of a challenge (i.e. "I will wait

21. Teillet, "L'*Historia Wambae*," is the fundamental statement on the panegyric as model; Collins, "Julian of Toledo and the Education of Kings," 12, argues that the work "[i]s also not, in the formal sense, a panegyric," perhaps limiting the formal sense to a very few generic traits, and points (ibid., 12–13) to Sallust, and specifically the *Bellum Iugurthinum*, as a preferable model.

22. Cf. Fontaine, "Quelques observations," 653: "Il semble donc que ces deux analyses paléographiques, sans nous permettre de longues spéculations sur l'histoire du texte, a fortiori sur sa provenance, nous autorisent néanmoins a tourner desormais nos regards de l'Espagne vers les Pyrénées, voire au delà, en direction de la *Francia* carolingienne ou précarolingienne. Il suffira de rappeler l'importance de la diaspora wisigothique, dans l'Europe d'après 711, pour concevoir qu'une telle perspective n'est pas incompatible avec les quelques affinités isidoriennes de la culture de notre auteur; . . ."

for you here" or "Wait for me there"). Wamba is of course not a young prince amusing himself with sports, and Paul disfigures the original conceit by making him compete with bears and boars in voracity and with serpents in venomousness.[23]

b. *Historia* and *Insultatio*

The author most frequently cited by Julian, though never by name, is Orosius. He is quoted repeatedly in the *Historia* and *Insultatio*, and at least once in the *Iudicium*. The late antique genre of *historia* is strongly defined by its Orosian outlook on world history.[24] And yet Orosius, though indisputably a source, and for far more than just the phrases identified by Levison in his notes to the HWR, has never been thought a possible model for the design of either the *Historia* or the *Insultatio* as wholes. The immense, world-historical scope of his work could not have inspired Julian's closeup of a short-lived rebellion, with its careful tracing of the origins, unfolding, and conclusion of the uprising and its dramatic recreation of decisive moments. In addition, the characteristic insistence of Orosian *historia* on the leaders of church and state as joint guides of the Christian community is ignored in the HWR, if not roundly contradicted. The *Ars grammatica* now attributed to a student or students of Julian's, composed or compiled after he had become bishop of Toledo in 680, quotes numerous poets, and especially Vergil, but neither Sallust nor the panegyrics. It is reassuring that it does not quote Orosius either, and the explanation may be that in his teaching Julian chose to draw grammatical examples mainly from literature in verse.[25]

23. This is possibly a sarcastic inversion of Pliny's "cum callidis astu" (see above note 17).

24. The late antique and early medieval tradition of *historia* is best described in Werner, "Gott, Herrscher und Historiograph."

25. See the index of authors cited in *Ars Iuliani episcopi Toletani* (ed. Maestre Yenes, 243–244).

A passage in *Hist.* 19 has long been considered a quotation from the *Bellum Catilinae.*[26] Describing the battlefield after the final encounter between Catiline's forces and the armies of the republic led by Marcus Petreius, Sallust writes: "Catiline however was found far from his men among the corpses of his enemies, still breathing slightly and retaining in his face that ferocity of spirit that he had while alive."[27] Julian draws the following picture of the streets of Nîmes towards the end of the siege: "One could see the bodies of men lying on the streets of the city, with a still menacing face and a savage ferocity, as if standing yet among the troops . . ." The basic idea of a face that remains fierce in death is indeed the same; otherwise the *Historia* echoes Sallust only in a few quite common words: *"voltu"* and *"vultu," "ferocitate"* and *"ferociamque animi,"* and both pasages can be classified as instances of the topos of landscape after a battle of which many other specimens might be cited.[28] Manitius pointed out long ago that Julian's "they open a path for themselves by the sword" (*"viam sibi ferro aperiunt"*) (*Hist.* 18) was "echt sallustisch," thinking no doubt of *"ferro iter aperiundum est"* (*Bellum Catilinae* 58, 7), but the phrase appears to have been a commonplace and can be found elsewhere, e.g. in an anonymous panegyric of

26. Cf. Levison, 517 note 3.

27. *Bellum* Catilinae 61, 4 (ed. Rolfe, 126): "Catilina vero longe a suis inter hostium cadavera repertus est, paululum etiam spirans ferociamque animi, quam habuerat vivos, in voltu retinens."

28. There are numerous examples in the panegyrics; see for instance, the anonymous panegyric of Constantius Chlorus presented at Trier in 297, chapter 16, 3–4 (*Panégyriques*, vol. 1, 95): "Omnes enim illos, ut audio, campos atque colles non nisi taeterrimorum hostium corpora fusa texerunt. Illa barbara aut imitatione barbariae olim cultu uestis et prolixo crine rutilantia, tunc uero puluere et cruore foedata et in diuersos situs tracta, sicuti dolorem ulnerum fuerant secuta, iacuerunt . . ." See also in Pacatus's oration in praise of Theodosius, chapter 34, 2–3 (*Panégyriques*, vol. 3, 101): ". . . tegit totos strages una campos continuisque funeribus cuncta late operiuntur. Iam qui ad muros differenda morte properauerant aut fossas cadaueribus aequabant aut obuiis sudibus induebantur aut portas quas eruptione patefecerant morte claudebant."

Constantine: "had you not opened a path for yourself by slaughter" ("*nisi tibi uiam caedibus aperuisses*").[29]

Aside from these possible quotations, however, there are good
grounds for seeing Sallust's monographs, and in particular the *Bellum Catilinae*, as the fundamental model followed by Julian in the
Hist. In the first place, Sallust's format, announced by the program-
matic decision to tell Rome's history "*carptim*," i.e. "in parts" or "in
sections," would account best for the limited scope of the *Hist*.,
which is otherwise unexampled in early medieval historiography.[30]
In the second place, after a few chapters on the value of historical
writing (*Catiline* 1–4, *Iugurtha* 1–4), which match *Hist*. 1 rather closely, Sallust's texts are, like Julian's, narrative throughout, without the
many discursive passages that often make up the greater part of
panegyrics. Finally, in their monographic structure *Catiline* and
Iugurtha share a highly specific device of composition with the *Historia*. Both begin their narratives with sections that can be considered the prehistory of the conflicts that will follow, but remain
clearly distinct from them. In the *Bellum Catilinae*, these are the chapters on the milieu of Catiline and his associates and on the political
and financial pressures that drove them to conspire against the state
(roughly, chapters 5–19); in the *Bellum Iugurthinum* they are the chapters on the dynastic troubles of the royal house of Numidia, King
Micipsa's adoption of his nephew Jugurtha, and the latter's eventual usurpation (chapters 5–12). These sections are discontinuous in
time with the central events, and do not share the emphasis of the
ensuing narratives on military and political events at a national and
international level. What they allow Sallust to do is to thematize

29. Cf. Manitius, *Geschichte*, vol. 1, 131 note 2, and the anonymous panegyric
of Constantine presented in 313, chapter 9 (*Panégyriques*, vol. 2, 131).

30. *Bellum Catilinae* 4, 2 (ed. Rolfe, 8). On the *Iugurtha* as "deliberate fragment," see Levene, "Sallust's *Jugurtha*: An 'Historical Fragment.'" The author's
contention that "the reader is invited to focus his attention away from the
writer's 'fragment,' and direct it instead towards the putative unwritten whole"
(p. 53) could by no means be applied to Julian's *Historia*.

certain features or qualities that are dominant in them and then to project these by way of interpretation on the monograph as a whole. This is especially evident in the *Catiline*, where the rebellion is presented, in the light of the introductory chapters, as a symptom of the decline of republican society, which is shown to be rotting from the head, i.e., starting from the upper classes.[31] Something very close to this can be found in *Hist.* 2–4, chapters that describe events that preceded the rebellion in Gallia by up to six months, without connecting them with what follows in any textually explicit manner. Julian's own incipit for the *Historia* identifies it as being about Wamba's campaign and victory and says nothing about his election and his unction in Toledo, which are the subject of this introductory section. The juxtaposition of chapters 2–4 and 5–30, however, of the sacred formalities that define Wamba's legitimacy to the account of his expedition and its success, allows Julian to project throughout his narrative of the campaign an interpretation of the events as the clash between legitimacy and usurpation (*tyrannis*), with a foreseeable outcome. A striking difference, on the other hand, may be found in the fact that, whereas Sallust tells a great deal about who Catiline and Jugurtha were before they came in conflict with the Roman republic, Julian, pointedly, has not a single word of information about Wamba before he became king or about Paul before he was sent to Gallia.

The second term of the alternative, panegyrics, covers a large number of texts. Prose panegyrics are represented chiefly by the Gallic corpus of twelve *panegyrici latini*, with their strong ties to the fourth-century rhetorical schools of Autun and Bordeaux, and may be considered part of the shared literary, legal, and religious culture

31. See Giancotti, *Strutture delle monografie di Sallustio e di Tacito*, and Steidle, *Sallusts historische Monographien*, 1–16. Cf. Steidle, 4: "Auf diese Weise entsteht eine enge gedankliche Verbindung von Exkurs und folgende Erzählung, denn es ist geradezu ein Element der Erzählung, nämlich die allgemeine Charakteristik der Mitverschworenen, im Exkurs vorweggenommen; . . ."

of Southern Gaul and Spain in the late empire.[32] To these must be added verse panegyrics, which constitute almost a different genre, equipped with an elaborate allegorical and mythological apparatus and often conceived along epic lines: here the productions of Claudian and Sidonius, and Corippus's sixth-century panegyric of Justin the Younger are especially important.[33] The discursive nature of panegyrics, shaped as it is by the imperatives of performance and rhetorical display, would seem to make these works an unlikely inspiration for the narrative *Historia*, if not for the *Insultatio*. The later prose panegyrics, however, show a marked evolution towards narrative form, and works in verse follow a similar development prompted by their epic pretensions.[34] Many, though not all, of these compositions dramatize the clash between the subject of the oration and a usurper or other rival in the struggle for power. Particularly interesting among the works in prose are the panegyrics of Constantine delivered in 310 (conflict with Maximian), 313 (Maxentius), and 321 (Maxentius again), and even more so Pacatus's panegyric of Theodosius of 389, which gives a full account of the emperor's conflict with the usurper Maximus. Of the orations in verse, Claudian's panegyric on the consulship of Stilicho, recited in Milan and Rome early in 400, and the one on the sixth consulship of Honorius, presented in Rome in 404, offer a highly dramatic narrative of Stilicho's dealings with Alaric. Other productions of

32. See Matthews, *Western Aristocracies*, chapters 6 and 12.

33. Other prose compositions, such as Ennodius of Pavia's panegyric of Theoderic and the remains of Cassiodorus's orations, have less to offer as possible generic models for the HWR or the *Hist.* alone. On them, see McCormack, "Latin Prose Panegyrics," 187–192.

34. Cf. McCormack, "Latin Prose Panegyrics," 186: "Description, rather than narrative in the historical manner, was particularly suitable for panegyrics, the more so if it could evoke not only a visual experience in the imagination, but could also bring to mind works of imperial art and serve as a kind of commentary on them. However, the orators of the late fourth century returned to narrative in the historical manner: they spoke about facts and events rather than states of affairs and tableaux."

Claudian, also obvious vehicles for the glorification of Stilicho, are framed as mini-epics rather than panegyrics, but they must also be taken into consideration. The 398 *De bello Gildonico* on the defeat of the Moor Gildo, and the 402 *De bello Gothico,* on the defeat of Alaric at Pollentia earlier that year, show that foreign enemies—since neither Gildo nor Alaric could be counted as a usurper or a rival of the emperor—could nevertheless be characterized along the lines of the *tyrannus.* In one important respect at least these episodes provide a closer match for Julian's account of the struggle with Paul than do the works of Sallust. Neither the *Catiline* nor the *Jugurtha* singles out one representative of Roman greatness and legitimacy to stand in opposition to the conspirator/usurper. Instead, Sallust brings on stage several great men from senate and army to confront each of these enemies of Rome (e.g. Cicero, Cato, and Caesar vs. Catiline). The panegyrics, on the other hand, as is their nature, reduce the conflict to two figures, a simple binary opposition of the splendid and noble subject of the oration and his rival, destitute of any claims on which to ground his ambition.

A crucial scene of the *Hist.*, the refusal of imperial power or *recusatio imperii* (*Hist.* 2), can be matched in the panegyrics, where such episodes are frequent, but in the nature of things not in Sallust's republican histories.[35] Julian's portrayal of the usurper *in extremis,* abandoned by his followers, driven mad by Providence, and waiting every minute to be betrayed and handed over by his own people, can also be paired easily and in detail with episodes in many of the verse and prose panegyrics.[36] Claudian's two ferocious poems of invective, the *In Rufinum* of 397 and the *In Eutropium* of 399, against the praetorian prefect and the chamberlain of the Eastern Empire

---

35. Cf. Wallace-Hadrill, *"Civilis princeps,"* 37: "Equally important, there is nothing republican about the practice of refusal. Honours were fought for tooth and nail and did not fall into the laps of the unwilling."

36. Sallust's description of Jugurtha's increasing guilt and paranoia (*Bellum Iugurthinum* 62, 71–72), far more realistic and psychological, shows a wholly different approach to a comparable subject.

respectively, also repay study. These are works closely akin to panegyric: both glorify Stilicho at the expense of their subjects and in
general follow a biographical structure similar to that of the panegyric, replacing good qualities with slander.[37] Claudian's invectives,
which make a rich use of the mythological and allegorical conven-
tions of his other works, can explain what the *Insultatio* is doing
alongside the *Historia*, as a Sallustian model plainly cannot.

Many elements of the HWR in vocabulary, imagery, thematic
and scenic repertory can be traced back to panegyrics and related
forms, but these few will suffice to indicate that these orations and
poems of praise and vilification constitute a real alternative to the
Sallustian monographs. An especially interesting consequence is
that the case for a controlling influence of panegyrics would support a late-antique rather than a classical inspiration for Julian's
composition. Of course, the alternatives are in no way mutually exclusive: we should assume that Julian of Toledo knew Sallust,
whose works were among the standard schoolroom texts of the early middle ages.[38] The question is only the extent to which they in-
fluenced the Toledan cleric's single venture into historiography.

c. *Iudicium*

In the language of seventh-century Spanish legislation, the use
of *"iudicium"* to mean the written account of a judicial sentence is
well established, as is the obligation of judges to make copies of
such records available to both parties in a case of any importance.[39]

37. See Levy, "Claudian's *In Rufinum*," esp. 57–58; Cameron, *Claudian*, 83–84;
and Long, *Claudian's "In Eutropium*," 90–96, on how the panegyric uses invective
to characterize the enemies of its hero, and particularly the *tyrannus*.

38. See Smalley, "Sallust in the Middle Ages." On Sallust's influence on the
characterization of conspirators and related types in late antique literature, see
Courcelle, "Le jeune Augustin, second Catilina," and, with special relevance to
the Latin literature of Spain, Fontaine, "L'affaire Priscillien, ou l'ère des nouveaux Catilina."

39. Cf. for instance LV 2, 1, 25 (Chindasvind) (ed. Zeumer, 71): ". . . iudex,

Many features of the *Iudicium* are barely removed from the language and organization of the court document on which it is based: the insistence on treason or *perfidia* (in chapter 1 alone "guilty of breaking their oath of loyalty," "ill-fated treason displayed itself openly," "broke the bond of his voluntary oath," "violating his own spontaneous promise of loyalty"), the dogged enumeration of Paul's accomplices, listing many more than are mentioned in the *Hist.* (cf. *Iud.* 3 and 4), the pedantic quotation of laws from Reccesvind's code and canons from council acts (*Iud.* 7) in contrast to Julian's deliberately casual attribution of citations to "a wise man" in his own texts (cf. *Hist.* 9 and 26, *Ins.* 9), for example.

That such a document really éxisted is indicated, as mentioned above, by the abundance of information contained in the *Iud.* in comparison with the longer *Hist.* Characteristic of the original author of the *Iud.* is his special indignation at the rebels' custom of referring to Wamba as an "ill-starred king" *("infaustus rex")*, about which Julian, in the *Hist.*, has not a word to spare.[40] That the original document was written some time before the HWR as a whole was put together is suggested by its references to blinding as a mitigation of the death penalty, which reflect the options left by a law of Chindasvind,[41] where *Hist.* 27 and 30 speaks only of decalvation, the sentence finally applied.[42] Julian drew not only the basic outline

---

presentibus utrisque partibus, duo iudicia de re discussa conscribat, que simili textu et suscriptione roborata litigantium partes accipiant."

40. Cf. *Iud.* 2: ". . . ut gloriosum domnum nostrum Wambanem principem infaustum regem nominare auderet, . . ." and *Iud.* 6: ". . . infaustum regem iamdictum, gloriosum domnum nostrum Wambanem regem, ut supra praemissum est, in ipsis conditionibus nominantes . . ."

41. Cf. *Iud.* 1: ". . . quibus ex clementia princeps dederit vivere, effosionem luminum non evadant, . . ." and *Iud.* 7: "Quodsi forsam eis a principe condonata fuerit vita, non aliter quam evulsis luminibus reserventur, ut vivant."

42. Unlike García López, "La cronología," however, I would not therefore conclude that decalvation implies the use of Ervig's revision of Chindasvind's law, since it was used to punish usurpers in Spain long before Chindasvind (see above, "History," at note 96).

of his narrative from this source, but also an occasional scene with its motivation: Bishop Gumildus of Maguelone flees his city when he sees it encircled by land and sea (*Hist.* 13 and *Iud.* 4). Julian's refashioning of the document, very slight if we keep in mind that he fails to correct a misattributed scriptural quotation in *Iud.* 1 (Isaiah for Jeremiah) is apparent in diction and phrasing, but also perhaps in certain rhetorical embellishments applied to judicial enactments of the text, such as the naming of witnesses in *Iud.* 1, which is transferred to the earth and the sky: "The earth, ravaged by their destructions, is witness to what we say; the sky is a witness too . . ." No other record of a political trial like this one is extant with which the *Iudicium* might be compared directly.

In an important study of Visigothic political assemblies published in 1946, Claudio Sánchez-Albornoz made a mistaken and surprising assumption that, fortunately, appears to have had no impact on later scholarship on the subject.[43] According to him, the trial of the rebels described in *Iud.* 5–7 took place after Wamba's triumphant return to the *urbs regia* and hence in Toledo and with Julian as an eyewitness. This would make Julian the sole author of the *Iud.* and eliminate the need for a former documentary source. It is not easy to guess the eminent scholar's reasons for reading the HWR in this manner, as if the sequence of texts followed a linear chronology and the *Iudicium,* coming after the *Historia,* must needs refer to subsequent events, and as if there had been two trials, one near Nîmes "before the whole army" (*Hist.* 27) and another in Toledo "in the presence of the entire army" (*Iud.* 5). Wamba had allowed the army to disband while still in Gallia (*Hist.* 29: ". . . while still in Gallia, staying in a place called Canaba, he rewarded the entire army with the pleasing news that they had evacuated the region successfully and released them all at once, from that very place"), and the reason is presumably that the trial had already taken place.

---

43. Sánchez-Albornoz, "El aula regia," 11–12.

He clearly had no plans to reconvene his forces in Toledo in the immediate future.

4. Words and Images

The most salient formal quality of the HWR is its abstraction. Taking as it does most of its elements from earlier works that reflect a Roman and imperial reality, it reduces them to almost purely conceptual values and representations that permeate the text and color the narrative by virtue of their small number and high frequency. Most pervasive is the effect of certain words and groups of images: though distributed unequally in the various sections of the HWR, they occur so often and in so many different combinations that they function as a running interpretation of the events and arguments presented by Julian, operating almost subliminally to condition the reception of his work. Their very abstraction makes it difficult to distinguish words from images, since both often come down to simple nouns. The crucial words are terms with legal or political meanings and no sensory connotations: *"perfidia"*/*"perfidus,"* with the related terms *"infidelitas"* and *"periurium,"* and *"tyrannus"*/ *"tyrannis."*

"Perfidia"/*"perfidus,"* derived from *"fides"*/*"fidus,"* occur chiefly in the *Hist.* and *Iud.*; Julian is drawing here on Visigothic usage in law and political philosophy.[44] Throughout the HWR the words mean 'treason'/'traitor' in the specific sense of breaking a solemn and formal oath, the oath sworn to Wamba at the time of his accession: the *Iud.* has the explicit paraphrase "breaking their oath of loyalty" (*"fidei violare promissum"*) (*Iud.* 1).[45] Without being equally precise as

44. *"Perfidus"* is not used in the *Insultatio.* The noted first canon of Toledo VII, the council summoned by Chindasvind in 646, bears the title "De refugis atque perfidis clericis sive laicis" and in its text uses *"perfidus"* twice, in the sense of treason as breaking of an oath (Vives, 249–253). Chindasvind's law on the same subject, LV 2, 1, 8 (ed. Zeumer, 57) uses it only once: "Nam si humanitatis aliquid cuicumque perfido rex largiri voluerit . . ."

45. What is implied here is the oath of allegiance sworn by the *fideles* at the

to the form taken by treason, this is also the meaning of *"perfidia"* found in the panegyrics and related works: "having saved our lives we curse treason, and would not allow ourselves to commit it" (Claudian, *De bello Gildonico*, 264–265);[46] "And now he [Stilicho] rejoices that timely treason has broken out with a surge of rebellion [against Alaric] . . ." (Claudian, *De sexto consulato Honorii Augusti*, 213–214);[47] the anonymous author of the panegyric of Constantine of 310 writes of the "treachery of the barbarians" *("perfidia barbarorum")* unleashed as soon as Constantine moves away from the borders of Germany.[48]

"Perfidia" in particular also has a religious sense well documented in late antique and medieval theology: unbelief, with a possible connotation of perverse obstinacy and a tendency to persecute the true faith.[49] It is often used of Jews and, among the Visigoths, also of Arians.[50] Here the basic meaning of *"fides"* is no longer an oath, but doctrine or belief. It would be a mistake to think that this sense is entirely absent from the HWR, particularly given the religious halo with which Julian surrounds Wamba, the "pious prince," and the violently anti-Judaic content of the *Hist.* and the *Ins.*, with their

---

time of the ruler's accession; cf. *Iud.* 6: "Unde prolatae sunt conditiones, ubi spontanea promissione in electioni gloriosi domni nostri Wambani regis ipse nefandissimus Paulus vel socii sui una pariter nobiscum consenserunt et inviolabiliter se ei vel patriae fidem observaturos sub divini numinis sponsione testati sunt . . ." The evolution of this oath is traced in Claude, "The Oath of Allegiance and the Oath of the King."

46. (Ed. Platnauer, vol. 1, 116–117): "damnamus luce reperta / perfidiam nec nos patimur committere tali."

47. (Ed. Platnauer, vol. 2, 88): "iamque opportunam motu strepuisse rebelli / gaudet perfidiam . . ."

48. See chapter 21 (*Panégyriques*, vol. 2, 71).

49. Blumenkranz, *"Perfidia,"* 163–164, gives examples from various Visigothic authors, including Julian.

50. Cf. Isidore's description of Leovigild as "Arrianae perfidiae furore repletus" (*Historia Gothorum* 50, ed. Mommsen, 282), and Reccared in his *tomus* for Toledo III (Vives, 110): ". . . et haereses pertinaciori animositate propriae niterentur perfidiae."

charge that the Jews of Gallia were behind the original rebellion.[51]

Although the oath-breaking that constitutes treason can only be understood as an individual act, Julian presents it with insistence as a principle of association, the germ of criminal communities. He writes of a *"conventiculum perfidorum"* (*Hist.* 8) or gathering of traitors, of armies (*"cum cetero agmine perfidorum"* [*Hist.* 11]), garrisons (*"multiplici perfidorum presidio"* [*Hist.* 12]), troops (*"caterva illa perfida"* [*Hist.* 24]), and military formations (*"cuneos perfidorum"* [*Iud.* 1]) of traitors. *"Perfidia"* seeks to communicate and reproduce itself, to draw others to the disgrace of treason (*"ad perfidiae notam trahere"* [*Hist.* 6]), to procure partners for itself (*"perfidiae suae socium"* [*Hist.* 6], *"perfidiae suae sociis"* [*Hist.* 7], *"perfidiae suae socios"* and *"suae perfidiae sociavit"* [*Hist.* 8]). It is a factor of unity and solidarity among its votaries (*"in una concordantes perfidia"* [*Iud.* 3], *"eius perfidia instantissime adhaeserunt"* [*Iud.* 4]). The effect of treason is sometimes visualized as that of an epidemic and as flowing from a center (*"semina virulenta perfidiae"* [*Hist.* 6], *"fontem perfidiae"* [*Ins.* 2]), which restores individual agency to treason, if only implicitly, and likens the spread of treachery to contagion, and to the deliberate propagation of a plague.[52]

The historical form treason takes in the HWR is usurpation, and Paul breaks his oath to Wamba when he accepts the kingship in Gallia and requires his new subjects to swear equivalent oaths to him (*"iurare etiam sibimet omnes coegit"* [*Hist.* 8]).[53] Accordingly, *"tyran-*

---

51. Cf. Toledo VI, canon 3 (Vives, 236): "Inflexibilis iudaeorum perfidia . . ." and *Ins.* 2: ". . . ad Hebraeorum probati sunt transisse perfidiam."

52. Cf. Sallust, *Bellum Catilinae* 36, 5 (ed. Rolfe, 62), explaining the loyalty of Catiline's followers, not one of whom betrayed the conspiracy: ". . . tanta vis morbi aeque uti tabes plerosque civium animos invaserat." See also Claudian, *In Rufinum* 1, 30–35 (ed. Platnauer, vol. 1, 48), on the political impact of his villainous protagonist: "ac velut infecto morbus crudescere caelo / incipiens primos pecudum depascitur artus, / mox populos urbesque rapit ventisque perustis / corruptos Stygiam pestem desudat in manes: / sic avidus praedo iam non per singula saevit."

53. Cf. *Iud.* 2: ". . . populos in hac nefaria electione sibimet iurare coegit."

nus," "*tyrannis*," and the less frequent adjective "*tyrannicus*" are next in importance to "*perfidia*" and "*perfidus*" in the terminology of the HWR. They are especially problematic words, given the uncertainty of the principle of succession to the throne, which made it possible for today's usurper to become tomorrow's most sacred prince.[54] The definition of usurpation implicit in Visigothic literature requires that the usurper take power by force, either through open rebellion or a palace coup: hereditary succession, even though it flouted the elective principle consecrated at Toledo IV, was not considered usurpation.[55] Military conspiracies and pronunciamientos had been the scourge of the late empire in the West, undermining political institutions more radically than the barbarian invasions, so "*tyrannus*" and related words introduce late antique anxieties and theoretical speculations into the HWR.

From Greek, "*tyrannus*" had inherited a subsidiary sense of 'usurper' in addition to its basic meaning 'ruler, king' dominant in classical Latin, where the word is often a synonym for "*rex*." From Plato, Latin had also inherited the meaning 'cruel, abusive, unjust ruler' that is prevalent in rhetorical orations and Stoic writings.[56] The use of "*tyrannus*" for 'usurper' with strict reference to the legality of accession is characteristically late-imperial and can be traced to the inscription on the arch of Constantine which describes Maxentius as a *tyrannus*, and thus to the year 312.[57] The older meaning 'unjust ruler' was familiar to Isidore and can be found in his writings about kingship,[58] but the late antique definition of "*tyran-*

---

54. As pointed out by Orlandis, "En torno a la noción visigoda," 36, however, Visigothic usage considered only how a ruler had come to power and saw no contradiction in attributing piety and other fine royal qualities to a *tyrannus*.

55. Orlandis, "En torno a la noción visigoda," 40.

56. See Béranger, "*Tyrannus*," esp. 85–88.

57. See Springer, "*Tyrannus*," chapter 4 (101–111), and Neri, "L'Usurpatore come tiranno," 81.

58. *Etymologiae* IX, 3, 20 (ed. Lindsay): "Iam postea in usum accidit tyrannos vocari pessimos atque improbos reges, luxuriosae dominationis cupiditatem et crudelissimam dominationem in populis exercentes."

nus" is dominant in his *Historia Gothorum* and in contemporary Spanish documents.[59]

Julian's preference for abstraction leads him to use *"tyrannis"* 'usurpation' more frequently than *"tyrannus,"* and to present usurpation as an object, a thing that can be desired (*"tyrannidis ambitione"* [*Hist.* 20]), fought for (*"vindicare tyrannidem"* [*Hist.* 9]),[60] resisted (*"eius tyrannidi resistere"* [*Hist.* 9]) and seized (*"hanc tyrannidem sumeres"* [*Iud.* 5]). Compensating for the bare, schematic quality of Julian's usurper are vestiges of some of the personal qualities attributed in antiquity to the earlier 'abusive ruler,' among them cruelty (*"tyrannidis inmanitate deposita"* [*Hist.* 20]) and impiety (*"tyrannidi adiungeret sacrilegium"* [*Hist.* 26]).[61]

Neither *"perfidia"* and *"perfidus"* nor *"tyrannus"* and *"tyrannis"* has sensory correlations, and they cannot be considered images. The conceptual orientation of Julian's style emerges even more distinctly from his use of *"signum"* and the related *"vexillum."*[62] *"Signum"* in

---

59. Cf. *Historia Gothorum* 49 (ed. Mommsen, 287): ". . . Hermenegildum deinde filium imperiis suis tyrannizantem obsessum exsuperavit." Ibid. 57 (ed. Mommsen, 290): ". . . Wittericus sumpta tyrannide innocuum [regem] regno deiecit . . ." See also Count Bulgar, *epistola* 14 (*Epistolae Wisigothicae*, ed. Gundlach, 682) on Witteric: ". . . ab impii iussione tyranni . . . "; John of Biclaro, *Chronicon*, anni viii Mavricii imperatoris, 3 (ed. Mommsen, 219) on Argimundus: ". . . dux nomine Argimundus adversus Reccaredum regem tyrannidem assumere cupiens . . ."; Toledo IV, canon 75 (Vives, 219): "Quiquumque . . . praesumtione tyrannica regni fastigium usurpaverit, anathema in conspectu Christi et apostolorum eius sit . . ."; and Toledo VII, canon 1 (Vives, 249–250): "Quis enim nesciat quanta sint hactenus per tyrannos et refugas transferendo se in externas partes inlicite perpetrata . . ."

60. Cf. "praeruptumque regni fastigium vindicare" (*Hist.* 8), "tantae coniurationis . . . vindicandum existiment facinus" and "gloriae nostrae nomen vindicare debemus" (*Hist.* 9). These repetitions with shifting moral evaluation are a favorite device of Julian in the HWR.

61. On these traits of the older *tyrannus* see Jerphagnon, "Que le tyran est contre-nature," esp. 42–45, and Neri, "L'Usurpatore come tiranno," 80–82.

62. Cf. Teillet, *Des Goths*, 608, which discusses some of the meanings of these words.

classical Latin already had one important abstract possibility, which is 'sign' or 'mark,' in addition to the sense of 'standard or banner carried by troops into battle.' In medieval Latin, both *"signum"* and *"vexillum"* acquire the new meaning 'sign of the cross,' where *"vexillum"* before could only mean a standard. In the verse panegyrics of the late empire, however, military banners provided a highly colored picture: Claudian and Sidonius dwelt on the illusion that the totemic beasts—eagles and dragons—of the Roman army were actually swirling over the troops: in Claudian's panegyric on the third consulate of Honorius, "these [troops] bear flying eagles, those raise the painted heads of dragons, and many a serpent writhes among the clouds coming to life angrily when the wind animates them with its breath and by various exhalations pretends to hiss."[63] Sidonius, in his panegyric of Maiorianus, paints a comparable image of a banner in the wind: "Already the embroidered dragon rushes in and out of both armies, its throat swelling when the breezes blow into it; with yawning jaws the image counterfeits a raging hunger; the wind drives the fabric to a fury whenever it beats upon that supple back with its breath, and the hollow stomach can no longer take so much air."[64]

In the HWR, such imagery is replaced by the bare noun, especially in the discussion by the Nîmois looking down from their walls of what the absence of Wamba's banners could mean: "... a king could not go forth without his standards" (*"sine signis"*) (*Hist.* 16), "the king had come with his banners hidden" (*"bandorum signis*

---

63. *Panegyricus de tertio consulatu Honorii Augusti,*138–141 (ed. Platnauer, vol. 1, 280): "... hi volucres tollunt aquilas, hi picta draconum / colla levant, multusque tumet per nubila serpens / iratus stimulante Noto vivitque receptis / flatibus et vario mentitur sibila tractu."

64. *Panegyricvs dictvs domino imperatori Ivlio Valerio Maioriano Avgvsto* 402–407 (ed. Anderson, vol. 1, 96): "iam textilis anguis / discurrit per utramque aciem, cui guttur adactis / turgescit zephyris; patulo mentitur hiatu / iratam pictura famem, pannoque furorem / aura facit quotiens crassatur vertile tergum / flatibus et nimium iam non capit alvus inane."

absconditis") (ibid.), and in the phrase "the awe-inspiring standards of war" (*"bandorum signa terrentia"*) (*Hist.* 23). Plain unadorned designation also serves to name other kinds of signs, in particular divine signals and portents, such as the vapor and the bee that rise from Wamba's head at the ceremony of his unction: "a sign of favor" (*"signum hoc salutis"*) (*Hist.* 4) and "the omen of some future prosperity" (*"signum cuiusdam felicitatis secuturae"*) (ibid.) Religious and military meanings come together in the most visible standard of the campaign, the battle-crucifix containing a splinter of the true cross that is handed to the ruler on his departure from Toledo and that always accompanies the king in the middle of his armies: "Rally now to the standard of victory!" (*"Exurgite iam ad victoriae signum . . . !"*) (*Hist.* 9), cries Wamba after exhorting his troops to follow him east without disbanding.[65] The sign of Christ's victory is also a signal or omen of Wamba's victory over the rebels and, like any standard, it allows the troops to locate their leader visually so as to rally around him whenever necessary. There is a matching use of the word for the enemy and for evil: because they conspire, the Galli can be said to bear the sign or the emblem of treason (*"perfidiae signum"* [*Hist.* 5]), and all traitors, once defeated, are judged worthy of bearing the sign of their undoing (*"confusionis propriae signum"* [*Iud.* 1]). Characteristically, *"vexillum,"* which rarely means anything other than a real banner, becomes first an abstract figure of divine reward for righteousness ("the banner of victory [*triumphale vexillum*] was granted to us by God" [*Iud.* 1]) and then the spiritual mark or imprint made on Wamba by the rite of unction (*"sacrae unctionis vexilla"* [*Hist.* 3], *"sanctae unctionis vexilla"* [*Hist.* 4]).[66]

The central image of the HWR, however, is that of the head

65. Cf. Férotin, *Le Liber Ordinum*, col. 152, and McCormick, *Eternal Victory*, 308 note 51.

66. The anonymous panegyric of Constantius Chlorus presented in 297, chapter 16, 4 (*Panégyriques*, vol. 1, 95), describes the dead leader of a rebellion in Britain as "ipse vexillarius latrocinii."

and the limbs in the human body, although it does not occur in the *Iudicium*. It brings together the most important themes of Julian's narrative and connects them to each other by imagistic (i.e. basically visual) associations. The political and legal symbolism of this image was deeply rooted in Visigothic culture; a law of Reccesvind had outlined its implications with great clarity.[67] Julian assumes and implies this complex image without spelling out what it stands for; it had become thoroughly familiar before his time, and not just in law. In 565, a full century before Reccesvind's code, the poet Corippus in Constantinople composed a verse panegyric to celebrate the accession of Justin II and his consort Sophia. After his coronation, described in Book II of the poem, the new emperor makes a speech from the throne before the senate of the eastern capital. Among his initial words are the following: "One animal is made up of several limbs, but it is the head that rules them. Therefore God the Creator, in making man [lacuna in the text] so that the head may govern all the limbs. That they may be ruled, wisdom is allotted to the head which, occupying the summit of the body, may observe the limbs with tranquil eyes, so that whatever extremities of the body below the wise one should see by this watchful light to be afflicted with illness, it may heal, expelling with medicine the harmful contagion. The Roman empire is rightly compared to a single body composed of many members, it is proper to say. We are therefore the head of this united body."[68] The striking

---

67. See above, "History," at note 72.

68. *In laudem Iustini* 2, 186–196 (ed. Cameron, 53): "pluribus ex membris animal componitur unum, / sed caput est quod membra regit. deus ergo creator / conponens hominem + natus+ [lacuna] / omnibus ut membris caput inperet, utque regantur, / coniuncta est capiti sapientia, corporis arcem / quae retinens oculis speculetur membra serenis, / ut quoscumque videt vigilanti lumine sollers / peste laborantes subiecti corporis artus, / sanet, et infestos pellat medicamine morbos. / Romanum imperium corpus bene ponitur unum / conpositum multis, quod fas est dire, membris. / nos sumus ergo caput solidati corporis huius."

similarity of figures and ideas between this passage and Reccesvind's law suggests strongly that these particular themes circulated widely in Latin literary culture throughout the sixth and seventh
centuries, and that they were well known in Corippus's native
Africa as well as in Constantinople and Toledo. The physical head
of the head of state in the HWR is singled out by the God-sent
signa of the bee and the column of vapor (*"evaporatio . . . sese erexit in
capite,""a loco ipso capitis apis visa est"* [*Hist.* 4]). But so is that of his rival
the usurper Paul, described as the viper-like leader or head of the
conspiracy (*"vipereum caput perfidiae"* [*Hist.* 7]), first by the sacrilegious coronation he undergoes with a votive crown "which Paul
dared to place upon his own crazed head" (*"quam . . . Paulus insano
capite suo imponere ausus est"* [*Hist.* 26]) and later by decalvation.[69] The
description of kingship as a summit or a great height implies that
the usurper is attempting to rise to an undue elevation (in Wamba's
question to Paul at the trial, for instance, whether there was any
fault on his side "moved by which you . . . tried to take over the
government of the kingdom" (*"huius regni apicem suscipere attemptares"*
[*Iud.* 5]) and connects both the head and its position to a vocabulary of elevation that is scattered all over the HWR: *"fastigium,"
"culmen," "fastus," "supercilium,"* even *"cothurnus."*[70] The appropriate
movement for a usurper's head is the opposite, i.e. bending down,
humiliating itself at the rightful king's feet, which is how *calcatio colli*, the political ritual by which the victor treads on his rival's neck, is
brought into the picture: "Paul, curving his back, offers his neck to
the royal feet" (*"Tunc . . . curba spina dorsi vestigiis regalibus sua colla sub-
mittit"* [*Hist.* 27]).

69. Wamba's first rival, Count Hildericus of Nîmes, is referred to as "huius
. . . caput tyrannidis" (*Hist.* 6) and "his . . . criminis caput" (ibid.).

70. Some of these words are discussed in Teillet, *Des Goths*, 542. See also
Corippus, *In laudem Iustini* 1, 1–3 (ed. Cameron, 36): "Imperii culmen . . . cano."
Toledo V canon 3 (Vives, 228) decrees the exclusion from candidacy to the
throne of those who without being qualified by birth or merit "putant . . . ad
regiae potestatis pervenire fastigia."

The interdependence of head and limbs as fundamental law of the body politic is firmly anchored in Visigothic secular and canon law, to the point that when the king ceases to fulfill his proper function he can be characterized as no longer a head but a voracious stomach that starves the other *membra*, reversing the classical parable of the revolt of the limbs against the belly.[71] According to Reccesvind's simile, the role of a good king operating as the head of the political organism is protective (the eyes are there to spot "any approaching dangers" [*"quecumque noxia concurrissent"*]), but also therapeutic, as indicated by the reference to physicians and their priorities. The head's responsibility for the health of the limbs is emphasized even more strongly by Corippus, and Julian applies the figure to the rebellion led by Paul when he compares the Spanish army in their concern for treacherous Gallia to "a sane head taking pity on a sickly limb" (*"sanum caput languenti membro compatiens"* [Ins. 7]). The sickness of the faithless province is envisioned at one point as a sore that requires the harsh surgery of the *Insultatio* to be healed properly, lest "an ulcer develop in the healed wound" (*"ne ulcus in sanata iam plaga appareat"* [Ins. 9]).[72]

Julian's original contribution to this set system of images is to diagnose the affliction of the limbs primarily as a fever. The vocabulary of high, burning temperatures that he uses, here too limited to *Historia* and *Insultatio* and absent from the *Iudicium*, includes the nouns *"febris," "ignis," "incendium," "calor," "accensio," "incensio," "succensio"*

71. See above, "History," at note 60. The parable of the belly and the limbs is told by Menenius Agrippa in Livy 2, 32.

72. The same topos of the danger of superficial treatment is used by Julian in the preface to *De comprobatione sextae aetatis* (ed. Hillgarth, 145): "Peritorum mos est iste medicorum, ubilibet uulnus serpit in corpore, ferro uulneris materiam praeuenire, et purulentas primum radicitus amputare putredines, antequam sanas ulcus inficiat partes." On *"ulcus,"* see Toledo XVI, canon 10 (Vives, 509): "Sicut ulcus quod granditer serpit in corpore non nisi gravioribus medicaminibus aut ferro curatur, ita perfidorum obstinatio . . ." This council was held in 693 under Egica, three years after Julian's death. The rhetoric, however, is much the same.

and the verbs *"accendere," "inflammare," "incalescere," "incandere,"* and *"effervescere."* Temperature, because it is not directly observable and so manifests itself chiefly through secondary symptoms, allows Julian to attribute the political ills of Spain to a deep-seated and invisible factor which acts as a motivating force in the various instances of treason, betrayal, and rebellion he must represent. Gallia, never a part of Spain itself but at best an extremity, a limb attached to the national community, is "driven by an inconceivable fever of treason" (*"inextimabili infidelitatis febre vexata"* [*Hist.* 5]) and for a long time tossed to and fro by shifting temperatures (*"dum multo iam tempore his febrium diversitatibus ageretur"* [ibid.]). The territory of the province is described as panting with fever (*"terrae magnis febribus hanelanti"* [*Hist.* 28]) and in its final personification in the *Insultatio* Gallia is said to be acting frenziedly because driven by fever: "You, therefore, if after madness you have recovered your memory, would do well to remember what words you used to cry out in your fever . . ." (*"Tu ergo si post frenesim memoriam recepisti, recordare te convenit quibus inter febres vocibus perestrepabas . . ."* [*Ins.* 6]) and is addressed as a convalescent. But emotional heat also motivates the real actors of the HWR, the nameless troops: "the spirits of all take fire" (*"incalescunt animi omnium"* [*Hist.* 10]), "tempers instantly became heated" (*"nostrae partis multitudo . . . subita cordium accensione incanduit"* [*Hist.* 12]), "the wish to fight was fervent on either side" (*"efferbuit . . . ab utraque parte incentivum belli"* [*Hist.* 17]),[73] and Wamba himself in his response to Bishop Argebadus: "roused by some firing of his spirit, he became angry . . ." (*"quadam animi succensione efferbuit"* [*Hist.* 22]) and in his final attack on the Nîmes amphitheatre, "moved by an incredible kindling of his spirit" (*"incredibili animi accensione permotus"* [*Hist.* 24]). The king, as healthy head taking action to cure a diseased limb, is

---

73. Julian uses a curious juxtaposition of figurative and literal fires: "At ubi incalescunt nostrorum animi . . . portas incendunt . . ." (*Hist.* 12) and "Unde ferociori quam fuerant incensione commoti . . . subposito igne portas incendunt . . ." (*Hist.* 18), as if the emotional heat were transformed into real flames.

moved by the same forces as the ailing members; in crushing his enemies he experiences analogous firings of his temperature. The fever of war is contagious, and as a warrior he is not immune to anger. The natural disposition of men, even that of the public presupposed by Julian, is cold and phlegmatic (*"frigida remanet et torpescit"* [*Hist.* 1]) and needs the febrile heat of heroic tales to be moved to accomplish deeds worthy of fame.

5. The *Historia*

a. Design

More than two-thirds of the *Hist.* (chapters 9–30) is dedicated to Wamba's actual campaign against the rebels, and for this part of the narrative Julian followed the account of the original document on which the *Iudicium* is based, and specifically the section corresponding to *Iud.* 2–4. The emphasis is on Wamba's itinerary, and thus on place-names (cities and strongholds), the schedule of the campaign (times and distances), and strategy. His close dependence on this source, to which he added more anecdotal information from other, possibly oral, versions, is probably the main reason why the *Hist.* shows no clear pattern of composition, none of those parallelisms, symmetries, and antitheses that serve to underscore meaning in early medieval histories and to ease the audience into a particular interpretation and point of view.

The dominant contrasts are thematic and not structural: they do not determine the shape of the narrative as text. To his linear chronicle of sieges and battles the author has added an introduction in three parts: (i) his wholly discursive preamble on the exemplary and inspirational purpose of the work (*Hist* 1); (ii) the account of Wamba's election at Gérticos and unction at Toledo (*Hist.* 2–4); (iii) the story of the Gallic conspiracy of Hildericus, the count of Nîmes, and how Paul, the commander sent by Wamba to crush the rebels, lured them instead into a larger rebellion that involved part of the Tarraconensis (*Hist.* 5–8).

This triple introduction serves a vital expository function, but it also announces themes that will remain dominant throughout the *Hist.* In particular, the elaborate dramatic account of Wamba's acclamation, his ritual refusal of power, forced acceptance, and eventual unction at Toledo, the ceremonial center of the kingdom, ensures that the new king, about whom nothing else is known, will embody royal legitimacy for the rest of the narrative. There is simply no other meaning for him to bear. These sections contrast with the ones in which Paul, himself also a mere name when he is sent out from Toledo to put down Hildericus's rebellion, manages instead to get himself elected king of the East (*Hist.* 7–8). Every detail of the election is devious and invalid, and Julian's comment that Paul achieved his wishes "with divers fraudulent reasonings" (*"diverso fraudis argumento"* [*Hist.* 8]) introduces the trait by which the new *tyrannus* will be distinguished from now on: he always lies, and will repeatedly be shown lying to his own followers. At first he succeeds, however, in what would seem to be an impossible task: in spite of the regionalism of Spain, which had so far prevented different provinces from joining forces against the new ruler, he manages to bring together elements from both sides of the Pyrenees, and *Hist.* 5–8 summarizes the complicated story of two conspiracies that become one. These episodes explain and deliberately contrast with the later chapters in which the rebels fall out with each other (*Hist.* 19–20): when they do so, it is very much along regional/national lines (*Galli* vs. *Spani*), and the fragile unity built on Paul's falsehoods disintegrates when confronted with the truth of Wamba's claim and the authentic unity of his army. By leaving out entirely the previous lives and the physical and moral portraits of the protagonists, characteristic of panegyric, Julian reduces the opposition of king and usurper to an abstract, almost allegorical disjunction.[74] In preventing his army from disbanding after fighting

74. The alternatives open to Julian range from the realistic portrayal of Julian the Apostate on his eastward course after his victory at Strassburg in

the Basques (*Hist.* 9), in dividing it into three parts to cross the Pyrenees and take the *clausurae* and then bringing it together again ("the multitude of troops gathered from various parts assembled as one army" [*"e diversis partibus collecta in unum exercituum multitudo percrebuit"* (*Hist.* 12)]), Wamba proves twice that he can create a unity among the people that Paul's devices are unable to sustain. After the scene of his election in Narbonne, the usurper is always presented at odds with his own subjects, who either contradict him (*Hist.* 16–17) or openly disobey his commands, which by the end have become supplications (*Hist.* 19–20).

In the description of the campaign two factors are stressed. The first is the movement and speed of the operation. After coming together again on the slopes of the Pyrenees, the army of the Goths, also referred to here as that of the Spaniards or of Spain,[75] proceeds northward in a straight line across eastern Gallia. To their advance corresponds a withdrawal of the chief conspirators, who join

---

chapter 6 of Mamertinus's panegyric of 362, which incorporates the point of view of the barbarian beholders of imperial grandeur (*Panégyriques*, vol. 3, 21: "Virgines, pueri, feminae, tremulae anus, titubantes senes non sine magno attoniti horrore cernebant imperatorem longam uiam sub grauium armorum onere currentem, properantis anhelitum sine sensu lassitudinis crebriorem, sudorum riuos per fortia colla manantes et inter illum pulueris qui barbam et capillum onerarat micantia sidereis ignibus lumina") to the hieratic/enumerative icon of Theoderic that closes Ennodius's panegyric of the Gothic ruler (ed. Vogel, 214: "Statura est quae resignet prolixitate regnantem; nix genarum habet concordiam cum rubore; vernant lumina serenitate continua; dignae manus quae exitia rebellibus tribuant, honorum vota subiectis. nullus intempestive positum iactet, quia quod agunt in diis dominis diademata, hoc in rege meo operata est deo fabricante natura. illos faciunt tot divitiarum adiumenta conspicuos, sed hunc edidit simplex et indemutabilis figura meliorem").

75. This is an important point in the argumentation of Teillet that the HWR marks the ideological birth of the Spanish nation, cf. *Des Goths*, 633: "Il (i.e. Julian) exalte comme superieure à celle des Francs l'armée des Goths, qui n'est plus designée dans l'*Historia* sous le nom traditionel d'*exercitus Gothorum*— dont les historiens précités exaltaient la victoire sur l'armée romaine—mais sous le nom d'*exercitus Hispaniae*—armée déja 'nationale'—opposée comme telle a l'armée de *Francia*, alliée aux rebelles gaulois."

Paul first in Narbonne, later at Nîmes, where they await a final confrontation. Geographically and strategically, Nîmes is the limit of their retreat, the point beyond which they may not go without crossing the border into Francia and thus making themselves exiles or *refugae*. It is clear, by the time the army reaches Nîmes, that no other city remains in the power of the rebels: the border fortresses have been taken, together with Narbonne and Maguelone. What Julian emphasizes throughout is the celerity and enthusiasm of the operation, evidence of the "unanimity of minds" (*"consensio animorum"* [*Hist.* 23]) that impels Wamba's men. From the beginning, "no delay was made" (*"standi mora nulla fuit"* [*Hist.* 12]) and the king "allowed no delay in the matter" (*"nulla de reliquo mora fit"* [*Hist.* 15]). The troops renounce sleep to reach their aim more rapidly: "they covered the distance marching the whole night at an accelerated pace" and "travel[ed] wide awake all that night … to complete their headlong journey" (*"cum nocte tota cursum festinati confecissent"* [*Hist.* 13] and *"nocte tota pervigiles maturatum iter conficerent"* [*Hist.* 15]), so that they appear before the enemy as if by a miracle, with unbelievable and demoralizing swiftness: "suddenly, as the surging light of dawn shone forth, our troops appeared together, well provided with both weapons and courage" (*"subito, cum vergentis diei lux orta prodiret, apparuere simul nostrorum acies, armorum pariter et animorum apparatu dispositae"* [*Hist.* 13]). They long not only to rush ahead but to obtain victory forthwith: "[they] considered themselves beaten in every way unless they were victorious immediately" (*"victos se per omnia deputantes, si cito non vincerent"* [*Hist.* 18]) and the impulse that leads them to triumph at Nîmes remains with them afterwards when they chase Lupus of Aquitaine and his forces "at increasing speed" (*"concita velocitate"* [*Hist.* 27]).

The second factor on which Julian insists is the self-deceit of the rebels, the erroneous appraisal of their own plight that characterizes everything they do and say. Throughout, Paul's cohorts are presented resisting from behind walls, besieged and surrounded, trusting in fortifications rather than courage on the field: they are "rebel soldiers fighting on the walls" (*"in muro pugnantes seditiosos"* [*Hist.* 12]) who "choose to give battle within the city from their walls" (*"eligunt potius intra urbem suis de muris bellum conficere"* [*Hist.* 13]) and can be described as "finding their hopes of victory rather in walls than in courage" (*"plus in muris quam in viribus confidentiam vincendi locantes"* [*Hist.* 17]). The very deliberate irony stems from the fact that their confidence is genuine and expresses itself by defiant boasts and insults (*Hist.* 12–13). A notable instance is *Hist.* 14, which consists almost entirely of the proud speech of an anonymous warrior from the walls of Nîmes, uttered in defiance of the besieging *Spani.* As a full and rather formal heroic speech in *oratio recta* with no other dramatic circumstances sketched in, it corresponds to a more classicizing or late-antique narrative style than most other scenes of the *Hist.* What is remarkable is that it reverses the logic of this sort of taunt, which would make sense only coming from the other side of the wall. Words of menace and challenge have a function if intended to shame the enemy from the safety of his walls, as when in *Aeneid* 9 Numanus insults the Trojans precisely because they are cowering behind a palisade while their leader is away,[76] but not from the lips of those who will not venture beyond their protection. In addition, Julian makes the nameless rebel boast not of future prowess but of fighting that others will do for him: the burden of his speech, the epic form of which serves as deliberate parody, is that the Franks will soon be there to annihilate the besiegers. Confident in this expectation, he prophesies that the defeated Goths will have to hide "in hollows in the rocks" (*"praerupta petrarum"*).[77] The irony is marked by Julian when later on, after Wamba's men have entered the amphitheater at Nîmes, the rebels have to be

76. Cf. lines 598–599 (ed. Page, vol. 2, 62): "non pudet obsidione iterum valloque teneri, / bis capti Phryges, et morti praetendere muros?"

77. Later, in *Hist.* 16, Paul himself, also speaking from the walls, will repeat this image: "ad definita illico evolabunt latibula."

forced out "from the caves of the amphitheater" (*"a cavernis are-nunum"* [*Hist.* 24]) and "from their hiding-places in the arena" (*"de abditis arenarum"* [ibid.]) and even more sharply when Lupus of Aquitaine and the awaited Frankish rescuers on whom such hopes had been placed are chased by the *Spani* across the border and the inhabitants of Francia find themselves forced to hide in "unfamiliar haunts" (*"incertis sedibus"* [*Hist.* 27]) and "well-concealed hiding-places" (*"latebrosis compendiis"* [ibid.]). The speaker's final boast is that his side, once victorious, will exhibit Wamba humiliated and loaded with chains: "I will show you your king, for whom you came to fight, in fetters. I will cover him with insults and deride him with invective" (*"Principem illum vestrum, pro quo pugnaturi venistis, alligatum vo-bis ostendam, conviciis addicam, insultatione inludam"*). This too turns out to be the exact opposite of what happens, as Julian reminds his audience when Paul is later presented to the army "loaded with irons" (*"onustus ferro"* [*Hist.* 27]) and must bend his neck under the king's foot.

Within this diagram of quick advance and faint-hearted withdrawal, unanimous courage and disastrous self-delusion, the narrative turning-points are presented as dramatic scenes with considerable formal autonomy and, in each case, antecedents in literary tradition. The first important scene, however, belongs to the prehistory of the campaign.

b. The Refusal of Power (*Hist.* 2–3 and 8)

Incidents in which a leading Roman, acclaimed as emperor, declines the supreme dignity offered him have a long history in Latin literature and go back to Augustus himself. The first question they bring up is whether the refusal is a mere commonplace of historiography and panegyric or whether it corresponds to a public attitude of modesty and self-denial that was expected in real life.[78] It is

---

78. Cf. Béranger, "Le refus du pouvoir," 179: "Le prétexte du lieu commun ne dispense pas de l'enquête. Qu'est ce que le 'topos,' sinon l'expression devenue

in fact certain that *recusatio* was more than a literary convention: on the one hand, such refusals were sometimes accepted;[79] on the other, contradictory accounts of one and the same imperial elevation suggest that, while the gesture was often insincere and might be contradicted by the self-interested lobbying of the imperial candidate, it was nevertheless expected, performed, and presented to the world as evidence of the new emperor's lack of personal ambition.[80] The ideological significance of the refusal is also fairly clear: as an indication that the candidate does not desire the accumulated powers of empire unless they are thrust upon him, i.e., that he is no dictator, it represents an homage to the fossilized republican values that the Roman empire preserved almost uninterruptedly until its end. It belongs together with the deference shown by most emperors to the senate, with annual consulships and the corresponding *fasti* of East and West.[81] Such "republican" formalities, which could flourish only after the republic itself had become a pious memory, were strongly senatorial in character, and the *recusatio* of new or future emperors should be placed alongside the ritualized reluctance with which members of the senatorial aristocracy accepted public office in imperial times, to intimate that only the sense of duty of their class led them to sacrifice private *otium* to the *negotia* of the public realm.[82] A symmetrical, though ideologically distinct, form

---

banale d'une grande verité? A l'historien d'examiner dans quelle mesure elle est vivante et inspire des actes."

79. See, for example, the case of the praetorian prefect Salutius, offered the empire after the death of Julian the Apostate (Ammianus 25, 5).

80. An example is the account, given by Tacitus, *Historiae* 2, 74–78, of Vespasian's intriguing for power in Syria and Judea when compared with that of Flavius Josephus, a political ally, who portrays him as accepting the imperial dignity only under extreme pressure, after his troops threaten to kill him if he refuses (*Jewish War* 4, 602–604).

81. Cf. Price, "From noble funerals to divine cult," 58: "The novel supremacy of one man in a state that prized its traditions was intolerable if expressed bluntly."

82. Matthews, *Western Aristocracies*, 9–12.

of renunciation might be the rejection of ordination or the episcopal office by monks and holy men; this too is presented as proof of disinterest and self-denial, though not in republican or political terms.[83]

In records of imperial elevation, refusal is so wholly expected that it can be most often indicated by a phrase or two, especially in the panegyrics. Already Pliny reminds Trajan that "you refused to rule; you refused, which meant you would rule well. Therefore you had to be forced."[84] And Pacatus, three centuries later and with an evident awareness of the cynicism that has developed around such abnegations, reminds Theodosius that ". . . you rejected the empire offered you, and did not do so only for appearance's sake, so that you would be seen to accept it under duress, but resolutely, and long, and like one who intends to have his way."[85] In his panegyric of Avitus of 456, Sidonius, with a measure of originality, combines the theme of the senatorial sacrifice of *otium* for the welfare of Rome with a tentative imperial elevation brokered by, of all proponents, the Visigothic king Theoderic II and his senate, acting as allies of the empire. Avitus, who, after serving as praetorian prefect of Gaul, had retired to his country estate, was forced to visit Theoderic at Toulouse in the role of an ambassador of peace: the errand is referred to as a heavy obligation, "he bore the burden of an honor imposed on him,"[86] but he is well received because the Visigoths have known him long, as he had once been Theoderic's tutor in Latin literature and law. Surrounded by a council of skin-clad Gothic elders, Theoderic expatiates on his love for Rome and

83. See above, "History," note 141.

84. *Panegyricvs* 5, 5–6 (ed. Durry, 100): "recusabas enim imperare, recusabas, quod erat bene imperaturi. Igitur cogendus fuisti."

85. Cf. 12, 11 (*Panégyriques*, vol. 3, 78): ". . . oblatum imperium deprecatus es; nec id ad speciem tantumque ut cogi videreris, sed obnixe et diu et uelut impetraturus egisti."

86. *Panegyricvs dictvs Avito* 388 (ed. Anderson, vol. 1, 150): ". . . ingesti pondus suscepit honoris."

his desire to make up for his ancestor Alaric's depredations, and ends by proposing that Avitus himself should become the new emperor. The reaction is an implied gestural *recusatio*: ". . . if you, noble leader, should only accept the name of Augustus. Why do you avert your eyes? Unwillingness does you all the more honor. We do not force this upon you, but make this plea: with you as commander, I will be a friend of Rome; with you as emperor I will be its soldier."[87] Avitus, we are told, departed in sadness, because he knew that as soon as the Gauls heard of Theoderic's proposal they would compel him to accept it: "You depart sadly, Avitus, knowing that it would not remain hidden from the Gauls that the Goths might serve the empire if you became emperor."[88]

Less unusually staged, and considerably closer to Wamba's *recusatio*, is Corippus's account in his verse panegyric of 565 of the elevation to imperial dignity of Justin II. On the night of Justinian's death, his nephew awakes from a dream in which the Virgin arrays him in the imperial robes and tells him that he has been chosen for that office by God and the dying emperor. Justin is explaining the dream to his wife Sophia in their palace apartments when members of the senate beat on his door: they come to announce Justinian's passing and to acclaim Justin as his successor. There are many expressions of mourning—"the palace then rang with the sound of great weeping"[89]—and the emperor-elect seems concerned only with his bereavement. When the senator Callinicus, speaking for himself and his colleagues, exhorts him to accept the purple, Justin, in tears, refuses it because it is incompatible with his grief:

87. Ibid. 508–510 (ed. Anderson, vol. 1, 160–162): ". . . si tu, dux inclite solum / Augusti subeas nomen. quid lumina flectis? / invitum plus esse decet. non cogimus istud, / sed contestamur: Romae sum te duce amicus, / principe te miles."

88. Ibid. 519–520 (ed. Anderson, 162): "discedis, Avite, / maestus, qui Gallos scires non posse latere / quod possint servire Getae te principe."

89. *In laudem Iustini* 1, 121–122 (ed. Cameron, 40): "magno tunc regia fletu / ingemuit."

"He, however, shaken by the fate of the blessed father, refused the scepter with tears, washing his cheeks with an abundant stream so that the man's face and clothing were drenched, so great was his love of his elder. 'Desist!' he said. 'You ask for a hard thing and plead in vain, my friends. Shall I adorn this head by placing on it the crown when it is proper for Justin to be sad?'"[90] But the senators exhibit their *consensus*[91] by falling to their knees and kissing his feet, and the crowd lies prostrate before him in proskynesis, begging him to take pity. Eventually, he relents: "At last, moved by these words, he yielded."[92]

Justin's rejection of the throne and the badges of imperial office takes place when he already knows, by his dream, that he is the choice of the Almighty and of his uncle and when, according to Corippus, he has been offered the support of the senate. The only reason given for his refusal, that he is distraught with grief, is hardly serious, especially since Justinian had been known to be at death's door. We are therefore not surprised to read that, after some collective and ritualized supplication, Justin yields. Clearly, his refusal is a formality, an attitude expected of him at this point. Wamba's equivalent gesture, though very similarly conceived, immediately after the death of Reccesvind and in the midst of ceremonial mourning (*"dum . . . exequiale funus solveret et lamenta"* [*Hist.* 2]), is much more seriously meant, since it takes a threat of violent death to overcome. We are reminded after Wamba's unction that he took on the burden of government "not only unwillingly" (*"non solum nolens"* [*Hist.*

90. Ibid. 1, 160–166 (ed. Cameron, 41): "ipse autem patris concussus sorte beati / sceptra recusabat lacrimans, largoque rigabat / imbre genas, vultusque viri vestesque madebant: / tantus amor senioris erat. 'desistite!' dixit. / 'duram rem petitis frustraque instatis, amici. / ergo super posita caput hoc ornabo corona / quando Iustinum tristem decet esse?'"

91. On the force of *consensus*, see Béranger, "Le refus du pouvoir," 187–188, which shows, without mentioning Corippus, how firmly anchored this Byzantine poem is in the ideology of Roman panegyric.

92. *In laudem Iustini* 1, 187 (ed. Cameron, 42): "vocibus his flexus cessit tandem."

4]) but after rising in order through the ranks.[93] The lack of ca-
reerist ambition that had characterized him as a member of the
palatine office, made evident by his patience in waiting for promo-
tions, is confirmed and heightened by his refusal of the kingship·

Place and time are decisive for *recusatio.* Justin is in a favorite
room of his own palace, distant from the setting of his uncle's
death. He is first presented in this private sphere, guarded by a jeal-
ous doorkeeper, where he sits relating to his wife what the Virgin
has told him. From this intimate stage he is drawn, with some appearance of reluctance and distress, and brought to the imperial
palace to assume his new dignity. The old Roman notion of the
sacrifice of private leisure to political duty is strongly implied in
this displacement. The election of Wamba occurs, by contrast, in
the setting of his predecessor's passing. There are no private spaces;
the entire narrative sequence unfolds in public. However, Reccesvind dies not in the palace at Toledo but at a country estate, and
Wamba's presence there amid a crowd of palatine officials marks
him as part of a very small elite, one of those few who come into
consideration for the kingship on the death of the childless incum-
bent. Since Julian invents no premonitory dreams and the late king
has, significantly, not appointed a successor, some sign from above
is required to pick out the so far anonymous and featureless
courtier from among the mourners. Leaving the more conspicuous
omens of royal power for the moment of unction, Julian reaches
back into literary tradition for the involuntary acclamations,
"moved less by one emotion than by a common cry" ("*non tam animo
quam oris affectu pariter provocati*" [*Hist.* 2]) that had revealed to the
world that Trajan should be the successor of Nerva, and that the
layman Ambrose should become bishop of Milan.[94]

93. This last rather bureaucratic consideration should not matter if Wamba's election, as Julian pretends, is believed to be dictated by divine choice. But
it is not omitted.

94. Cf. Pliny, *Panegyricus* 5, 2–3 (ed. Durry, 99–100): "An fas erat nihil

Justin's acclamation and *recusatio* take place at night, a time of increased privacy, and his foot touches the threshold of the imperial palace at exactly the moment of dawn.[95] In the case of Wamba, Julian stresses the fact that one and the same day brought the death of one ruler and the elevation of the next, and phrases it so as to place it among the chronological coincidences that panegyrics count as signs of a providential intervention.[96]

A flood of tears together with formal postures of supplication add a heightened emotional tone to either scene. As he refuses the insignia, Justin weeps so copiously as to drench his clothes,[97] while Wamba is "choked by tearful sobs" (*"lacrimosis singultibus interclusus"* [*Hist.* 2]). Here Corippus and Julian of Toledo move in a tradition

---

differre inter imperatorem quem homines et quem di fecissent? quorum quidem in te, Caesar Auguste, iudicium et fauor tunc statim cum ad exercitum proficiscereris, et quidem inusitate notuit. Nam ceteros principes aut largus cruor hostiarum aut sinister uolatus auium consulentibus nuntiauit; tibi ascendenti de more Capitolium quamquam non id agentium ciuium clamor ut iam principi occurrit . . ." and Rufinus, *Historia ecclesiastica* XI, 11 (ed. Mommsen, vol. 2, 1018): "cumque inibi multa secundum leges et publicam disciplinam pro quiete et tranquillitate perorasset, pugnantis inter se et dissidentis populi subito clamor et vox una consurgit Ambrosium episcopum postulantes: baptizari hunc protinus clamant, erat enim catechumenus, et sibi episcopum dari, nex aliter unum populum fore atque unam fidem, nisi Ambrosius sibi daretur sacerdos." On unanimous acclamations as divinely inspired, see Roueché, "Acclamations in the Later Roman Empire," esp. 187–188.

95. Corippus, *In laudem Iustini* I, 197–201 (ed. Cameron, 42): "limen ut Augustae sacro pede contigit aulae, / omnia gallorum strepuerunt culmina cantu. / exactam noctem primi sensere volucres, / et laetum cecinere diem, alarumque dedere / plausibus adsiduis et acuta voce favorem."

96. For instance, according to an anonymous panegyric of Constantine presented in 313, chapter 16, 2 (*Panégyriques*, vol. 2, 136), Maxentius dies on the sixth anniversary of his accession "ne septenarium illum numerum sacrum et religiosum uel inchoandum uiolaret." Claudian, in his preface to the second book of *In Eutropium*, 10–12 (ed. Platnauer, vol. 1, 178), stresses the significance of the fact that Eutropius's consulship was followed by exile that same year: "annus qui trabeas hic dedit exilium. / infaustum populis in se quoque vertitur omen; / saevit in auctorem prodigiosus honos."

97. *In laudem Iustini* I, 161–162, quoted above in note 90.

that had deviated long before them from the disapproval of tears in grown men expressed by Sallust in the *Bellum Iugurthinum* when the Roman general Metellus weeps on learning that his rival Marius has been handed control of Numidia by the senate: "Shaken by these developments beyond what is right and decent, he neither held back his tears nor tempered his tongue; though an outstanding man in other respects, he bore these setbacks in an unmanly way."[98] Already Claudian shows us whole armies weeping openly, and with no overt or implied criticism, as when Stilicho's troops are separated from their commander: "When the army saw itself divided and left behind, they gave a mighty groan and made wet their helmets with the tears they shed; the constricting sighs that smothered their voices shook the powerful fastenings of their breastplates."[99] Clearly, emotion is not only permitted but required, and hence also displayed. This expectation still applied to the Visigothic kings, who had to demonstrate to clergy and court that they had "entrails of compassion" *("viscera pietatis")*. Thus Ervig, in his *tomus* for Toledo XII, represents himself as appearing before the assembled bishops "while shedding tears."[100]

Ritual prostrations admit of little variety; the crowd of dignitaries in Justin's rooms repeats the accustomed gestures: "on bended knee the senate scattered numerous kisses on the sacred feet," "lying prostrate at his feet, the entire crowd implores at once 'You are pious: have mercy on your suppliants, holy one. Assist us in these perils.'"[101] In Wamba's case "whole companies fling them-

98. *Bellum Iugurthinum* 82, 2 (ed. Rolfe, 304): "Quibus rebus supra bonum aut honestum perculsus, neque lacrumas tenere neque moderari linguam, vir egregius in aliis artibus nimis molliter aegritudinem pati."

99. *In Rufinum* 2, 257–260 (ed. Platnauer, vol. 1, 76): "ut sese legio vidit disiuncta relinqui, / ingentem tollit gemitum galeasque solutis / umectat lacrimis pressamque morantia vocem / thoracum validos pulsant suspiria nexus . . ."

100. (Vives, 382): ". . . ob hoc venerabilem paternitatis vestrae coetum cum lacrymarum effusione convenio . . ."

101. *In laudem Iustini* 1, 156–158 (ed. Cameron, 41): ". . . senatus / creber adorabat dominos, et poplite flexo / plurima divinis supplex dabat oscula plan-

selves at his feet so that he will not refuse what they demand"
(*"catervatim, ne postulantibus abnueret, suis pedibus obvolvuntur"* [*Hist.* 2]).
The problem with these pious gesticulations as introduced by Julian, and it is not a small one, is that one sentence later they are replaced by brutal threats and the suggestion of a drawn sword. In
the nature of things, physical compulsion of this sort, however ultimately flattering to its objects, is not mentioned in panegyrics. It
does occur in episodes of *recusatio* described in historiography—for
instance, the elevation of Vespasian as told by Flavius Josephus, and
that of Julian the Apostate as described by Ammianus—but in
those cases, naturally, there are neither tears nor kissing of imperial
feet.[102] Julian of Toledo's combination of both in one short scene
betrays the archaizing and mechanical nature of his borrowing of
late imperial staging for an early medieval episode that lacks all the
ideological presuppositions of *recusatio*, and in particular the vestig-
ial "republican" fear of a power-hungry despot.

Other elements of Wamba's refusal of kingship add to the
scene's unconvincing and paradoxical character. The tearful figure
who invokes his advanced age and the parlous condition of the
realm proceeds, within the *Historia* itself, to lead a lightning campaign against the Basques, to prevent by his unaided initiative the

---

tis . . ." and 173–175 (ibid.): "talia dicentis pedibus prostrata iacensque / omnis
turba simul 'pius es, miserere' perorat / 'supplicibus, vir sancte, tuis: succurre
periclis.'"

102. Flavius Josephus, *Jewish War* 4, 603 (trans. Williamson, 270): "But when
he turned down their invitation the officers were the more insistent, and the
rank and file surrounded him sword in hand, and threatened to kill him if he
refused the life that was his due." In the case of Julian the Apostate, the threat
of violence occurs in his own account of the events in a letter to Constantius
transcribed or recreated in Ammianus, 20, 8–10 (ed. Seyfarth, vol. 2, 108):
"unde solito saeuius efferati nocte in unum collecti / palatium obsidere Augus-
tum Iulianum uocibus magnis appellantes et crebris. cohorrui, fateor, et secessi
amendatusque, dum potui, salutem occultatione quaeritabam et latebris. (. . .)
sed exarsere mirum in modum eo usque prouecti, ut, quoniam precibus uincere
pertinaciam conabar, instanter mortem contiguis assultibus intentarent."

dispersion of the army, and then to lead those same troops to a re-
sounding victory over the rebels. Julian cannot have written his narrative so soon after the events that he would not have heard of the
king's draconian and unprecedented army law, given in 673. But the
sincerity of Wamba's *recusatio* was essential, and it is possible that
Julian, conscious of the discontinuity between the timorous character of the beginning and the ruthless, single-minded leader of the
rest of the *Historia*, made an attempt to explain this mutation in the
personality of his protagonist. At the end of *Hist.* 4, immediately
after the royal unction, he reminds his audience and posterity of
"how manfully" (*"quam viriliter"*) this king ruled his realm, who
reached the summit of power not only unwillingly but also rising in
order through so many ranks and compelled (*"coactus"*) by the enthusiasm of the entire nation. A transformation of the man,
brought about by the sacred power of unction, appears to be indicated by Julian's stress on the unexpected, surprising aspect of
Wamba's virile leadership after his initial scruples and his courtly
patience in waiting for his turn, and among the evidence to support
it we might count the fact, pointed out by S. Teillet, that Wamba is
referred to as a man (*"vir"*) only before being anointed and never after that.[103] An analogous change in character as the effect of accession, made manifest in a before-and-after pattern by contrast with
the initial timidity displayed in *recusatio*, is shown by Avitus in Sidonius's panegyric. Jupiter, speaking to Rome, says about the new emperor: "How often he will bring foreign peoples under thy yoke,
striking them with your eagle-standards—he who, as a private citizen, fled from the highest omens of empire when once, as he was
traveling, that imperial bird brushed off from him his common
cloak!"[104]

103. Cf. Teillet, *Des Goths*, 601–602, and "L'*Historia Wambae*," 419.
104. *Panegyricvs dictvs Avito* 591–594 (ed. Anderson, vol. 1, 168): "O quas tibi
saepe iugabit / inflictis gentes aquilis, qui maxima regni / omina privatus fugit,
cum forte vianti / excuteret praepes plebeium motus amictum."

The sincerity or truthfulness of Wamba's refusal matters because it will contrast with a later scene, that of Paul's proclamation as king of the rebels, which emphasizes throughout the usurper's use of deception, particularly in the implicit *recusatio* (*Hist.* 7) that follows Paul's departure from Toledo and his various efforts to undermine the expedition entrusted to him by Wamba. Julian stresses secrecy and dissimulation: Paul, in terms borrowed from Orosius, "secretly joins a . . . usurpation" (*"tyrannidem . . . secrete invadit"*), "proceeds by hidden measures" (*"agit haec arcano quodam consilio"*), and pretends that he intends to fight the rebels (*"simulate se pugnaturum contra seditiosos enuntiat"*). Only when confronted with Argebadus of Narbonne, who has somehow found out the truth and attempts to close off the approach to the city, does he finally emerge in his true character as "the viper-like leader of treason" (*"vipereum caput perfidiae"*) as he stands rebuking the loyal bishop.[105]

In the scene that follows, which takes place in Narbonne (*Hist.* 8), Paul is ready to make public his true political colors (*"tyrannidis suae consilium proditurus"*) but certainly not to stop lying. He still proceeds "with divers fraudulent reasonings" (*"diverso fraudis argumento"*) and, having betrayed his lord, acts now to make dupes of his new associates. Once all have agreed that they cannot accept Wamba as their ruler, Paul tells them: "Choose a head of government from among yourselves, to whom the crowd will yield in agreement and who may seem fit to rule over us" (*"Caput regiminis ex vobis ipsis eligite, cui conventus omnis multitudo cedat, et quem in nobis principari appareat"*). These are the only words quoted as direct speech in this scene of political deliberation, and they are meant to be noticed. Julian has already told us that Paul desires to be king: he is "drawn by the desire to reign" (*"regni ambitione illectus"* [*Hist.* 7]) and guided by "the royal rank he aspires to" (*"affectatum fastigium regni"* [ibid.]), so this

105. Julian is very likely thinking of Vergil's vipers which, whether literal or figurative, always lurk in hiding before they emerge suddenly and with terrifying effect; cf. *Aeneid* 2, 379–382 and 471–475, and *Georgics* 3, 414–439.

attempt to appear disinterested is only further proof of his hypoc-risy and a marked contrast to Wamba's honest refusal.

The next man to speak is Ranosindus, a military commander from the Tarraconensis, who was recruited to the rebellion by Paul and crossed the Pyrenees with him. Like Paul, Ranosindus has so far no connection to the original rebellion of Gallia, initiated by the count of Nîmes. The two stand in Narbonne, the capital of Gallia, and Ranosindus proposes Paul for the new king, refusing to consider any other. Once the Galli accept this foreigner as their leader, Paul and Ranosindus can be said to have coopted their up-rising. The gain to these outsiders is too considerable for Ranosin-dus's intervention to appear spontaneous and unprepared. The pos-sibility that he has been prompted by Paul is strongly suggested.

c. The King at the Head of His Armies (*Hist.* 9 and 10)

A trait of late antique narrative taken over by early medieval historians was the prominence given to ritual and ceremony. Among the reasons for this are the abundant gestural cues that ritu-al supplied to scenic/dramatic narrative, and the fact that ritual came, so to speak, already interpreted, both in the symbolism of its individual movements and in their sequence.[106] Julian of Toledo might be taken for one of these ritualistic narrators, since the *Histo-ria* famously provides the earliest extant account of a European roy-al unction in the scene of Wamba's anointment by Bishop Quiricus (*Hist.* 4). In fact, however, despite the ideological importance of the unction, which becomes the chief mark of Wamba's legitimacy and makes it a sacrilege to rebel against him, Julian spends a single sen-tence on the actions involved, to which he adds, in another sen-tence, the miracles or omens of the vapor and the bee that arose from the new king's head. An even more eloquent proof of Julian's lack of interest in ceremonial staging is that we are never shown the

---

106. Cf. Martínez Pizarro, *A Rhetoric of the Scene,* 109–150.

ruler's departure from Toledo. Last seen sending out Paul from the
urbs regia to take care of the rebels (*Hist. 7*), he is reintroduced when
already "in the region of Cantabria" ("*in partibus ... Cantabriae*"
[*Hist.* 9]), where he is informed of Paul's betrayal. The Visigothic
liturgy has preserved an elaborate protocol to be enacted in the
church of St. Peter and St. Paul whenever the king rode out to battle.[107] Julian has omitted the entire ceremony and the pageant of
the king departing from his capital.[108]

What the author of the *Historia* must establish at this point is
Wamba's suitability as a military leader, since, predictably, shortly
after his election he is confronting armed challenge and a threat of
secession from the realm. For Visigothic kings of the seventh century, their role at the head of the *exercitus Gothorum* remained the primary one.[109] It was symbolized, following Roman tradition, by the
military belt or *cingulum*,[110] and it is on this account that the bishops
of Toledo XII, when they resolve that the sacrament of penance is
irreversible, add very pointedly that it is not compatible with the
belt that stands for military duty: "We enjoin that they never again
return to [the wearing of] the military belt."[111] With these words
they implicitly identify royal office, from which Wamba is being

107. See above, "History," at note 103, and in this chapter note 65.

108. Recently de Jong, "Adding Insult to Injury," has argued for the central-
ity of ritual to the HWR, as the systematic opposition of good and bad ritual
form allows Julian to build up a contrast between the legitimate king and his
enemies that is heavy with political significance. This would appear to be true,
but Julian's primary aim is to create this antithesis, not to discuss ritual form in
itself, about which he has little to say.

109. See Collins, *Early Medieval Spain*, 107–108.

110. The use of *"cingulum"* as a metonym for military service is well established in medieval Latin; cf. Blaise, *Lexicon latinitatis medii aevi* s.v.1: "ceinture militaire, service militaire"; Latham, *Dictionary of Medieval Latin* s.v.2: "belt as emblem
of military service or knighthood"; *Mittellateinisches Wörterbuch* s.v.Iγ: "spectat ad
praestationem cinguli militaris."

111. Toledo XII, canon 2 (Vives, 389): ". . . ne ulterius ad militare cinculum
redeant religamus."

ousted, with the ability to wear the belt. This is also why the defeated Paul, dragged to the presence of Wamba, "instantly cast himself in the dust and ungirded his belt" (*"statim se humo prostravit sibique cingulum solvit"* [*Hist.* 25]): in so doing he gave up his claim to royal dignity. In *Hist.* 9, however, Wamba is still untried, and there is the question of his age, which had been one of his arguments for refusing the throne. The *Historia* will later make clear that he rides behind a very solid vanguard of his troops and stays away from battles and sieges. On the way to Nîmes he remains thirty miles behind the troops that will besiege the city [*Hist.* 13]; these same troops must later send messengers to him requesting additional forces [*Hist.* 15], and Paul, lying to his followers that Wamba must be present at the siege [*Hist.* 16], makes his opponent's absence especially conspicuous. This protected position is most likely a matter of sensible strategy, of not exposing the supreme commander of the army in front-line fighting, where he is less valuable.[112] Nevertheless, his contribution to the victory over Paul needs to be stressed, and in particular his authority over the extremely "protofeudal" army, which has to be asserted anew before every engagement. No second-in-command is ever named who might detract from his glory. His presence alone, in the symbolic itinerary from the ceremonial center of the *urbs regia* to the disputed periphery of Cantabria and from there to the rebellious limb, the "remote corner of the earth" (*Hist.* 9: *"extremo terrae angulo"*) that is Gallia, works as a reclamation under

---

112. Although the panegyrics often praise rulers for leading their men in battle (cf. Pacatus 10, 3, *Panégyriques*, vol. 3, 77–78), they also provide various arguments for not doing so. Claudian, *De bello Gildonico* 380–387 (ed. Platnauer, vol. 1, 126), shows Stilicho persuading Honorius that he need not lead in person the struggle against the rebellious Moor: ". . . plus nominis horror / quam tuus ensis aget. minuit praesentia famam. / qui stetit aequatur campo, collataque nescit / maiestatem acies." The anonymous panegyric of Constantine of 313, 9, 3–6 (*Panégyriques* vol. 2, 131), faults the emperor's heroic behavior at Verona for more familiar political reasons: "cur ipse pugnasti? cur te densissimis hostium globis miscuisti? cur salutem rei publicae in pericula tanta misisti?" See Nixon and Rodgers, *In Praise of Later Roman Emperors*, 309–310 note 66.

royal authority of the entire territory of the realm at the beginning of his reign. That too is the purpose of Wamba's address to the troops in Cantabria and of the punishment he later imposes on soldiers guilty of violence against the local population.

The oration before the army is Wamba's longest speech by far, and it is successful: he gets the men to do what he wants. He talks about occasions "when the spirit is fired" *("[d]um calor est animi")* and spirits become heated accordingly *("[a]d quod dictum incalescunt animi omnium")*. Remarkable about the speech as a scene are the absence of visual cues and the curious rhetoric of national and regional stereotypes. All Julian tells us about the setting is that the action takes place in the country of the Basques. The moment, too, is ill-defined, and even the audience remains uncertain. Wamba sees palatine officials paralyzed by the dilemma whether to march on directly to Gallia or to first disband the army and then reassemble it with more numerous forces and richer supplies: when he perceives them "bewildered by this quandary" *("bicipiti consilio nutantes")*, he begins his speech, but in such a way ("he addressed them all together as follows" [*"hic communi admonitione alloquitur"*]) that in one sentence he is both opening his mind to the *primates palatii* and addressing the troops in general. The locality is wholly unspecified and the king's words are not accompanied by gestures or actions.[113] An oration framed in this abstract manner is very classical and recalls the addresses of Roman leaders to their troops before decisive battles, for instance Catiline's final speech before encountering Petreius and his forces.[114] The lengthy, highly rhetorical cast of Wamba's oration resembles nothing if not the recreated speeches of classical Roman historiography.[115]

113. The exhortation "Exurgite iam ad victoriae signum!" could conceivably imply that he is holding the war-cross in his hand as he speaks.

114. *Bellum Catilinae* 58 (ed. Rolfe, 118–122). It also resembles, in its abstract and discursive character, the defiant speech by an anonymous rebel from the walls of Nîmes discussed above (*Hist.* 14).

115. On the tradition of such speeches in the historical writing of antiquity,

The relation of what the king says to the particular occasion in which he speaks is not uncomplicated and must be studied as part of the rhetoric of the speech: he disregards the struggle against the Basques, in which his men are engaged at the moment, and talks to them about the fighting they will have to do later against the Galli and Paul. He is not exhorting the troops to fight bravely, the usual burden of such addresses, but persuading them to do so without first disbanding, thereby turning to the soldiers themselves for a decision usually taken by the high command. The king does encourage his men to fight ("Destroy the very name of the traitors!" [*"nomen disperdite perfidorum!"*]), but this is future fighting, not the combat in which they are engaged at the time of speaking. He remains entirely self-effacing, focusing only on the troops, their glory, and the prestige of their nation, with many references to the weak and contemptible character of the enemy, who are presented as either foreigners (the Franks) or rebellious subjects of the Goths (the Galli).[116] Clearly, though, what matters is to get the troops themselves to override the hesitation of their commanders, to refuse to be disbanded (*"non igitur opus est retro verti militem"*), and thereby to keep Wamba from having to negotiate with the nobility in order to reassemble the various contingents of his army. So the speech is far more political and less martial than it pretends to be, and it is with an odd twist that the king turns finally to the matter at hand, reminding his forces that they have work to finish before

---

see Fornara, *The Nature of History in Ancient Greece and Rome,* chapter 4, and Potter, *Literary texts and the Roman Historian,* 130–138.

116. On early national stereotypes in the HWR, see Teillet, *Des Goths,* 625–632. The panegyrics of Constantine often contain invective against the Franks, with whom he had fought frequently before becoming emperor: cf. the panegyric of 310, chapter 21, 2 (*Panégyriques,* vol. 2, 71): "Ecce enim, dum a limite paulisper abscesseras, quibus se terroribus barbarorum perfidia iactauerat . . ." Mamertinus's panegyric of Maximian, presented in 289, chapter 11, 4 (*Panégyriques,* vol. 1, 34), describes the Franks as "lubrica illa fallaxque gens barbarorum."

they can move on to more important matters: "Let us first, therefore, bring destruction to the Basques . . ." *("Abhinc ergo Vasconibus cla-
dem inlaturi accedamus").*

When, the Basques once defeated, the army begins to move east
to the Tarraconensis and we are told that Wamba later divided his
forces into three sections *("in tres turmas exercitum dividit")* that would
cross the Pyrenees into Gallia by different routes, anticipation appears to have become the law of the narrative, since at this point
(Hist.. 10) the *exercitus,* which is marching past Calahorra and
Huesca, still needs to stay united to take Barcelona and Gerona before it can think of crossing over. It is not surprising then that,
when the time really comes for the army to split up, Julian tells us
again, with a reminder that this was said before and adding the
names of the fortresses that defend the various passes: "he split it,
as has been told, into three divisions" *("per tres, ut dictum est, directiones
exercitus Pirinei montis dorsa ordinavit"* [*Hist.* 11]). Why was this division
mentioned ahead of time? The passage is conspicuous in the neatly
composed *Historia,* where unnecessary repetition is systematically
avoided. One possibility is that, because the incident that follows
the anticipated reference to the division into three is stylized according to Old Testament models, and because Abimelech, Saul,
and David introduce similar divisions among their forces,[117] Julian
sought to model the entire sequence of *Hist.* 10 along Old Testament lines, with Wamba in the role of one of the old, divinely chosen kings of Israel and Judah, the wise and righteous leader of his
armies.[118]

117. Judges 9.43: "[Abimelech] tulit exercitum suum et divisit in tres turmas." 1 Samuel 11.11: "Constituit Saul populum in tres partes." 2 Samuel 18.12:
"[David] dedit populi tertiam partem sub manu Ioab, et tertiam partem sub
manu Abisai . . . et tertiam partem sub manu Ethai . . ." See Teillet, "L'*Historia
Wambae,*" 419 and 423 note 26.

118. Certainly, there are also non-scriptural instances: the emperor Theodosius did likewise on setting out against Maximus, according to the panegyric of
Pacatus, 32, 3 (*Panégyriques,* vol. 3, 98): "Tunc copias tuas trifariam dividis ut et

The little use made by Visigothic authors of Old Testament models, and particularly of the figure of David, has often been noticed,[119] but in this case all doubts are settled by Wamba's invocation later in the same chapter of an episode from 1 Samuel to explain and justify his own behavior. When soldiers marching east become guilty of arson and rape, Wamba has them circumcised. Julian describes this measure as the most extreme punishment, "harsher . . . than if they had been fighting against him" *("graviora in his supplicia . . . quam si hostiliter contra illum egissent")* and accounts for it by having Wamba cite the story of the high priest Eli and the destruction that came upon him because he failed to chastise his sons (1 Samuel 2.12–4.18). Many impulses shape this incident, not all of them scriptural. There are simple political considerations: the outrages have been inflicted on the local population, with whom peace has been made, and Wamba does not want them to turn against his army. In addition, the maxim that the king's chief moral obligation was to correct his subjects had long been a commonplace of political thought, as expressed by Isidore of Seville: "He does not rule

hostis audaciam multiplicato terrore percelleres et fugam circumfusus ambires." This was also the strategy of Radagaisus when he invaded Italy in 406, according to the Gallic Chronicle of 452 (ed. Burgess, 73). But both of these, in so far as they are not simply accurate reports, could be inspired by the biblical examples.

119. Claude, *Adel, Kirche und Königtum,* 130, dates the first comparison of Visigothic to Old Testament kings to Braulio of Zaragoza's letter to Chindasvind asking the king to raise his son Reccesvind to the throne, and hence to the late 640s. Reydellet, *La royauté,* 562, remarks on "le rôle à peu pres nul que joue David dans les idées politiques de l'époque" and presents Wamba's unction as "[l]e seul emprunt direct à l'Ancien Testament." See Hillgarth, "Historiography," 280–281. Note, however, LV IV, 2, 13 (ed. Zeumer, 180–182), an unattributed *novella* ascribed to Wamba by Zeumer, "Geschichte IV," 115–119, and by King, *Law and Society,* 37 note 2. The law, which concerns legal guardianship over children whose mother has died, and the administration of her estate, departs from Reccesvind's earlier law on this issue and justifies the change by quoting Solomon seven times (Proverbs and Ecclesiastes) and *"hymnidicus ille . . . David"* once (Psalms).

who fails to correct."[120] The crime being punished involves a form of unchastity, as Wamba himself makes clear, and it is presented as a sin that defiles the army at a time when it is in special need of divine favor and protection. The panegyrics, too, had often portrayed emperors, even non-Christian ones, as the protectors of virtue and modesty in whatever cities their armies entered or took by force, from Trajan, "whose arrival never terrified a father or a husband,"[121] to Constantine who, entering Milan, elicited feelings of "much security among the matrons and virgins who looked upon him."[122] Most troublesome, however, is the extraordinary punishment chosen by Wamba. At least two scholars have opted for interpreting it as the more familiar penalty of castration,[123] but there is no way of getting around those "severed foreskins of the rapists" *("praecisa adulterorum praeputia")* that testify to the justice of the *religiosus princeps*. The choice of circumcision may be connected to the violent anti-Judaism of the *Historia* and the *Insultatio* and to the classification of *"circumcisus"* in a late addendum to the Visigothic law as a verbal insult punishable by 150 lashes in public.[124] The model, however, is exclusively biblical, namely the bride-price required by Saul of David for his daughter Michal: "a hundred Philistine foreskins, to take vengeance against the king's enemies."[125] David dou-

---

120. *Etymologiae* IX, 3, 4 (ed. Lindsay): "Non autem regit, qui non corrigit." Isidore uses the case of Eli repeatedly as an illustration of the failure to chastise and its consequences, cf. *Questiones in Regum I*, 1, 8 (PL 83, col. 393) and *Sententiae* 3, 46, 1 (ed. Cazier, 290).

121. Pliny, *Panegyricus* 20, 2 (ed. Durry, 112): "Nec uero ego in laudibus tuis ponam quod aduentum tuum non pater quisquam, non maritus expauit . . ."

122. This according to the anonymous panegyric of 313, 7, 5 (*Panégyriques*, vol. 2, 129): "quae securitas intuentium te matrum, te uirginum! quae duplici fructu fruebantur, cum pulcherrimi imperatoris formam uiderent et licentiam non timerent."

123. Adams, "Toledo's Visigothic Metamorphosis," 130: ". . . any soldier found guilty of rape was to be castrated." García López, "La cronología," 134, note 39: ". . . solo 'algunos' culpables son castrados . . ."

124. See McCormick, *Eternal Victory*, 312, note 69.

125. 1 Samuel 18.25: "centum praeputia Philistinorum, ut fiat ultio de inimi-

bled the number: "and he struck down among the Philistines two hundred men, and David brought their foreskins . . ."[126] although later (2 Samuel 3.14) they are referred to again as one hundred. Wamba becomes a figure of David, exacting the Lord's revenge. This is a startling instance of the liberties Julian is willing to take with historical plausibility in order to use a prestigious narrative model. The practice of circumcision was punishable by death under Reccesvind and later, under Ervig, by castration and disfigurement.[127] We may assume that Christians would not have known how to perform this ritual and would have considered themselves defiled by it. That the king would have considered imposing this forbidden and alien surgery on Christian soldiers as the punishment for rape strains credibility and is best accounted for as an illustration of how far Julian will go for the sake of biblical stylization. Wamba may well have punished rapists harshly in some other way, but what we have here is a quotation from Scripture in the form of a fantastic and unbelievable episode.

Though intermittent, the identification of Wamba with Saul and David was established at his unction, when he became the *unctus Dei* or *christus Domini*.[128] Writing almost certainly after the proclamation of the new military law, Julian might also have had in mind the critique of kingship contained in 1 Samuel, with its insistence on the heavy conscription that kings will impose on the sons

cis regis." The English translation quoted above is from the recent version by Robert Alter, *The David Story*, 116–117.

126. 1 Samuel 18.27: "Et percussit ex Philistiim ducentos viros, et attulit eorum praeputia."

127. Cf. LV 12, 2, 7 and 11 (ed. Zeumer, 415 and 417), and LV 12, 3, 4 (ed. Zeumer, 433). See also Saitta, *L'antisemitismo*, 68 and 78.

128. Cf. 1 Samuel 24.7 and 11; 1 Samuel 26.9 and 23; 2 Samuel 1.14. The *Altercatio ecclesiae et synagogae* ascribed to Severus of Minorca and dated to the early fifth century has been proposed by Hillgarth as a source for the HWR (cf. Hillgarth, "Historiography," 301–302, and the notes to his reprint of Levison's edition in *Opera* 1). The work (ed. Segui and Hillgarth) shows a marked interest in the *unctus Dei:* cf. lines 177, 393, 403, 431.

of Israel: "This will be the practice of the king who will reign over you: Your sons he will take and set for himself in his chariots and in his cavalry, and some will run before his chariots" and ". . . when Saul saw any warrior or valiant fellow, he would gather him to himself."[129]

d. The End of Usurpers (*Hist.* 16 and 19–20)

Paul, met most recently as a cunning and successful schemer who persuaded the men of Gallia to place him at the head of their rebellion, reappears now in a wholly different role. The shift in focus from Wamba to him creates, if not a symmetry, at least a rough balance in the contrast of legitimate ruler and usurper. Since neither *princeps* nor *tyrannus* has been given a biography or a personal portrait, they are defined exclusively by their actions, and the radical change in their characterization by *Hist.* 16 is due to the moral and political leadership of the army demonstrated by Wamba and, in the case of his opponent, to his uninterrupted retreat northwards across Gallia and to the admitted reliance of his forces on the military assistance of foreigners, i.e. the Franks—or Aquitainians—of Duke Lupus. High on the walls of Nîmes looking down on the army of the Goths, Paul now embodies the usurper who confronts the common fate of his kind.

Usurpations, which had been countless in the late empire of the West, eventually gave rise to a new character in historiography and political literature, and to a new meaning of the term *"tyrannus."* Since usurpers could have the most varied social backgrounds and individual qualities, often seeming, by the testimony of their contemporaries, clearly preferable to the rightful emperors, *"tyrannus"*

---

129. 1 Samuel 8, 11: "Hoc erit ius regis, qui imperaturus est vobis: filios vestros tollet, et ponet in curribus suis, facietque sibi equites et praecusores quadrigarum suarum." 1 Samuel 14, 52: "Nam quemcumque videbat Saul virum fortem, et aptum ad praelium, sociabat eum sibi." The translations quoted are taken from Alter, *The David Story*, 42–43 and 86.

lost the character traits of the abusive ruler it had once designated. It referred now only to the manner of seizing, or attempting to seize, power. The human mask of the usurper was left blank, since anyone—a senator, a commander of the army, a rhetorician, or a simple soldier—could find himself involved in a conspiracy and become its head. The only personal note attached to the word at this point was a sense of inevitable failure, since successful usurpers tended to be remembered as legitimate rulers, or to benefit from a political amnesia.[130] Accordingly, the literary character or role of the *tyrannus* as he appears in the histories and panegyrics of late antiquity is defined by pathos. He has gambled and lost, and since he could be almost anyone, it is not difficult to identify with him. He is shown facing an imminent fall, and usually alone or isolated, unable to share his fears with his accomplices, who either goaded him to rebellion or were seduced by him to join their fortunes to his enterprise. He is often presented at night, unable to sleep, anxious and full of terrible premonitions.[131] His men turn against him and hand him over to the enemy; otherwise they ignore him and confirm his worst fears by treating him in advance like one defeated, or already dead. In the last book of his *History,* Orosius reflects on the

130. Nixon and Rodgers, *In Praise of Later Roman Emperors,* 413 note 86, point out, on the subject of Mamertinus's speech of thanks to Julian, 13 (cf. *Panégyriques,* vol. 3, 26–27), an interesting digression on usurpers, who "in propria furentes adfectati regni supplicia pependerunt," that the passage is "a charming novelty in a speech delivered to a successful usurper." John of Biclaro and Isidore of Seville kept a more accurate record: cf. John of Biclaro, *Chronica* 579? 3 (ed. Mommsen, 215): "Hermenegildus . . . tyrannidem assumens . . ."; Isidore, *Historia Gothorum* 57 (ed. Mommsen, 290): "Wittericus sumpta tyrannide inocuum [i.e. Liuva II] regno deiecit . . ."

131. Cf. Sallust, *Bellum Iugurthinum* 72, 2 (ed. Rolfe, 286): "Neque post id locorum Iugurthae dies aut nox ulla quieta fuit . . ." and Ammianus's account of the agony of Procopius, *Historiae* 26, 9, 9 (ed. Seyfarth, vol. 4, 42–43): "maiore itaque noctis parte consumpta, cum a uespertino ortu luna praelucens in diem metum augeret, undique facultate euadendi exempta consiliorum inops Procopius, ut in arduis necessitatibus solet, cum Fortuna expostulabat luctuosa et graui . . ."

usurpers who threatened the long reign of Honorius, discussing them not as individuals but as specimens, familiar manifestations of a predictable and doomed phenomenon. His thoughts can be read as the deepest and most concentrated expression of the late antique experience of usurpation as that experience turns into types and literary formulae; they add up to a *catalogus tyrannorum*, a pageant of failure, humiliation, and betrayal:

> From this point, I will go over the catalogue of usurpers as succinctly as possible: Gerontius, a worthless rather than evil man, murdered Constans the son of Constantine, whose attendant he was, at Vienne and set in his place a certain Maximus. As for Gerontius himself, he was killed by his soldiers. Maximus, stripped of the purple and abandoned by the soldiers from Gaul who were transferred to Africa and then recalled to Italy, lives now in exile and poverty in Spain, among barbarians. Next Jovinus, the man of highest nobility in Gaul, fell as soon as he elevated himself by usurpation. His brother Sebastian made a single choice: to die as a usurper; and indeed, he was put down as soon as he became one.[132]

The usurper Attalus (406–416), "made, unmade, remade, and deposed" *("imperatore facto, infecto, refecto ac defecto")* by Alaric, who "laughed over the mime and watched the comedy of imperial power" *("mimum risit et ludum spectauit imperii")*, is described, in phrases that summarize the author's vision, as "a hollow likeness of em-

132. Orosius, *Historiae*, 7, 42, 4–6 (ed. Arnaud-Lindet, vol. 3, 124): "Iam hinc, ut de catalogo tyrannorum quam breuissime loquar, Constantem Constantini filium Gerontius comes suus, uir nequam magis quam inprobus, apud Viennam interfecit atque in eius locum Maximum quendam substituit; ipse uero Gerontius a suis militibus occisus est. Maximus exutus purpura destitutusque a militibus Gallicanis, qui in Africa traiecti, deinde in Italiam reuocati sunt, nunc inter barbaros in Hispania egens exulat. Iouinus postea, uir Galliarum nobilissimus, in tyrannidem mox ut adsurrexit et cecidit. Sebastianus frater eiusdem hoc solum ut tyrannus moreretur elegit: nam continuo ut creato occisus est."

pire" ("*inane imperii simulacrum*") and as one who "had borne the shadow of empire" ("*umbram gestaret imperii*").[133]

Panegyrics elaborate single traits of this general and abstract figure to fit individual *tyranni*. Thus, for example, Claudian's poem of 404 on the sixth consulate of Honorius makes the defeated Alaric after the battle of Pollentia a usurper by association. He is terrified ("*tremens*") and besieged by the enemy ("*obsessus*"), his soldiers curse him openly and soon begin to desert: "Already frequent desertions reduce his diminished forces, and within single days the count of his army decreases."[134] He begs them not to leave, but in vain, and then with tearful eyes ("*oculis umentibus*") breaks into a monologue in which, among many other regrets, he describes the well-known fate of the *tyrannus*, who is marked out for betrayal: "Is there not one of my followers left? My companions are hostile, my intimates loathe me. Why do I tarry, when life is hateful? Where shall I hide the fragments of my wrecked life?"[135]

In his prose panegyric of Theodosius, Pacatus had attempted a more comprehensive treatment: beginning with a general indictment of usurpers, he brought to the portrait of Maximus, the *tyrannus* of Gaul, elements of Christian damnation missing in the poems of the pagan Claudian. Early on, the panegyrist apostrophizes usurpers as a class: "Hear this, murderers of your country,

133. Ibid. 7, 42, 7–10 (ed. Arnaud-Lindet, vol. 3, 124–125). Cf. Sidonius, *Panegyricvs dictvs Avgvsto 538–541* (ed. Anderson, vol. 1, 164): "sed dum per verba parentum / ignavas colimus leges sanctumque putamus / rem veterem per damna sequi, portavimus umbram / imperii..." The phrase is used here by a spokesman of the Gallic nobility to describe the role of Valentinian III.

134. (Ed. Platnauer, vol. 2, 92) 250–251: "iamque frequens rarum decerpere transfuga robur / coeperat inque dies numerus decrescere castris . . ."

135. Ibid. (ed. Platnauer, vol. 2, 96) 314–317: "nullusne clientum / permanet? Offensi comites, odere propinqui. / quid moror invisam lucem? Qua sede recondam / naufragii fragmenta mei?" In the mini-epic *De bello Gothico*, Alaric is again described as "desertus ab omni / gente sua" (ed. Platnauer, vol. 2, 132; 88–89). Both poems, as expected, swell the claims of Claudian's patron Stilicho. The pathetic Alaric they describe would return in 410 to sack Rome.

who obtained the scepter by defiling it with the blood of your masters and who, at a risk not smaller than the crime, bargaining with your lives for imperial power, bought the title of ruler at the price of blood."[136] In line with this characterization of the entire category of usurpers, which reminds them grimly of the odds they have accepted and will eventually pay, Maximus can later be described as a "purple-clad executioner" (*"purpuratus carnifex"*). When destiny catches up with him, Maximus shows terror and expresses, in the customary interior monologue of his role, a sense of having no allies left and no place of refuge open: "Meanwhile Maximus escaped, looking behind him to watch out for you, in the manner of one demented and terrified. He had no plans, no ideas, and not even hope, which is the last thing to abandon men . . . 'Where shall I flee? Should I try to make war? And will I be able to resist with part of my forces him whom I could not stand up to with all of them? Should I close off the Cottian Alps, now that the Julian Alps have served me so well? Shall I seek Africa, which I exhausted? Revisit Britain, which I abandoned? Entrust myself to Gaul? But I am hated there? Have confidence in Spain? But I am known there.'"[137] But if Maximus is mad, this is, according to Pacatus, the work of God and of Theodosius's imperial good fortune, which drive the usurper to take insane measures that bring about his fall and his punishment. "Finally, God turned his eyes once more in our direction . . . and cast madness upon that cursed head so that he tore up

---

136. *Panegyricvs Theodosio Avgvsto dictvs* 12, 2 (*Panégyriques*, vol. 3, 79): "Audite hoc, publici parricidae, qui oblita caede dominorum sceptra cepistis et periculo non minore quam scelere, imperium uita paciscentes, sanguinis pretio regni nomen emistis . . ."

137. Ibid. 38, 1–2 (*Panégyriques*, vol. 3, 104–105): "Ibat interim Maximus ac te post terga respectans in modum amentis attonitus auolabat. Nec ullum ille consilium ullamue rationem aut denique spem, quae postrema homines deserit, sequebantur; (. . .) 'Quo fugio? bellumne temptabo? ut quem uiribus totis ferre non potui parte sustineam? Alpes Cottias obserabo, quia Iuliae profuerunt? peto Africam quam exhausi? repeto Britanniam quam reliqui? credo me Galliae? sed inuisus sum. Hispaniae committo? sed notus sum.'"

the treaty, violated fetial law, and was not afraid to declare war."[138] "But who can have doubts that Fortune had a part in his lack of reason? It was she, she who blinded the counsels of the usurper, she who blunted both his courage and his sword, she who struck and held back the hand already stretched out to kill himself."[139]

Julian of Toledo's account of Paul *in extremis* should be read as a late and particularly rich instance of this late antique literary tradition of the fall of usurpers. It is unusual in that it consists almost entirely of dramatic narrative, with little of the moralizing commentary that serves as binding element in the panegyrics. In addition, it brings the dimension of time to what is elsewhere the description of a single climactic moment of downfall: the sequence *Hist.* 16–21 covers more than two successive days, at the beginning of which (*Hist.* 16) we find Paul still in command, although his men no longer take his word for truth and they contradict him openly. After Nîmes falls and the rebels make their final move into the protection of the amphitheater, we learn that "a new rebellion now breaks out among the rebels themselves" ("*[s]urgit etiam nova inter seditiosos ipsos seditio*" [*Hist.* 19]) as the Galli turn against their foreign leader and the men he had brought from Spain. A significant deviation from the traditional portrait of the usurper meeting his doom is that Paul, though ignored and despised, is not betrayed by the Galli, who instead fear he may make his peace with Wamba by betraying them.

---

138. Ibid. 30, 1 (*Panégyriques*, vol. 3, 96): "Tandem in nos oculos deus retulit . . . et hunc sacerrimo capite obiecit furorem ut foedus abrumpere, ius fetiale uiolare, bellum edicere non timeret." "*Ius fetiale*," i.e. fetial law or fetial custom, refers to the prerogatives of the college of fetial priests, who in Rome were in charge of the formalities involved in declaring war and in sanctioning peace treaties.

139. Ibid. 42, 2 (*Panégyriques*, vol. 3, 109): ". . . num cui dubium est in eo quod non habuit rationem fuisse Fortunam? Illa, illa tyranni consilia caecauit, illa et animum eius obtudit et gladium, illa expeditam in uulnus manum percussit et tenuit."

Absent since *Hist.* 8, Paul reappears on the battlements of Nîmes in a scene derived from epic poetry: a teichoscopy, or view from the city walls. The scenic type, which can be traced as far back as *Iliad* III and Helen's explication of the Greek camp to the Trojan elders, is fittingly introduced by a Vergilian formula about Dawn's saffron couch.[140] The crowd within the city is already standing on the walls at the dawn of day, eager to inspect the condition of the besieging army. As in the most traditional teichoscopies, the activity of those who watch is characterized as interpretation: they must make sense of the possibly misleading sights the daylight reveals. They see many more campfires than on the previous day and conclude rightly that the army has grown overnight. Paul now appears on his way to a high watchtower for a privileged view of the field. He will occupy a physical equivalent of the *fastigium regni* to which he aspires, the elevation of arrogance and ambition. The panegyrics occasionally present usurpers on the walls in this same attitude, though the figure looking out is more often the hero of the piece. Claudian has the evil Rufinus gaze in exultation from the walls of besieged Constantinople: "But fierce Rufinus rejoices in the city under siege; he exults in its sorrows, and from the summit of the highest tower he inspects the terrible scenes in the surrounding countryside."[141] In his later short epic on the Gothic war, however, he describes—in the first person plural of an eyewitness—the population of Milan together with the emperor Honorius himself staring from the city walls as they pray for relief from the impending Gothic siege. A cloud of dust on the horizon may conceal a friend or an enemy, but then Stilicho's head emerges from it, and those on the walls recognize his white hair and know that they are

---

140. On early medieval versions of teichoscopy, see Courcelle, "Une 'τειχοσκοπια' chez Grégoire de Tours."

141. *In Rufinum* 2 (ed. Platnauer, vol. 1, 62) 61–63: "obsessa tamen ille ferus laetatur in urbe / exultatque malis summaeque ex culmine turris / impia vicini cernit spectacula campi . . ."

saved.[142] The pathos of the doomed usurper and the peculiar effect of sympathy that may make of him a victim in the end, even if a deserving one, is especially clear in a later scene of this general type, Gregory of Tours's narrative of the siege of the pretender Gundovald at Comminges by the forces of King Guntram.[143] When Gundovald appears on the walls "on top of the town gate" to answer the scurrilous personal attacks of the besiegers with what sounds like a sincere account of his life, it is easy to believe that Gregory of Tours considered his claims to be genuine and saw him as a pawn of the ambitious conspirators who had lured him from Constantinople and were to hand him over to Guntram's men shortly thereafter. Since the scene involves neither seeing nor interpretation, it cannot be considered a proper teichoscopy, but it expresses powerfully the conflicting emotions evoked by the literary *tyrannus*.[144]

When Paul speaks, his words are addressed to those behind the walls. He has nothing to say to the Goths, but he still can, and

142. *De bello Gothico* (ed. Platnauer, vol. 2, 158) 455–461: "pulveris ambiguam nubem speculamur ab altis / turribus, incerti socios adportet an hostes / ille globus. mentem suspensa silentia librant, / donec pulvereo sub turbine sideris instar / emicuit Stilichonis apex et cognita fulsit / canities. gavisa repens per moenia clamor / tollitur 'ipse venit.'"

143. *Historiae* 7, 36 (ed. Krusch and Levison, 357): "Ascendebant enim multi per collem et cum Gundovaldo saepius loquebantur, inferentes ei convitia ac dicentes: 'Tune es pictur ille, qui tempore Chlotacharii regis per oraturia parietis adque camaras caraxabas? Tune es ille, quen Ballomerem nomine saepius Galliarum incolae vocitabant?' . . . At ille, cum haec audiret, proprius super portam adstans dicebat: 'Quod me Chlotacharius pater meus exosum habuerit, habetur incognitum nulli; quod autem ab eo vel deinceps a fratribus sim tonsoratus, manifestum est omnibus. . . . Tamen, si tanto odio nostro mens vestra crassatur, vel ad regem vestrum deducar, et si me cognuscit fratrem, quod voluerit faciat. Certe, si nec hoc volueritis, vel liceat mihi regredi, unde prius egressus sum. Abibo enim et nulli quicquam iniuriae inferam.'"

144. On Gregory of Tours's attitude to Gundovald's claims see Wood, "The secret histories," 264–266, and on the strategy of the siege at Comminges, Bachrach, *The Anatomy of a Little War*, 133–148.

must, lie to his own people. The argument he comes up with to re-
vive their courage is based on a double falsehood: that the Goths
are not to be dreaded as warriors, their prowess being wholly a
thing of the past, and that the Gothic army is now complete and
there are thus no further reinforcements to fear. This second lie
forces him to the conclusion that Wamba must be present on the
field before the wall, even if he does not show himself or his banner. But Paul's followers are now less docile and question his falsehoods: many of his men (*"plerique ex suis"*) object that a king cannot
go forth without his banners. Paul's reply, that Wamba is intentionally keeping down his standards to make the rebels think he is elsewhere and may arrive with fresh troops at any moment, is clearly
the last argument left to him and destined to be discounted or put
in doubt.

Hist. 17–18 marks a pause and a transition in Julian's portrayal of
the usurper confronting his fate: for a moment, the focus moves
away from him to describe actual fighting (though for the rebels it
is, as always, fighting from the walls) and the final step in the collective withdrawal of the *tyrannus* and his men before the victorious
Goths as they give up Nîmes itself for the more strongly fortified
castrum arenarum. Paul by now is entirely passive and defeated, even
before his followers, and the blame begins to shift to them because
of their enduring hostility to Spain, which they display by attacks
on their former leader and the men he has brought over from beyond the Pyrenees. When they come to him to complain that his
opinion of Gothic courage is false, as proved by the wounds they
have just now received, Julian refers to them as "many of the foreign warriors" (*"plerique de externae gentis hominibus"* [*Hist.* 17]), choos-
ing a significant moment to remember that they are foreigners.[145]

---

145. They are wounded, and therefore must have been fighting, so they have
to be foreigners. In this rather oblique way, Julian strengthens his claim that the
Galli do not do their own fighting.

The incident provides further evidence that what Paul tells them is neither believed nor respected any more.

In the narrowed compass of the amphitheater, the ill-made alliance created by Paul among the troops he has brought from Toledo, the noblemen from the Tarraconensis, the rebels of Gallia and their Frankish helpers breaks down along its natural fault lines, i.e. the conflicting allegiances of these groups, exacerbated by defeat and the certainty of punishment. Paul is never betrayed because the Galli are not in a position to do so: as a Spaniard of high rank, he has advantages over Galli and *externae gentes* whatever his position. But they do turn on him with insults, contempt, and suspicion, and the fact that they are his former associates places Paul in a predicament very similar to that of the usurper betrayed by his own people, a fact stressed in the scenes that follow by insistent play with possessive adjectives and pronouns: "despised by his own," "to rise against your own people," "surrounded (threateningly) by his own people."[146]

In *Hist.* 19 and 20 Paul reaches the extreme of isolation: already rejected by his former allies, who rebel against him (this is the "new rebellion among the rebels themselves"), he is now deprived of the most intimate ties, the ones created by kinship and by personal service, when he sees the rebels kill one of his servants *("vernulus suus")* and then a member of his family *("vir quidem, e sua ortus familia")* and he is unable to do anything to help them. This second victim places the guilt squarely on Paul's head before dying: the usurper has armed himself against his own people (whether the Spaniards or the Goths) and is unable to protect himself or his dependants—his family, friends, and servants—from the violence he

146. Cf. "quendam e suis e suorum manibus ante se iugulari prospiciens" (*Hist.* 19), "suum esse vernulum . . . clamaret" (ibid.), "e suis ipsis contemnitur" (ibid.), "e sua ortus familia" (*Hist.* 20), "contra tuos insurgere" (ibid.), "cum nec tibi nec tuis nunc valeas . . . prodesse" (ibid.), "circumventus a suis iugulatus obcubuit" (ibid.).

has unleashed. Paul, already pale and trembling (*"exsanguis ac treme-bundus effectus"* [*Hist.* 19]), speaks only in the gentlest and most plain-tive tones (*"ab illo blandis hortaretur sermonibus"* [*Hist.* 20]) and with wholly uncharacteristic moderation. When his relative falls from the marble steps of the amphitheater to his death at the hands of Paul's former subjects, the usurper is witness to a literal illustration of what, more allegorically, is happening to himself. The other's fall places Paul, by implication, once more on a high point, a summit that he will not occupy for long; to this end, the mention of marble steps takes account, for once in the *Historia,* of the internal archi-tecture of the amphitheater at Nîmes. To the hostile witnesses of his last moments as "king of the East," Paul is almost as if a corpse already (*"quasi et ipse continuo moriturus"*); he does not count and need not be listened to. He has become the empty husk described by Orosius as "a hollow likeness of empire" and it is possibly for that reason that he must complete the ritual of humiliation on his own, by taking off the royal garments he had adopted.[147] There is no one to either force or help him to do it, because he is completely alone. In the panegyrics, this moment is variously realized. Pacatus makes it a ritual humiliation for the defeated Maximus: ". . . the diadem is struck down from his head, the tunic torn from his shoulders, the ornaments plucked from his feet, and the whole man arrayed ac-cording to his desserts. The plunderer of public wealth is stripped in public, his rapacious hands bound, the fugitive's legs laid bare, and he is placed before your eyes as it is fitting that the captive be presented to the victor, the slave to his master, the usurper to the emperor."[148] The panegyrist of Constantius Chlorus in 297 turns

---

147. Note, however, that he does not remove the *cingulum,* which he only takes off later, in the presence of Wamba (*Hist.* 25). Though it is not counted among the insignia of kingship, this points to its extraordinary symbolic im-portance. See above at notes 110 and 111 to this chapter.

148. *Panegyricvs Theodosio Avgvsto dictvs* 43, 22, 2–3 (*Panégyriques,* vol. 3, 109): ". . . capiti diadema decutitur, humeris uestis aufertur, pedibus ornatus euellitur, totus denique homo aptatur ad meritum. Publice publicus spoliator exuitur,

the gesture into a voluntary admission of defeat from the leader of an uprising in Britain, who lies dead "having renounced voluntarily those (imperial) garments that he had profaned while he lived."[149] In a brief but highly stylized piece of ceremonial staging, Paul is also the one to confirm, by a change of costume, his new status as already-dead or almost-dead: he keeps on the robe he wears to take communion the next day, which he expects will serve him as a shroud, as traitors were often denied interment (*Hist.* 21).

e. Politics of Clemency (*Hist.* 21–25)

The final chapter of the rebellion is at hand; all that remains is to negotiate the terms of surrender. Although the scene presented by Julian of Toledo appears to involve only abject self-abasement on the part of the rebels and the offer of a very qualified mercy by the victorious Wamba, it in fact conceals much calculation and maneuvering on either side, the unspoken political dimension of the granting of pardons.

The episode, at the center of which Julian placed the interview of Wamba with Bishop Argebadus, is framed by tableaux of the army, now headed by the king in person, as it appears before Nîmes to enforce the surrender. The first part, culminating in the meeting of bishop and king, takes place four miles from the city (*"quarto fere ab urbe miliario"*); then Wamba and his forces, described again with a flattering *praeteritio*, move forward until they are only one stadium distant from their goal (*"eminus ab urbe fere uno stadio positus"*). The sequence first moves outward from the city with Argebadus, who sets forth as delegate of the rebels. This is important because the initial appearance of the king leading his men implies the point of view

---

nectuntur manus rapaces, nudantur crura fugitiuo, talis denique tuis offertur oculis qualem offerri decebat uictori captum, domino seruum, imperatori tyrannum."

149. *Panegyricvs Constantio dictvs* 16, 4 (*Panégyriques,* vol. 1, 95): ". . . cultu illo quem uiuus uiolauerat sponte deposito."

of the suppliant bishop who sees them arrive. Wamba in fact *reappears,* having last been seen in *Hist.* 11. After his marked absence during the fighting, underscored by Paul's lies to his own people, the king now makes an entrance in a wholly new attitude designed to increase the alarm and apprehension of his enemies: he is on horseback at the head of a large army. It is notable that Wamba's deportment in this scene, where he is very much the bearer of the military belt, involves no hieratic rigidity:[150] he remarks Argebadus, dismounted and crouching in the dust by the way, and his dialogue with the bishop is accompanied first by copious tears on the part of both and then by a sudden burst of anger.

Unanswered questions about Argebadus's participation in the rebellion add to the political ambiguity of this episode. Originally (*Hist.* 7), he had been loyal to Wamba and attempted to block the road to Narbonne against Paul's army, for which he had been denounced and insulted by the usurper. But now, begging the king's mercy for his defeated rival, he refers to the rebels with an inclusive *"nos."* This could express his emotional solidarity with the men on whose behalf he is speaking, but it could also be an indication that he had, at some point previously, yielded to their pressure and joined their conspiracy.[151] Particularly suspicious is his presence at Nîmes. If he is the bishop of Narbonne, why did he not stay in that city, in the custody of Witimirus? Why has he followed the leaders of the rebellion in their retreat across Gallia?

The sequence as a whole makes its point by playing against familiar narrative stereotypes. A king arrives in a city of his realm, and he does so in full force, with elements of pageantry and dis-

---

150. A stony impassibility was dictated by the ceremonial style of late antiquity, inspired possibly by the Persian court; see Charlesworth, "Imperial Deportment." On the religious sense of this ritual demeanor, see Fontaine, "Un cliché de la spiritualité antique tardive."

151. Cf. Thompson, *Goths in Spain,* 220: ". . . the Bishop seems later to have compromised himself with the insurgents."

play: we would expect the description of an *adventus*.[152] But Wamba is not visiting Nîmes: he comes ready to take it by force. And no one emerges to welcome him to the famished and half-destroyed city: a single petitioner on the road cannot replace the customary procession of welcome. Wamba is compelled to do the exact opposite of a king shown in the act of arrival: he has to send his own men into Nîmes to bring out the defeated rebels to meet him where he stands, one stadium from the gates. But the sense of this contrast is precisely that we do not have an *adventus* here, and hence none of the festive tone and the emotions of political wholeness evoked by that ceremony.

The encounter of bishop and ruler is as familiar as *adventus* and refers us to countless episodes in early medieval historiography in which *sacerdotium* meets *regnum* and where, if the saint or prelate has anything to ask of the secular lord, he most often "receives everything he requested," as a token of the deference of earthly rulers to the spiritual powers.[153] The scheme, ultimately derived from the conflicts and collaborations of kings with high priests and prophets in the Old Testament, hovers over Argebadus and Wamba as they meet on the road to the city. But Argebadus is not speaking for the church, so it cannot be said that he represents it, and he is not pleading for Nîmes, because he is not its bishop. The *"nos"* he uses with Wamba refers only to the rebel leaders, and he stands before the king as their spokesman and nothing else. Admittedly, the role of intercessor before armed secular power fits exactly into a bishop's attributions in such episodes, but why is he at Nîmes, pleading only for the king's enemies, and not taking care of his own flock in Narbonne? Another feature of the scene that distinguishes it from the usual church/state encounter is Argebadus's extreme self-abasement

152. On the practice and meaning of *adventus* see McCormack, "Change and Continuity in Late Antiquity."

153. On scenes of this type see Martínez Pizarro, "Images of Church and State."

when he grovels in the dust before the mounted king. He must begin by admitting to guilt (though perhaps only from empathy with the men he speaks for), so he cannot take the usual righteous stance of the representative of the priesthood, but his posture is still shocking, as evidenced by the reaction of Wamba who, while he stays on horseback, has the prelate brought to his feet. Mounted figures are rare but not unheard of in such scenes: the *Historia tripartita* of Epiphanius and Cassiodorus, well known to Visigothic historians and a specially rich source of church/state episodes,[154] describes, in a passage taken from Theodoret, the encounter between two emissaries of the emperor Theodosius, the *magister militum* Hellebichus and the *magister officiorum* Caesarius, and some Syrian monks. The imperial dignitaries were bringing to Antioch the emperor's threats of punishment because the Antiochenes had rebelled against a new tax and dragged a statue of the empress in the dust:

> When they then arrived . . . who conveyed the emperor's threats, all were moved to terror; but the men who inhabited the desert and who struggled for holiness, many and excellent men, offered countless warnings and prayers to the emperor's envoys. The holy man Macedonius, however, who knew nothing about the present life and was even deeply ignorant of divine writ, but lived in the summit of the mountains offering by day and by night pure prayers to the savior of all, was not induced to show reverence to the emperor or to the judges he had sent, but in the middle of the city seizing the tunics of either, commanded them to dismount from their horses. And seeing this minuscule old man covered with wretched rags, they were at first outraged. But when some men who exhorted them to comply had explained to them the (spiritual) power of the man, they quickly leaped from their horses and, touching his knee, humbly begged his indulgence.[155]

154. See Hillgarth, "Historiography," 278–279.
155. *Historia tripartita* 9, 32, 6–7 (ed. Jacob and Hanslik, 548–549): "Cum igitur venissent, qui portabant minas imperatoris, Hellebichus magister mili-

The change in posture of Hellebichus and Caesarius, who start
out high on their mounts and indignant at the monk's insolence
and end at his feet touching his knee, in the conventional attitude
of supplication, restores the true scale of values by acknowledging
the superiority of spiritual *virtus*, and that is the usual outcome of
such encounters in ecclesiastical histories. It does not matter that
the secular officials are on a perfectly justifiable mission, that the rebellion is a genuine uprising against imperial authority, or that the
empress, affronted in effigy, has been portrayed in the previous
chapter (also borrowed from Theodoret) as a pious and charitable
woman.[156] Wamba, on the other hand, never descends from his
horse, even if he has Argebadus raised from the dust. He rebukes
the bishop angrily for his escalating demands and refuses to grant
the general pardon that he requests for the rebels. The point is
clearly that Argebadus did not obtain everything he asked for, and
the king rides on, moved, as we are told, by a sudden anger *("percito
furore commotus")* and roused by a firing or kindling of his spirit
("quadam animi succensione"), as if the fevers and high temperatures
that fueled the insurrection were making a last appearance, cours-
ing this time not through the conspirators or the Spanish troops,
but through the spirits of the ruler himself.

If the scene is not an *adventus* and diverges in all these ways from
the traditional models for church/state encounters, we may ask

---

tum et Caesarius magister officiorum, erant omnes sub formidine constituti.
Porro viri heremum habitantes, virtutis propugnatores, multi tunc et optimi
viri, plurima monita simul et preces eis, qui a principi missi fuerant, offerebant.
Macedonius autem vir sanctus, nihil huius vitae sciens, sed etiam divinorum li-
brorum penitus inexpertus, in summitatibus habitans montium, noctibus ac
diebus salvatori omnium puras offerens preces, non imperatoris indignatione
permotus, non iudicum ab eo missorum, in media civitate utriusque clamydem
conprehendens, ab equis suis ut descenderent, imperabat. At illi parvulum sen-
em pannis obsitum vilissimis intuentes primitus indignati sunt. Cum vero
quidam obsequia perhibentium virtutem viri illius indicassent, repente ab equis
exilientes et genua tenentes eius veniam suppliciter implorabant."

156. Ibid. 9, 31–32 (ed. Jacob and Hanslik, 546–548).

what it really is and, more importantly, what narrative function it fulfills. The most plausible answer would seem to be that it is a public petition, that is to say an episode designed to frame a display of royal *clementia*. The nature of *clementia*, much discussed in Hellenistic and early imperial political philosophy,[157] is an ideologically critical question because it defines the standing of the ruler —whether emperor or king—in relation to the law. Since *clementia* prompts the sovereign to qualify and mitigate the harshness of codified justice, it makes it possible to argue that in certain respects he stands above the law, for he can prevent its strict application. The panegyrics echo these debates and betray their importance: already Pliny announces to Trajan, "What I now hear and learn for the first time is not 'the ruler is above the laws,' but 'the laws are above the ruler.' When Caesar is consul, the same things are forbidden to him as to others."[158] Claudian lets Theodosius instruct the young Honorius as follows: "If you give a decree to be obeyed by all, or pass a law of general application, submit to it first yourself. The people are more inclined to comply with the law, and do not refuse to keep it, when they see its author obey it."[159] A law of Reccesvind had proclaimed the same principle, with the significant qualification that "subjects are compelled to respect the law by necessity, rulers by [their] will."[160] The clemency of a prince flows from emotions of *misericordia* and *pietas*, attributed with praise to the

157. See Adams, *Clementia principis.*

158. *Panegyricvs* 65, 1 (ed. Durry, 155): "Quod ego nunc primum audio, nunc primum disco, non est 'Princeps super leges,' sed 'Leges super principem' idemque Caesari consuli quod ceteris non licet."

159. *Panegyricus de quarto consulatu Honorii Augusti* 296–299 (ed. Platnauer, vol. 1, 308): "In commune iubes si quid censesque tenendum, / primus iussa subi: tunc observantior aequi / fit populus nec ferre negat, cum viderit ipsum / auctorem parere sibi."

160. LV 2, 1, 2 (ed. Zeumer, 46): ". . . quatenus subiectos ad reverentiam legis inpellat necessitas, principis voluntas." On this law see King, *Law and Society*, 44–45.

ruler by Visigothic church councils; it also confers upon the head of state the superiority that comes from being in full control of his anger and not yielding to vengeful and punitive impulses. In the flattering language of the panegyrics, however, the ruler's mercy and his innate disposition to forgive are made out to be much harder to restrain than his wrath. Theodosius, having defeated Maximus, is on the point of granting the usurper his life when, according to Pacatus, his own people intervene to save the emperor from becoming the victim of his generous impulses: "Indeed, you had already started to hesitate as to his dying, and cast down your eyes, suffused your face with blushing, and spoke mercifully. But it is good that you cannot do everything you wish. Your men avenge you even when you are unwilling. He is quickly removed from your sight and, to bar clemency from any intervention, he is borne to his death by countless hands."[161]

Petition scenes, since they allow the king to exhibit so many fine qualities, may fall under the suspicion of being rehearsed and wholly insincere, the terms of mercy discussed and agreed upon privately before the formal granting of the request takes place in public. Medieval instances increase our doubts that these pardons and concessions were dictated by the emotions of the moment.[162] Here both the unprecedented step taken by Argebadus in adding to his petition once the initial request had been accorded, and the king's abrupt and furious refusal guarantee the unprepared, genuine quality of the incident. The bishop's bold attempt has failed, and the question arises of the purpose served by presenting his failure so dramatically, together with Wamba's brief but intense flash of temper. The most convincing explanation is likely to be

161. *Panegyricvs Theodosio Avgvsto dictvs* 44, 2 (*Panégyriques,* vol. 3, 110): "Quin iam coeperas de eius morte dubitare et deieceras oculos et uultum rubore suffuderas et cum misericordia loquebaris. Sed bene est quod non omnia potes. Tui te uindicant et inuitum. Rapitur ergo ex oculis et, ne quid posset licere clementiae, inter innumeras manus fertur ad mortem."

162. See Althoff, "Demonstration und Inszenierung," 43–45.

political, i.e. to be based on the function of the HWR in the Toledo of the mid-670s: Wamba's dramatic reaction serves to cover up the fact that he has already granted as much as he possibly can. The rebels were guilty of usurpation and treason against the country, and of inviting foreign nations into Spain to help them out. Chindasvind had passed laws against such *refugae* and *insulentes*, making their crime punishable by death or—with royal mercy—blinding, laws which were invoked at Nîmes during the trial of Paul and his accomplices (*Iud.* 7).[163] Argebadus's demand that the king, having promised immunity from these penalties to all the rebel leaders, should also agree not to punish them at all is so excessive that it can only be understood as a distraction from the vastness of what Wamba has already conceded. It is important to show that the ruler can say no, most probably because he really cannot, because this early in his reign he does not wield the power to have men of the rank of Paul and the leaders of the rebellion in Gallia put to death. He must be content with mere decalvation,[164] and with the pageant of disgrace described in *Hist.* 30. The confiscation of their property decreed in *Iud.* 7 does not appear to have reduced the conspirators to political insignificance, because in 683 they were still influential enough to compel Ervig to return their estates under the blanket measure of restoring their right to testify.[165] This consideration would also make sense of Julian's detailed account of the ritual humiliation of the defeated, first by the *calcatio colli* (*Hist.* 27) and later by a parade of dishonor in Toledo: in a narrative that pays little attention to the forms of ritual and ceremony,

163. LV 2, 1, 8 (ed. Zeumer, 53–57); cf. the comments of Zeumer, "Geschichte II," 57–68 (on Wamba's application of the law see especially p. 67).

164. *Hist.* 27: "Sed nulla mortis super eos inlata sententia, decalvationis tantum, ut praecipitur, sustinere vindictam."

165. Cf. Toledo XIII, *tomus* and canon 1 (Vives, 411–416). Ervig describes this measure using the familiar metaphor of the body politic: ". . . divulsam per tyrannidem nostri corporis partem in societatis nostrae gremio conamur reducere" (ibid. 412).

these descriptions have been included to disguise the king's relative impotence in victory as a bold statement of power over his enemies.

6. The *Insultatio*

a. Design

The *Insultatio* is so different from what comes before and after it that it has often been discussed as a separate and independent work, closely related to the *Historia* and the *Iudicium* but with a purpose and design of its own. It can be characterized as a highly rhetorical oration: as such it has a speaker, the "humble historian" *("vilis storicus")* of its incipit, who addresses the personified Gallia. Accordingly, the entire composition is in the second person singular. Equally new and remarkable is the almost complete absence of narrative: real, individual characters vanish from the scene, even Wamba himself is mentioned only in passing as *"unctus" (Ins.* 5: *"anima uncti sui")* and *"ordinatus princeps" (Ins.* 7), while no reference at all is made to Paul or to Hildericus, the originator of the rebellion in Gallia. No individual actions are narrated or discussed, only collective responsibilities of the Galli and the Spaniards and allegorical activities of the personified province. A less obvious but important feature of the *Insultatio* is its time-frame, which presupposes the events of the *Historia* as the speaker addresses an already defeated Gallia, but also reaches back beyond the origins of the rebellion to survey the entire previous history of relations between Visigothic Spain and its Gallic territories.

And yet, the aim of Julian of Toledo is to inscribe the *Insultatio* within the sequence of the HWR, and the work can be understood only in that context. The title of *storicus* identifies its speaker as the author of the *Historia.* After a fairly detailed account of the rebellion and its defeat, he is qualified to outline a balance-sheet of the guilt of Gallia; as a historian, he knows well whereof he speaks. Especially significant is *Hist.* 5, which introduces the allegorical character of the perverse nurse/mother, feverish with evil, who raises a monstrous child of reptilian features. Personification occurs nowhere else in the *Historia*, so when this same memorable figure reappears in the *Insultatio*, we may take it as an indication that the time has come to deal with the crimes of Gallia, and in the specific (figurative) terms introduced early in the *Historia* for this purpose.

The *Insultatio* is more concerned with formal invention and rhetorical display than the other parts of the HWR.[166] A province as such cannot appear in court, and when denouncing Gallia the *storicus* need make no effort to establish her responsibility for specific acts of betrayal. The allegory of Gallia, who is first a perverse woman who hurts herself and her benefactors, then the complacent mother of a monstrous child (the rebellion), then the mother of perverse and treacherous sons (the Galli), and finally a female sick with a deep-seated malady requiring harsh medical treatment, elaborates freely if somewhat chaotically on a model provided by Julian's sources. It frames a number of more or less ambitious devices, notably a protracted *ubi sunt* that outlines the evil, self-destructive nature of Gallia and a point-by-point comparison or *synkrisis* between her children the Galli, who take after her, and the Spaniards, their ill-used benefactors.

b. Personification: Mother and Monster

The character of Gallia has considerable originality. It has been connected to the personification of Spain in the *"Laus Spaniae"* that opens Isidore's history of the Goths.[167] There Spain is addressed as "mother of princes and nations" and as "queen of all provinces," as a mother and queen thus who was first chosen by the power of Rome (*"Romulea virtus"*) but later seized by the rising prosperity of the Goths.[168] In order to derive his Gallia from this model, or

166. Collins, "Julian of Toledo and the Royal Succession," 39, describes *Insultatio* and *Iudicium* as "more redolent of works composed for the schoolroom."
167. See McCormick, *Eternal Victory*, 326.
168. HG (ed. Mommsen, 267): "... o sacra semperque felix principum

rather to set her up in opposition to it, Julian would have had to turn positive into negative systematically, but also to add many details to Isidore's rather thin allegory.[169] Closer to the hostile and negative characterization of Gallia comes the personified Synagoga of an anonymous fifth-century *Altercatio ecclesiae et synagogae* that has been attributed to Severus of Minorca.[170] There Synagoga, treated as a defeated rival by Ecclesia, is described by her as a "once purple-clad queen," refers to herself as a mother of many sons ("I who had so many and such great sons . . . who was the mother of nations"), is accused of homicide ("you are charged with the crime of murder"), and is twice addressed as "wretched one" (*"misera"*), very much like Julian's Gallia.[171] But a more comprehensive model for the monstrous nurse or nursing mother of the *Insultatio* can be found in Claudian's poems of invective, which combine the rhetorical scheme of *vituperatio* (Greek *psogos*) with such features of late antique short epic as a narrative structure and allegorical personifications.[172] *Vituperatio* is in fact an inversion of panegyric, and this affinity brings the *In Rufinum* and *In Eutropium* very close to the genre

---

gentiumque mater Spania: iure tu nunc omnium regina provinciarum . . ." (Ibid.) "iure itaque te iam pridem Roma caput gentium concupivit et licet te sibimet eadem Romulea virtus primum victrix desponderit, denuo tamen Gothorum florentissima gens post multiplices in orbem victorias certatim rapuit et amavit . . ."

169. Isidore portrays Spain almost entirely in terms of natural resources and landscape, about which Julian, who probably never went to Gallia, had nothing to say. The "Gallia crine ferox" personified by Claudian with conventional allegorical props in the second book of his panegyric on the consulship of Stilicho (ed. Platnauer, vol. 2, 20), 241–243, is of course the Roman and not the Visigothic province and could hardly have been recycled for use here.

170. See Hillgarth, "Historiography," 301–302.

171. *Altercatio* (ed. Segui and Hillgarth), lines 74–75: "et ecce sub pedibus meis purpurata quondam regina versaris"; 482–483: ". . . ego quae tot et tantos filios habui et filiorum multitudine gloriata sum, et derelicta despicior, quae fui mater populis"; 523: "homicidii crimen admisseris"; 357: "Audi misera, audi infelicissima"; 394–395: "Ergo misera quod negare non potes confitere." This source would also agree with the anti-Judaic animus of the HWR.

172. See Levy, "Claudian's *In Rufinum*," 58–60.

that appears to have been the chief source of inspiration for the
HWR as a whole.

The direct ancestry of Julian's Gallia may be traced to the fury
Megaera, who appears early in the *In Rufinum* at a reunion of spirits
of hell *("innumerae pestes Erebi")* gathered to bewail the golden age
conferred upon Rome by Stilicho and Honorius. To this assembly
Megaera announces that she has a monster in reserve whom she has
personally nourished and brought up and who is capable, by himself, of bringing to an end the present peace and harmony of the
world. Although Megaera, unlike Gallia, is not directly characterized as *altrix, nutrix,* or *mater,* she presents herself as the wet-nurse of
this infant-monster, who is no other than Rufinus, the prefect of
the East: "I have a monster more terrible than all hydrae . . . whom
I was the first to take to my bosom as he left his mother's womb."[173]
The baby is not just nursed by the snakes that make up Megaera's
locks, but is himself serpent-like, in the movements with which he
crawls *("reptavit")* to her breasts and twines himself *("volutus")*
around her neck which, like Gallia's *"elata colla"* (*Ins.* 1), is high-raised
("ardua colla").[174] We are very close to the images of a viper-birth
("generatione viperea" [*Hist.* 5], *"viperina nativitate"* [*Ins.* 8]) and a monstrous birth *("genita monstruosa"* [*Ins.* 4], *"monstra ex se genita"* [ibid.])
with which Julian represents the rise of a conspiracy in this disaffected province.

Julian does more than simply copy Claudian's fury; he improves
on Megaera in a variety of ways. Cutting her off from her mythological and pagan origins, he multiplies her feminine roles and
makes her in addition to nurse ("nurse of scandal" [*Ins.* 2]) a mother ("mother of blasphemers" [ibid.]), stepmother ("stepmother of

173. *In Rufinum* 1, 89–93 (ed. Platnauer, vol. 1, 32): "'est mihi prodigium
cunctis inmanius hydris, / . . . quem prima meo de matre cadentem / suscepi
gremio.'"
174. Ibid., 93–96 (ed. Platnauer, vol. 1, 32): "parvus reptavit in isto / saepe
sinu teneroque per ardua colla volutus / ubera quaesivit fletu linquisque trisulcis / mollia lambentes finxerunt membra cerastae; . . .'"

traitors" [ibid.]), and stepdaughter ("stepdaughter of deceit" [ibid.]), tying her to the genealogy and thus to the causation of all imaginable crimes. In her infidelity to Wamba and to Spain, she proves also to be a whore ("to wallow among flocks of harlots in the manner of beasts" [*Ins.* 1]) and an adulteress ("Has even one woman been found who, having a husband, could desire the society of another . . . ?" [*Ins.* 3]). This too is an innovation in Julian's treatment of the classical fury who, as late as Claudian, is destructive and bloodthirsty but not lascivious, whereas Gallia appears to be as inclined to every form of debauch as she is to carnage and treason. More effectively, Julian gives his Gallia a body, movement, and almost a physiology—in any case, a reproductive system. Megaera, like Claudian's other allegories, had been characterized conventionally by props—in her case snaky tresses and a torch—and had grown into her role only by her own spoken account of her sentiments and actions. Gallia, on the other hand, does not speak; she is portrayed by the *storicus* through a series of rhetorical questions, charges, and imprecations. From these, part by part, an anatomy emerges: a wide-open mouth ("*spansa oris tui fastigia*" [*Ins.* 1]) from which haughty speech ("*elatae voces*" [ibid.]) proceeds, a lofty neck ("*elata colla*" [ibid.]), self-destructive hands ("*quum tuis te . . . manibus lacerares*" [ibid.]), breasts that are fountains of evil ("*Haec enim tota ex tuis uberibus promanasse . . .*" [*Ins.* 3], "*hoc . . . primum famosum malum apparuit, . . . inter media uberum tuorum*" [ibid.]), and a violent fist ("*uni pugillo tui*" [*Ins.* 4]). Like her words, her movements ("*motus illi tumentes*" [*Ins.* 1], "*elati motus*" [*Ins.* 4]) and her gait ("*superciliosus incessus*" [*Ins.* 4]) manifest the demented pride and ambition that animated the rebellion. Many of these behavioral rather than physical traits are listed in a second, shorter *ubi sunt* further into the *Insultatio* (*Ins.* 4), where Gallia is described with the vocabulary of elated arrogance and boastfulness that runs through the HWR. Somehow, the association with serpents enables Gallia to secrete poison ("*venena tua*" [*Ins.* 5], "*venena tui pectoris*" [*Ins.* 6]), and her bile is described as a deadly venom (*"fellis tui antidoto"* [*Ins.* 5]). Her female embodiment and her responsibility as intellectual author and begetter of the rebellion are combined in the metaphor of her mind as a womb (*"uterus mentis tuae"* [*Ins.* 3]). By providing her with this much physical reality, Julian ties her to the organological imagery of head and limbs that pervades the HWR, and integrates the conceits of rebellion as monstrous birth and of deep-seated illness ("what words you used to cry out in your fever" [*Ins.* 6], "you are altered by pallor and disfigured by emaciation" [*Ins.* 9]) as the cause of all this criminal behavior with the theme of fever, of the uprising as a soaring temperature of the body politic, making possible in this way the stern forgiveness offered Gallia in the end, contingent on her future health.

The portrait is time-bound; its elements introduced one by one with an *ubi sunt* (*Ins.* 1) are thereby relegated to the past. The present is marked by pallor and emaciation, and in light of this evolution accounted for by illness the traits of evil in Gallia's past incarnation can be read retrospectively as symptoms; thus the way is prepared for clemency. Two themes derived from the panegyrics are introduced to satisfy the claims of justice, though they are at odds with each other. In the first place, the illness, the fever, the madness turn out to be punishments inflicted on Gallia for her evil ways, to make sure that her machinations come to nothing ("What need had you to challenge to battle those stronger than yourself, to plot the destruction of men of greater power? Yet this you do not do undeservedly, but in order that, possessed by madness, you should not know whom you dare to attack" [*Ins.* 6]). This notion, according to which illness does not entirely explain away Gallia's evil, is very close to the belief often expressed by the panegyrists that God drives the usurper mad so that he may fail in his enterprise. Pacatus accounts in this manner for Maximus's errors of strategy.[175] The

175. See above at notes 138–139 to this chapter.

usurper is described later acting "in the manner of one demented and terrified."[176] Nazarius too, in his panegyric of Constantine of 321, attributes Maxentius's ill-chosen disposition of his troops on the battlefield to the usurper's mental derangement caused by a hostile divinity.[177] But Gallia is to be pardoned, and as the *storicus* has established that she was always favored by the Spaniards and by their king (*Ins.* 7 and 8), it remains but for him to interpret his own invective as a further kindness, a harsh but necessary treatment or surgery to cure her ailment. His words (*Ins.* 9) on the danger of a purely superficial healing, which add to the sense of Gallia's corporality with references to her scars (*"in cicatricum locum"*), sores (*"ulcus in sanata iam plaga"*), and compromised lungs (*"vitiatus pulmo"*), echo closely those of Claudian at the beginning of the second book of his *In Eutropium:* "when an ulcer has gone deep into the bones, one must heal it not with the light touch of the hand, but with steel and fire, lest the scar treated in vain burst out soon after. The flame must penetrate deep to allow the sick humors to flow out, leaving the veins empty of corrupted blood and enabling the very source of the illness to become dry."[178] If the illness is a well-earned punishment, perhaps it ought not to be cured; on the other hand, since Gallia has been defeated on all fronts, the penalty may have served its purpose, and mercy may have become politically expedient.

176. See above at note 137 to this chapter.

177. *Panegyricvs Constantino Avgvsto dictvs* 28, 1 (*Panégyriques,* vol. 2, 188): ". . . nisi animum iam metu deuium infestior deus et pereundi maturitas perpulisset; quod ipsa ratio disponendi exercitus docuit illum mente perdita implicatoque consilio . . ."

178. *In Eutropium* 2, 13–18 (ed. Platnauer, vol. 1, 184–186): "ulcera possessis alte suffusa medullis / non leviore manu, ferro sanantur et igni, / ne noceat frustra mox eruptura cicatrix. / ad vivum penetrant flammae, quo funditus umor / defluat et vacuis corrupto sanguine venis / arescat fons ipse mali . . ."

c. The Children of Gallia and Hispania

However vividly portrayed, Gallia stands for an abstraction; the Galli are real, and must be dealt with in other terms. Among the elements of panegyric borrowed and reinterpreted by invective are accounts of the subject's ancestry *(genos)* and upbringing *(anatrophé)* and an itemized comparison *(synkrisis)* with another figure who in panegyric serves as a foil (e.g. Domitian in Pliny's panegyric of Trajan) and in invective, consequently, must be ascribed every good quality.[179] A negative *genos* in invective, even if wholly imaginary, serves to confirm the base and abject character of the subject: his odious traits come from far back; they are deep-seated attributes of his family or nation. Hence Julian's emphasis on Gallia's maternity and on her two kinds of offspring. The monstrous child who should have been aborted or destroyed *(Ins. 4)* is the rebellion against Wamba. Apparently, Gallia pleads that it is not her own child, but came from abroad, which probably must be translated into the argument that the uprising came with Paul and his forces and should not be counted as her own work. While a prostitute and murderess—which Gallia has been made out to be—makes a disgraceful ancestor, the more real effect of *genos* here works in reverse: the province is dishonored by its treason, the mother shamed by her deformed child, the ancestress by her descendants. Her other children, introduced earlier, are the actual Galli who carried out the rebellion, and in presenting them Julian uses a briefly sketched *anatrophé*: because the mother was devoted to the blasphemous Jews, her sons have gone over to the Jewish 'infidelity' *("ad Hebraeorum probati sunt transisse perfidiam"* [*Ins.* 2]).[180]

179. These various parts did not have to be developed in full, or even at all, in every panegyric and invective. Levy, "Claudian's *In Rufinum*," 60, points out that Claudian has not a word to say about Rufinus's ancestry.

180. Here Julian expresses the obsessive fear of Jewish proselytism and Christian apostasy that pervades the Visigothic church councils as well as secular legislation on the Jews.

Perhaps because this judaizing brood of Galli has not been sufficiently characterized, the *synkrisis* or comparison, when it comes (*Ins.* 8) is between Gallia herself and the Spani or children of Spain.[181] It is also possible that, because the balance of their common history is drawn in terms of Gallic *crudelitas* repaid by Spanish *pietas*, the fury-like Gallia was chosen as a more convincing embodiment of that quality than her offspring. The comparison itself is structured very conventionally, as a systematic alternation of opposite characteristics or actions—what the *storicus* describes as "an extraordinary regularity on either side" (*"admirandus alternantium . . . partium ordo"* [*Ins.* 8]). In his panegyric of Theodosius, Pacatus had organized the *synkrisis* between the emperor and Maximus in exactly the same way, distributing the contrasting *notae* to *se* and *te* ("Would he not have reminded himself that you are the son of a victorious general, he of an unknown, you the heir of a most noble family, he a client . . . ?") and later between *secum* and *tecum* ("Finally, on your side loyalty, on his treason; on yours right, on his crime; on your justice, on his injustice . . .").[182] Julian builds his comparison on the contrast of *illi* (the children of Spain) and *tu* (Gallia) and plays with the various forms of parallelism allowed by the device, alternating contrary qualities and attitudes that can be nominalized ("They bring you peace and you give them deceit; they plan your defense, you their destruction" [*Ins.* 8]) with moral and political differences that can only be summed up in entire sentences

181. A further asymmetry: no personified Hispania has been elaborated to counterbalance Gallia. In Claudian's *De consulato Stilichonis* 2, 218–268 (ed. Platnauer, vol. 2, 18–22), the provinces of the empire gather at the temple of Roma, and the first two to speak are Hispania and Gallia (the latter understood in the old imperial sense, i.e. as Gaul).

182. *Panegyricvs Theolosio Avgvsto dictvs* 31, 1 (*Panégyriques*, vol. 3, 97): "Non sibi ipse obiecisset te esse triumphalis uiri filium, se patris incertum; te heredem nobilissimae familiae, se clientem . . . ?" Ibid. 31, 3 (ed. Galletier, vol. 3, 98): "Postremo tecum fidem, secum perfidiam; tecum fas, secum nefas; tecum ius, secum iniuriam . . ."

("When by chance they did not hasten here in arms [i.e. to defend you] they would buy your freedom for a price; you attempted to pay with presents for their destruction, since you could not bring it about by arms" [ibid.]).[183]

That Gallia and her sons (the latter collapsed, for rhetorical purposes, into their *altrix*) should be at war with Hispania and her own children implies that Gallia is not part of Spain and that her offspring are not Spani. Gallia is at best an enclave, a protectorate, and must remain dependent on a foreign army, the *exercitus Gothorum*, for its own defense and security. The *synkrisis*, with the passage leading to it (*Ins.* 7 and 8) uses the term *"Spani"* with remarkable frequency. In the *Historia*, Wamba's subjects had been referred to as *"Gothi."*[184] Only once are they referred to as *"Spani,"* and the occasion is significant: it is after Paul's followers, cornered in the *castrum arenarum*, have started to distrust each other, and the *incolae*, i.e. the native Galli, suspect Paul "and those who had come with him from Spain" of wanting to make peace with Wamba at their expense. Paul's followers from south of the Pyrenees, then, from Toledo to the Tarraconensis, are called *"Spani"*: "the Spani (were suspected by the Galli) of allowing death to be visited upon the natives and then going over to the king" (*". . . Spani vero, ne inrogata ab incolis morte transirent ad principem"* [*Hist.* 19]). The word, in its single occurrence in the *Historia*, reflects the point of view of the Galli: the Spani who fought for Paul are foreigners and as such have options, however desperate, that are not open to the natives. The *synkrisis* in the *Insultatio* uses *"Spani"* seven times, most often in *"exercitus Spanorum,"* but now clearly from the point of view of the opposite side. Through

183. "Illa tibi pacem, tu illis dolos, illi defensionem, tu peremptionem excogitas . . . Illi salutem tuam, et ubi forsam armis non currebant, pretiis emebant; tu necem illorum, quam armis patrare non poteras, muneribus definis comparandam."

184. E.g. "in Gothis principari" (*Hist.* 2); "nec Francos Gothis aliquando posse resistere" (*Hist.* 9); "illa famosissima virtus Gothorum" (*Hist.* 16); "illam quem dicebas in Gothis proeliandi segnitiam" (*Hist.* 17).

the *storicus*'s very pointed use of this term the victors can be heard telling the defeated rebels "We are Spaniards; you are not. You owe us submission and loyalty, because you are forever dependent on our arms and our good will."

7. *Iudicium:* The Scene of Justice

Julian of Toledo based the narrative of his *Historia* on the *Iudicium*, although he also used other sources of information, some of them possibly oral reports from participants in the campaign against Paul. At some point, however, most likely after completing the *Historia*, he subjected the *Iudicium* to a cursory revision and added it to the sequence of the HWR.[185] The revision was superficial, as Julian made no attempt to harmonize the account in the *Iudicium* with that of his own version: the *Iudicium* makes no mention of Wamba's initial campaign against the Basques, or of his success in preventing the troops from disbanding and returning home once that was over. The itinerary into Gallia retains some differences of detail and is more credible than that in the *Historia*. The much-emphasized division of the army into three is passed over in silence, unless the phrases *"per divisiones exercituum"* (*Iud.* 3) and *"simili ordine properantes"* (ibid.) may be considered to refer to it. Finally, the public trial of the rebels ends with a harsh sentence of death, commutable with blinding on the king's merciful initiative, added to which is total expropriation, a stark contrast to the penalty of decalvation decreed in the *Historia*. Julian simply put in a few favorite phrases and quotations.[186] The rather ambitious rhetoric of the opening (*Iud.* 1), with its syntactic parallelism and its series of jussive subjunctives, may owe something to his style; otherwise he appears to have left the document as he found it. Why did he include

185. The hypothesis that Julian revised the *Iudicium* as a first draft or version of the *Historia* is made untenable by the preservation of the *Iudicium* and its inclusion in the HWR.

186. See the discussion of authorship at the beginning of this chapter.

it in the HWR, however? What did he think the *Iudicium* could contribute to the sequence? One obvious reason for inclusion is that the *Iudicium* covers in some detail the trial of the rebels, mentioned but not described in the *Historia* (*Hist.* 27) and in that sense operates as a supplement to Julian's account. The probability is high that Julian omitted all information about the trial from his own account because he had already decided to preserve the *Iudicium*, possibly judging that the deliberations of the army tribunal could best be presented in the language of a court document. It is significant that only the *Historia* records the fact that the trial was held not in Nîmes but outside it, at some distance from the city.[187] This detail is of crucial importance, as it shows that the intended public for this vindication of Wamba's legitimacy were not the defeated Galli of Nîmes or Narbonne, but the leaders of the army themselves, the aristocratic Goths and palatine officials from whom the victorious king still had most to fear.[188] Julian, with his sharper sense of the underlying political dynamics of the campaign, mentions the fact and leaves out the trial itself. The *Iudicium*, perhaps intentionally blind to such unstated realities, stays within the limits of a document and a legal record.

The *Iudicium* also contributes to the formal variety of the HWR sequence, but the contrast of styles it introduces goes hand in hand with a difference in perspective and in intellectual grasp of the events memorialized. If its author writes like a member of the palatine office fully familiar with Visigothic law and conciliar legislation, it is because he thinks like one. The persona who writes or speaks the text identifies himself with a corporate *"nos"* and then, more specifically, as a member of the palatine office: "... after all of us had been summoned and brought together—that is to say, all the elders of the palace, all the *gardingi*, and all those in palatine service ..." ("... *convocatis adunatisque omnibus nobis, id est senioribus cunc-*

187. "eminus a Neumasense urbe in plana cum exercitu" (*Hist.* 27).
188. See McCormick, *Eternal Victory*, 315.

tis palatii, gardingis omnibus omnique palatino officio . . ." [*Iud.* 5]). Strictly speaking, this individual could still be one and the same with the *vilis storicus* of the *Historia* and *Insultatio*, but he uses such a different voice that any identity of the two appears implausible. His first person plural has a conspicuous affinity with the *"nos"* of other legal texts, for instance the *placitum* or pledge of the Toledan Jews under Reccesvind: "we all, Jews of the city of Toledo."[189] If the *Iudicium*, less than one fourth the length of the *Historia*, contains many more names, whole lists of them in fact, with a careful apportioning of responsibility and blame for the events of the rebellion, this is not only a feature of its bureaucratic documentary style but also an expression of the intellectual attitude of the text and the prosecutorial stance of its speaker, who is gathering evidence rather than telling a story.

The method of citation is conspicuous: the speaker/author, who is no biblical scholar and confuses Jeremiah with Isaiah (*Iud.* 1),[190] quotes canons by number from council acts, and book and title for the secular law (*Iud.* 7), and repeats charges almost verbatim whenever written evidence is brought before the court.[191] The contrast is marked with the ostentatiously belletristic preference for anonymous citation that characterizes the *Historia* and the *Insultatio*, with their "as someone said," "as a certain wise man said," "verses with which a wise man is said to have insulted death." The pedantic formalism of the *Iudicium*, which insists on locating the exact chapter and verse of a quoted text, betrays the presence of a radically different logic of composition from that which allows the *storicus*, with studied nonchalance, to strew unascribed *sententiae* over his epicized narrative.[192]

189. LV 12, 2, 17 (ed. Zeumer, 425): "omnes nos ex Hebreis Toletane civitatis."

190. See below note 168 to the translation.

191. See above at note 40 to this chapter.

192. Both are also different from the citations in Julian's later theological

The stylistic difference points to an ideological shift, and one concerned directly with the operation of legal texts. The scene of justice, the drama of the court, is displaced from its human protagonists to the documents of the case, which appear to speak by themselves with no need of interpretation. After a minimal confrontation between Wamba and Paul, with a single short speech on either side (*Iud.* 5 and 6), the remainder of the *Iudicium* is taken up by an account of *contropatio*, the Visigothic procedure for authenticating signatures,[193] applied to the mutually contradictory oaths or *conditiones* sworn by the rebels at Wamba's accession and later, after they went over to Paul, and then by the "bringing forth" of a canon from Toledo IV (". . . the sentence of the council of Toledo, canon 75, was quoted . . .") and from the Visigothic law (". . . the sentence of the law in Book 2, title 1, chapter 6 was referred to . . ."). The human mediation required to produce these texts in court is not specified, even though it is not easily believable that the members of Wamba's palatine office, starting out from Cantabria on a second campaign for which they had not been prepared on their initial departure from Toledo, would carry with them all this documentation. But more important is the effect of the texts and their legal manipulation on the speaker/author and his fellows: all possible doubt is removed, as by a perfect and infallible mechanism: "Taught by the precept of these holy rulings, we could no longer hesitate . . ." (*"Cuius sacri canonis praeceptione instructi, non ultra nobis est dubitandum . . ."* [*Iud.* 7]). The sentence of death or blinding follows with strict necessity. The movement of the *Iudicium* becomes circular at this point: texts (the council acts and law codes, at any rate) have an absolute value: they guarantee the legitimacy and the rightness of a legal decision with total certainty, leaving no room for ar-

---

works, which give no more than the name of the author quoted: "ut ait sanctus Augustinus," "Julianus Pomerius dicit," "In Cassiani voluminibus legimus," "De his ita Origenes doctor in suis dogmatibus docet."

193. See Zeumer, "Zum westgothischen Urkundenwesen."

gument. And the *Iudicium* itself, written in the style of court documents, shares some of their absolute value: the sentence it frames is immutable and beyond criticism.[194]

It is possible to speculate on the interest that this particular aspect of the *Iudicium* might have held for Julian. Confronted in his own *Historia* with the radical lack of accepted criteria of legitimacy that might apply to Wamba, and conscious of the fact that the king, by the manner of his election, represented a new standard, but also that, had he been defeated, Paul would have replaced him on the throne as a matter of course, in line with various successful usurpations in Visigothic history, Julian reaches, within his own text at least, for elements of absolute legitimacy and finds them in ceremonial forms and supernatural tokens. Wamba's acclamation and election and his unction at Toledo are juxtaposed to the devious election of Paul in Narbonne and his delusional coronation with a votive crown. The truth of Wamba's kingship, decreed in heaven before it is confirmed by ritual on earth, is marked by signs and miracles: the symbolic bee at his unction (*Hist.* 4), the host of angels flying over his army seen by an—ostensibly more objective—foreign witness later on (*Hist.* 23). To this positing of forms and signs as certainty against the ethical vacuum of Visigothic politics, Julian couples the *Iudicium,* with its equally optimistic claim for the value of legal texts, guarantors of their own interpretation and their literal truth.

8. Conclusion (largely conjectural): Julian at Work

The young priest, a native of the *urbs regia,* has made a promising start: a talented pupil of Eugenius II and already well connected at court, he is known to Wamba, late in whose reign he will be

---

194. For a comparable sense of the binding power of texts, see Toledo VIII, canon 2 (Vives, 268–277) and the dialectical contortions of the bishops trying to free themselves and the king from oaths they had taken solemnly. The most recent discussion of this episode is Stocking, *Bishops, Councils, and Consensus,* 1–4.

appointed to succeed Quiricus, the present bishop of Toledo, and to Count Ervig, the future king, to whom he has dedicated his (now lost) *Book of Divine Judgements.* His close friendship with the deacon Gudila suggests that he has no difficulty in socializing with Goths. He does, however, labor under a serious handicap: as a second-generation Christian, he is exposed to the constant doubt and suspicion of any rivals as to the sincerity and orthodoxy of his faith. Early in the reign of Wamba, it is not easy to foresee that this king will pass no new laws against the Jews; Reccesvind's legislation, almost as harsh to converted Jews as to their former coreligionists, remains valid and constitutes a daunting obstacle to any career at court or in the church.

When the new king is victorious over a secessionist rebellion in Gallia, Julian seizes on this subject as the occasion for a literary debut. Wamba, though at a sensitive and difficult moment early in his reign, when his kingship is still open to challenge, has taken over the power accumulated by Chindasvind and Reccesvind, and the unprecedented manner of his election, following in every respect the model established by the councils but never before obeyed, could be thought to herald a period of stability and increased royal authority. The HWR is Julian's response to this unique opportunity, and if the study of its sources allows us to trace most of its elements to classical and late antique models and to formal trends already pervasive in Visigothic Spain (such as the fashion for prose sequences), the combination of such diverse and uncommon parts already indicates the young author's stylistic adventurousness and wide reading. Sallust, whose monographs may have provided the generic model for the *Historia,* and the verse and prose panegyrics of the late empire, which served Julian as a quarry for type-scenes and commonplaces and for the theme of usurpation, had played little or no part in the literary culture of Isidore of Seville.[195] From these

---

195. See Fontaine, *Isidore de Seville,* vol. 1, 184–185. Isidore had in fact given a contemptuous definition of panegyric in *Etymologiae* VI, 8, 7 (ed. Lindsay):

unusual ingredients and some documents of the campaign, the young historian puts together a narrative that emphasizes the legitimacy of Wamba's kingship and his rival's preordained defeat and humiliation. Writing in Toledo soon after the king's triumphal return, Julian is fully aware of what this early victory means for the kingship. His insistence on Wamba's refusal to let the army disband from Cantabria and on the king's success in persuading the troops to follow him eastward directly, suggests that Julian is writing soon after the publication of Wamba's military law, which placed conscription and military service in the control of the crown. His otherwise baffling representation of the king's rebuke to Bishop Argebadus of Narbonne at Nîmes can only be understood in the context of the military duties imposed on the clergy by that same law, and of Wamba's unwillingness, for the remainder of his reign, to summon a general council of the church. Circa 674, Julian is betting on the king, although as diplomatically as possible. Where his personal situation is concerned no such moderation is called for, and the vehemence of his anti-Judaic sentiments must be considered strategic, responding not to an initiative of the present government but to deeply rooted, long-familiar political passions which could always resurface.

Julian is very fresh from the classroom and still gathering that vast literary culture in which he is second only to Isidore: the reading he draws on for the HWR is wholly distinct from the patristic culture of his theological works, and the grammatical treatise attributed to him, if it represents the substance of his teaching, is based on yet another set of texts, a conventional range of classical poets, Vergil chief among them. The variety of Julian's literary cultures, and his skilled manipulation of them to build up different aspects of his image—as learned theologian, as teacher to other talented clerics, as ambitious and brilliant young author taking his

---

"Panegyricum est licentiosum et lasciviosum genus dicendi in laudibus regum, in cuius compositione homines multis mendaciis adulantur."

first steps at the court of Toledo—constitutes an unimprovable il-lustration of the relation between literary knowledge and personal advancement in the early middle ages. The HWR, however, is a unique work even in the corpus of Julian's writings: nowhere else is the aim so literary and so closely tied to display; no other of his works is so deliberately and successfully classicizing.

There is an additional quality that points unmistakably to the author's youth and to the peculiar manner in which classical materi-als were available to the writers of late Visigothic Spain: Julian reaches for these prestigious sources with a minimal sense of their historical remoteness or of their being anchored in another religion and in the reality of a vanished empire.[196] Particularly striking are his comments on infanticide in *Ins.* 4, where he addresses Gallia as a mother of monstrous offspring: Why did she nourish and foster this misshapen product of her womb instead of destroying it? Is it not well known that righteous mothers kill their deformed chil-dren? Julian has somehow managed to forget the fulminations of Spanish church councils against abortion and infanticide.[197] Chris-tian authors had long praised the kindly spirit of parents who raised their retarded or malformed children with love and resigna-tion.[198] What Julian says here, however figurative, can only be ex-plained by an unmediated reference to pagan sources such as Seneca's comment in *De ira:* "We destroy malformed fetuses and

196. This can certainly be said of the panegyrics themselves which, even when composed by Christian authors or in praise of Christian emperors, con-vey pagan conceptions of the divinity of the emperor and the divinely appoint-ed mission of Rome.

197. See the texts collected in Pérez Prendes, "Neomalthusianismo his-pano-visigótico," conclusive in spite of the author's irrelevant Franco-era com-ments.

198. E.g. Gregory of Tours, *Virtutes S. Martini* 2, 24 (ed. Krusch, 167). A child conceived on a Sunday night is born fearfully deformed, to the point that "magis monstrum aliquod quam hominis speciem similabat." His mother raises him as if he were healthy: "[q]uem interemere non audens, ut mos matrum est, tamquam sanum puerum nutriebat." The boy is later healed by Saint Martin.

even drown children if they have been born weak or monstrous; it is not anger but reason that prompts us to separate the healthy from the useless."[199] The lack of any attempt to edit this heathen sentiment or to spare the sensibilities of a Christian audience suggests that the HWR and particularly the rhetorical *Insultatio* would have been judged as works in such a pure mode of literary display that they were not expected to realign their classical erudition with the realities of Christian and post-imperial life. Pagan justifications of infanticide had become, like anything else in the classics, available materials, ideas of an exalted provenance, ready for quotation.[200]

This instance ought to give the reader pause when going over the narrative of Paul's rebellion in the *Historia;* it is not likely to be the only case in which Julian attends to ancient models rather than to his own historical moment. We have seen above that in several important respects the work is molded by the political—and thus wholly contemporary—agenda of an ambitious young cleric at the beginning of what was to be a long and brilliant career. In many other points, however, the HWR coincides almost too perfectly with the panegyrics and their accounts of late antique conspiracies and rebellions led by doomed *tyranni.* It is highly probable that the resulting canvas, vibrant and original as it is, can tell us even more about the standards of literary performance in Toledo circa 674/675 and about young Julian at work at this decisive moment of his fortunes, than about the rebel leaders who rode into the *urbs regia* defeated and humiliated in September 673.

199. *De ira* 1, 15, 2 (ed. Bourgery, 18): "portentosos fetus exstinguimus, liberos quoque, si debiles monstrosique editi sunt, mergimus; nec ira sed ratio est a sanis inutilia secernere."

200. On this subject see Eyben, "Family-Planning in Graeco-Roman Antiquity," esp. 14–16 (with note 37) and 38–39.

Part II

Translation of Julian of Toledo's
Historia Wambae regis

❧ *Here begins the letter of Paul the Traitor, who unlawfully[1] led a rebellion in Gallia[2] against the Great King Wamba.*

In the name of the Lord, Flavius Paulus, anointed king of the East,[3] sends greetings to Wamba, king of the South. If you have al-

1. *tyrannice:* This adverbial form is rare. On the late antique use of *"tyrannis"* and *"tyrannus"* to denote not the abuse of legitimate power but the unlawful seizure of political authority, see Springer, *Tyrannus*, 101–111, and Béranger, *"Tyrannus."* Orlandis, "En torno a la noción visigoda," characterizes this as the meaning intellectually alive in Visigothic Spain, although instances of the more classical meaning, which is abuse or misuse of power, can also be found in the works of Isidore. With reference to Paul's rebellion against Wamba, *"tyrannis"* is used twice by Ervig, first in his *tomus* for Toledo XIII (Vives, 412), where he discusses the sentences passed earlier "in profanatoribus patriae, qui cum Paulo condam tyrannidem adsumerunt," and in his *lex in confirmatione concilii* for that same council (LV 12, 1, 3 [ed. Zeumer, 408]), alluding to those "quos profanatio infidelitatis cum Paulo traxit in societatem tyrannidis."

2. *in Gallias:* This is the name commonly used by Spanish writers for the Roman province of Gallia Narbonensis. *"Septimania"* is employed almost exclusively by those writing outside Spain. See James, "Septimania and its Frontier," 223. On the Visigothic distinction between *"Francia"* and *"Gallia"* see Teillet, *Des Goths,* 632. The history of the name *"Septimania"* is discussed in Fevrier and Barral i Altet, *Topographie Chrétienne,* 8 and 12, and by Demougeot, "La Septimanie dans le royaume wisigothique," 22.

3. *Flavius Paulus unctus rex orientalis:* The title *"Flavius,"* adopted by early medieval kings to establish symbolic continuity with Constantine, who in turn had borrowed it from the Flavian dynasty, had been used by Visigothic royalty since the days of Theudis (531–548), when the Visigoths were under an Ostrogothic protectorate. Wolfram, *Intitulatio* 1, 70–72 argues that it gives the *epistola* a touch of authenticity. He also notes, however, that *"unctus"* seems to betray the hand of Julian of Toledo, who in the *Historia* gave the first account of a royal unction. Salway, "What's in a Name?" 137–138, points out that *"Flavius"* is the most frequently attested high-status nomen in the late empire. For its use by Spanish kings in the Visigothic laws see Teillet, *Des Goths,* 540 note 21.

ready traversed the harsh and uninhabitable cliffs of the mountains, if you have already broken deep into the forest by narrow passes, like the lion of mighty breast, if you have utterly defeated the goats at running, the deer at springing, and the bears and wild pigs in voracity,[4] if you have already disgorged the venom of snakes and vipers, make this known to us, warrior, make this known to us, lord, friend of forests and crags. For if all these have collapsed before you and you are now hastening towards us in order to repeat for us at length the song of the nightingale,[5] and on that account, splendid man, your heart rises in self-assurance, then come down to Clausurae,[6] for there you will find a mighty champion[7] with whom you may legitimately fight.[8]

4. According to the pseudo-Isidorian *Institutionum Disciplinae* (ed. Fontaine, 655), which quotes here from Pliny's panegyric of Trajan, 81.2, the young nobleman should "certare cum fugacibus feris cursu, cum audacibus robore, cum callidis astu." Deer, boar, and serpent appear together in Sidonius's panegyric of Maiorianus 151–154 (ed. Anderson, vol. 1, 72): "ludum si forte retexam, / consumit quidquid iaculis fecisse putaris / istius una dies: tribus hunc tremuere sagittis / anguis, cervus, aper." They appear again in another poem dedicated by Sidonius to that emperor: *Carmina* 13, *Ad imperatorem Maiorianum* 15–18 (ed. Anderson, vol. 1, 214): "at tu Tirynthius alter, / sed princeps, magni maxima cura dei, / quem draco, cervus, aper paribus sensere sagittis, / cum dens, cum virus, cum fuga nil valuit . . ."

5. *ut nobis abundanter filomelae vocem retexeas:* The phrase shares the unclear sarcastic tone of the entire *epistola*, with its many animal comparisons. Is it perhaps implying that Wamba has adopted a plaintive tone to denounce the usurpation? Julian's teacher, Eugenius II of Toledo, composed several poems on the nightingale and its song (cf. *Carmina* 30–33 [ed. Vollmer, 253–254]), with no reference to the Ovidian tale of Philomela, but the repeated statement that the nightingale, who sings while others sleep, is watching over them to keep them safe; cf. *carmen* 31 (*"disticum philomelaicum"* [ed. Vollmer, 253]: "Insomnem philomela trahit dum carmine noctem, / nos dormire facit, se vigilare docet."

6. *descende usque ad Clausuras:* Clausurae was the name of a stronghold in the Pyrenees near Perthus (cf. "castrum quod vocatur Clausuras" [*Hist.* 11]). Today the commune of Les Cluses, distant some twenty-five kilometers from Perpignan, preserves Roman fortifications dated to the fourth century A.D. that overlook the Via Domitia. On these structures see Castellvi, "Clausurae." *"Clausurae"* could also be used in a more general sense for the system of fortifi-

cations protecting the southern border of Visigothic Gallia (Span. "las clausuras pirenaicas"). In his *tomus* to Toledo XVII (Vives, 525), King Egica refers to these forts as defining the border when he makes an exception for Gallia, decimated by a plague, in the application of his harsh laws against the Jews: "illis tantum hebraeis ad presens reservatis, qui Galliae provinciae videlicet infra clausuras noscuntur habitatores existere." The fortresses and their function are described in Vigil and Barbero, "Sobre los orígenes sociales de la Reconquista," 314–321. But since Paul is indicating a specific locality where Wamba may encounter him, it is likely that he refers to a specific stronghold.

7. *opopumpeum grandem:* The word is a Graecism derived originally from Septuagint (Leviticus 16.8) and most often translated as *"emissarius"* in Latin. See Levison, 500 note 2, and Berschin, *Biographie und Epochenstil* 2, 201.

8. Cf. in Jordanes, *Getica* 44 (ed. Mommsen, 116–117), the challenge of Riciarius, king of the Sweves, to the Visigoth Theoderic: "si hic murmuras, et me venire causaris: Tolosam, ubi tu sedes, veniam; ibi, si vales, resiste."

☘ *In the name of the Lord, here begins the Book of the History of*
Gallia which in the time of King Wamba of Sacred Memory[9]
was composed by the Lord Julian, Bishop of the See of
Toledo.[10]

☘ *In the name of the Holy Trinity, here begins the Story of The*
Most Excellent King Wamba and of His Expedition and
Victory by which he subdued with a celebrated triumph the
Province of Gallia, which had rebelled against him.

(1) An account of victories serves often as an aid to courage, drawing the spirits of young men to the banner of bravery, if

9. DIVAE MEMORIAE: According to Levison, 501 note 1, this part of the heading, with its reference to Wamba as dead, must be the work of a later editor, as it contradicts the second half of this *superscriptio*, where EXCELLEN-TISSIMI WAMBAE REGIS implies that he is alive. On *"divus"* as applied to the person or the memory of a dead ruler see King, *Law and Society*, 28 note 4. According to Ewig, "Zum christlichen Königsgedanken," 27–28, it is an ele-ment of imperial *Titulatur* not adopted in medieval Europe before the midddle of the seventh century. Teillet, *Des Goths*, 504–506, however, dates the adoption of imperial titles in general by the Visigothic kings to the conversion of Recca-red and Toledo III (589).

10. Julian was consecrated bishop of Toledo on January 29, 680; see Felix, *Vita Iuliani*, 12. But the same caution must be applied to this part of the heading as to "DIVAE MEMORIAE" above: it cannot be used to date the HWR as a whole. Only the second half of this title, i.e. the part that follows, is thought by Levison to be Julian's work, composed and published while Wamba was in power and before Julian's own rise to the episcopate.

something is told of the glory of men of old.[11] For human nature has a sluggish disposition to inner courage, and this is why it is found more inclined to vice than eager for feats of bravery, so that, unless it is constantly edified with the goad of useful examples, it will remain cold[12] and listless. To this end, in order that our narrative of bygone things may be able to cure phlegmatic spirits, we have presented deeds performed in our times, by which we may incite future ages to valor.

(2) In our days, indeed, arose the most noble prince Wamba, whom the Lord chose to rule worthily, who was proclaimed king by priestly unction, whom the consensus of people and fatherland[13] elected, who was sought out by the love of the people,[14] who before

11. Cf. the following advice from the *Institutionum Disciplinae* (ed. Fontaine, 654): "... oportet ... nihilque amatorium decantare vel turpe, sed magis praecinere carmina maiorum, quibus auditores prouocati ad gloriam excitentur." The idea is a commonplace in panegyrics, for instance in Claudian's poem on the fourth consulship of Honorius, 397–400 (ed. Platnauer, vol. 1, 314–316), where Theodosius recommends the following course of studies to his successor in the West: "... nec desinat umquam / tecum Graia loqui, tecum Romana vetustas. / antiquos evolve duces, adsuesce futurae / militiae, Latium retro te confer in aevum." It is also present in Sidonius's panegyric of Avitus, 175–177 (ed. Anderson, vol. 1, 132), where Jupiter describes to Rome the education of the future emperor: "didicit quoque facta tuorum / ante ducum; didicit pugnas libroque relegit / quae gereret campo."

12. *frigida remanet:* The phrase contrasts significantly with the vocabulary of high temperatures and combustion that runs through the HWR; see above in the chapter "Literature" the discussion "Words and Images."

13. *totius gentis et patriae communio:* See Teillet, *Des Goths*, 531–533 and 624–625, which traces the related formula "gens et patria Gothorum" to Isidore of Seville (cf. Toledo IV canon 75 [Vives, 218]: "... sacramentum fidei suae, quod patriae gentisque Gothorum statu ... pollicitus est").

14. Cf. Toledo XII canon 1 (Vives, 387), where Julian describes Ervig as "quem et divinum iudicium in regno praeelegit et decessor princeps successurum sibi instituit, et quod superest quem totius populi amabilitas exquisivit." On Julian's repeated use of this formula, see Teillet, "Un coup d'état," 106 note 39. An analogous formulation occurs in Pacatus's panegyric of Theodosius 31 (*Panégyriques*, vol. 3, 97): "Iam uero te principem in medio rei publicae sinu,

he rose to the summit of power was predicted a most brilliant reign by the prophecies and revelations of many. This illustrious man,[15] after King Reccesvind succumbed to death,[16] was performing the funeral rites and lamentations when suddenly all together in agreement, moved less by one emotion than by a common cry, proclaim with delight that they will gladly have him as ruler.[17] They vow thunderously, with united voices, that he and no other shall rule the Goths, and whole companies fling themselves at his feet so that he will not refuse what they demand. The man shuns them in every way, although choked by tearful sobs,[18] yields to no prayers and is persuaded by no popular entreaties. Now he claims that he will not take office with so many disasters impending, and now he argues that he is worn out by age. He is resisting fiercely when one of the commanders, as if about to act for everyone else, stands in the middle of the crowd and, fixing him with a threatening expression,

---

omnium suffragio militum, consensu prouinciarum, ipsius denique ambitu imperatoris optatum . . ." On royal election vs. dynastic succession in Visigothic Spain see Orlandis, "La sucesión al trono," esp. 91–97, and Collins, *Early Medieval Spain,* 112–113.

15. *Qui clarissimus vir:* Teillet, "L'*Historia Wambae,*" 419, points out that Wamba is called "*vir*" only before he is anointed, and after that only "*princeps*" (56 times). "Clarissimus vir," like "vir inluster," establishes his noble rank.

16. On the date of Reccesvind's death, see *Laterculus regum Visigothorum* (ed. Mommsen, 468), 41–42.

17. Claude, *Adel, Kirche und Königtum,* 157–158, describes Julian's account of the election of Wamba as "eine Inspirationswahl," stressing the supernatural coloring of the episode. Livermore, *Origins of Spain and Portugal,* 230, interprets the words "uno quodammodo non tam animo quam oris affectu pariter provocati" as "not from religious principle but from political convenience," for no clear reason.

18. *lacrimosis singultibus interclusus:* Powers 21–22 translates "surrounded by tearful lamentations," but cf. the same phrase used later (*Hist.* 25) to describe Wamba triumphing over Paul: "Haec et his similia fletibus interclusus princeps agebat," as well as for Bishop Argebadus of Narbonne imploring Wamba's mercy "lacrimarum singultibus interclusus" (*Hist.* 21). Julian also uses "intercludere" literally for 'to cut off, to block'; cf. *Hist.* 7 and Levison, 506 note 5, with comparable usage from Livy.

says: "Know that unless you consent to our wishes you will be cut down by the blade of my sword. Indeed, we will not leave before either our nation has received you as king or else, refusing, you have been swallowed by a bloody death today."

(3) Defeated by their threats rather than their prayers, he yielded, accepting kingship, and took them all into his favor[19] but postponed the rite of anointment until the nineteenth day from that date, so that he would not be consecrated king outside the ancient seat.[20] These events were taking place in a small estate in the region of Salamanca that from ancient times bore the name of Gérticos,[21] distant some hundred and twenty miles from the royal city. There, in one and the same day, and namely on the kalends of September (September 1), the dying king reached the term of his life and his

19. *ad suam pacem recepit:* Collins, "Julian of Toledo and the Education of Kings," 17: "In other words, any old scores that Wamba the count may have had to settle with his aristocratic peers and rivals would be wiped out when he became Wamba the king. Again, it is possible to suggest that this was a ritual element, which corresponded with reality only in so far as it served the new king's purposes." Sánchez-Albornoz, "La *Ordinatio principis,*" 9, refuses to interpret the passage: "Si [estas palabras] aludieran a un uso de estirpe visigoda, cabría sospechar el origen remoto de una promesa real asegurada mediante un juramento? No sé. Porque ignoro cómo el nuevo rey recibía en su paz a los palatinos."

20. *locum sedis antiquae:* Hillgarth, "Historiography," 284 note 83, translates this as "the accustomed place." On the ceremonial importance of Toledo see Ewig, "Résidence et capitale," esp. 34–36; Adams, "Toledo's Visigothic Metamorphosis," esp. 122–136; and Collins, "Julian of Toledo and the Education of Kings," esp. 18–19.

21. Gérticos: There is no agreement on the location of this royal estate, and little evidence to go on. A tradition of the later middle ages places it in the village of Bamba (now Wamba), west of Valladolid and some forty five kilometers from Baños de Cerrato, with its Visigothic basilica of San Juan de Baños, dedicated to St. John the Baptist by Reccesvind (see de Palol, *La basílica,* esp. 67–71). Collins, "Julian of Toledo and the Education of Kings," 2, speculates that the proximity of the possible site of Gérticos to this royal foundation suggests that much of the land in this region may have belonged to the crown and perhaps even, initially, to imperial land-holdings in Spain.

aforementioned successor was elected by the acclamation described above. Although, chosen by divine inspiration and later by the anxious acclaim and the veneration of the people,[22] this man had already been surrounded by the great pomp of royal ceremony, he would not suffer himself to be anointed by a priest's hand before he had come to the seat of royal government and had sought the chair of ancestral tradition, at which time only it would be fitting for him to receive the sign of holy unction[23] and to await most patiently the consent to his election of those living far away,[24] so that it would not be thought that, moved by a frenzied desire to reign, he had usurped or stolen rather than obtained from God a sign of such great glory. So, deferring it with cautious gravity, he entered the city of Toledo on the nineteenth day after receiving the kingship.

22. Claude, *Adel, Kirche und Königtum*, 155 note 2, distinguishes between *praeelectio* (by nobility and high clergy) and popular *acclamatio*, although what is described as happening at Reccesvind's estate cannot be considered an election, and acclamation by the people in Toledo can at best be called implicit in Julian's account. Teillet, *Des Goths*, 588, interprets *"praeelectio"* very differently, namely as "le mot . . . employé par Julien de préférence à *electio*, pour signifier l'acte qui a designé Wamba comme roi: un choix de Dieu, préexistant au choix des hommes."

23. *sacrae unctionis vexilla:* I translate *"vexilla"* here as a synonym of *"signum"* 'sign'; cf. *Hist.* 9: "Exurgite iam ad victoriae signum!" A variant, "sanctae unctionis vexilla," occurs at the beginning of *Hist.* 4.

24. *et longe positorum consensus ob praeelectionem sui patientissime sustinere:* Collins, "Julian of Toledo and the Education of Kings," 14, translates "and to receive the clearest assent of the men of standing *(positores)* to his election." Linehan, *History and the Historians*, 57, adopts Collins's reading, which fails to take *"longe"* and the medieval use of *"positus"* to mean 'resident' or 'domiciled at' into account. Cf. Claude, *Adel, Kirche und Königtum*, 155, and Teillet, *Des Goths*, 590. Cf. also Rufinus, *Historia ecclesiastica* X, 32 (ed. Mommsen, 994): ". . . ut et presentes et longe positos, quibus ipse per se disserere viva voce non poterat, perfectissima instructione corrigeret."

A comparable delay between proclamation and the actual *ordinatio principis* was probably observed by Chindasvind (642–653) also, who counted the beginning of his reign from April 30, 642, although he had been raised to the throne (by a successful usurpation) on April 17.

(4) And when he came to where he would receive the sign of holy unction in the palatine church,[25] that is to say the church of Saint Peter and Saint Paul, he stood, already adorned with the royal insignia, before God's altar and, according to ancient custom, pledged his faith to the people.[26] After this, he kneels and by the hand of the holy bishop Quiricus[27] the oil of benediction is poured on his head,[28] displaying its wealth of blessings when a sign of favor

25. *in praetoriensi ecclesia:* This title suggests the existence of a palace complex in Toledo, with a church in immediate proximity to the palace, to be used in the chief ceremonial occasions that involved the king. The model may have been Constantine's Church of the Apostles in Constantinople. At least six national councils of the Visigothic church met in this building. Férotin, *Le Liber Ordinum,* cols. 149–151, translates *"ecclesia praetoriensis"* as 'church of the royal guard,' which is also possible. Wamba later created a bishop for this church, a measure cancelled as abusive by Toledo XII canon 4 (Vives, 390–392).

26. *ex more fidem populis redidit:* Collins, "Julian of Toledo and the Education of Kings," 14, translates "as the custom is, he recited the creed to the people." Occasionally, the councils refer to the creed as a *"fides"* (in the sense of a profession of faith), but far more commonly as a *"symbolum."* Cf. Toledo III canon 2 (Vives, 125): "Ut in omnibus ecclesiis die dominica symbolum recitetur."

What the new king recited at this point is known to have been an oath before God and the assembled people; see Férotin, *Le Liber Ordinum,* cols. 500–501; Sánchez-Albornoz, "La *Ordinatio principis,*" 17; Orlandis, *La vida en España,* 88. The text of the oath has not survived, but it is likely that the king promised to rule with justice and to protect the church. As Teillet, *Des Goths,* 622, puts it, "il leur 'rend sa foi,' c'est à dire il leur prête serment en retour." The origin and composition of the oath are examined in Claude, "The Oath of Allegiance and the Oath of the King."

27. Quiricus: See *Prosopografía,* no. 250, and Rivera Recio, "Los arzobispos de Toledo," 203–205.

28. On Visigothic royal unction see Férotin, *Le Liber Ordinum,* cols. 501–502. Its origin and likely antiquity are studied in Müller, "Die Anfänge der Königssalbung," 333–340; Claude, *Adel, Kirche und Königtum,* 155–156; and King, *Law and Society,* 48 note 5. Although Wamba was quite possibly not the first Visigothic king to undergo this rite, the HWR provides the earliest extant account of the ceremony in Western Europe. Teillet, *Des Goths,* 607–611, stresses the Old Testament coloring of the episode and the representation of Wamba as the rightful, divinely elected ruler. The meaning of *"unctio"* had been strongly built up by Isidore with his etymology of *"Christus"*: *Etymologiae* VII, 2, 2 (ed. Lindsay): "Christus namque a chrismate est appellatus, hoc est unctus."

was immediately revealed. For soon from this very head, where the oil had been poured, certain fumes arose like smoke and stood there in the shape of a column, and a bee was seen to fly out from that same place on his head, which was certainly the omen of some future prosperity.[29] And to have placed this episode here in advance is perhaps not in vain, for it will bring home to posterity how manfully this king ruled his realm, who reached the summit of power not only unwillingly but also rising in order through so many ranks, one by one, and compelled by the enthusiasm of the entire nation.

(5) In his glorious time the land of Gallia, nurse of all treachery,[30] was charged by an infamous report that, driven by an inconceivable fever of treason, it nourished the faithless limbs it had be-

---

29. Symbolism of the bee: Closest to the meaning implied here come Isidore, *Etymologiae* XII, 8, 1 (ed. Lindsay): "regem et exercitum habent," and Cicero, *De divinatione* 1, 33, 73 (ed. Ax, 36), where a swarm of bees alighting on the mane of his horse serves as an omen that Dionysos will become ruler of Syracuse: "quod ostentum habuit hanc vim, ut Dionysius paucis post diebus regnare coeperit." The same general idea is present in panegyric literature, e.g. Claudian's *De quarto consulatu Honorii* 380–383 (ed. Platnauer, vol. 1, 314), where Theodosius, trying to prove that a ruler can be recognized from birth, tells his son that "sic mollibus olim / stridula ducturum pratis examina regem / nascentem venerantur apes et publica mellis / iura petunt traduntque favos . . ." Cf. Goulon, "Quelques aspects du symbolisme de l'abeille." A different but equally relevant interpretation is offered by Ammianus 17, 4, 11 (ed. Seyfarth, vol. 1, 216), who points out that among the Egyptians the hieroglyph for 'king' is a bee: "perque speciem apis mella conficientis indicant regem, moderatori cum iucunditate aculeos quoque innasci debere his insignibus ostendentes." According to Seneca, *De clementia* 3, 17, 3 (ed. Préchac, 39), however, the king of the bees has no sting: "rex ipse sine aculeo est; noluit illum natura nec saeuum esse nec ultionem magno constaturam petere telumque detraxit et iram eius inermem reliquit." It is this that makes him different from a tyrant.

30. *altrix perfidiae:* In Classical Latin, *"altrix"* is most often used figuratively, frequently coupled with *"terra"* to refer to the native land as mother or nurse of its population. The personification of Gallia here, later developed in full in the *Insultatio*, where the nurse becomes also an unnatural mother and an unfaithful wife, may derive from the *Laus Spaniae* of Isidore's *Historia Gothorum*, in which the author addresses Spain as a mother and later as a wife taken by force by the

gotten.[31] What indeed that is evil and lubricious could be missing there, where the conspiracies of plotters, the very banner of treachery, deceit in business, corruption in justice and, worse yet than all these things, the whorehouse of Jews who blaspheme against our Lord and Savior[32] are to be found? Indeed, this land prepared its ruin from its own brood, and with the generation of vipers[33] of its own womb it fed the engine of its destruction. When for a long time it had been tossed by these various fevers, suddenly by the fault of a single accursed leader a whole whirlwind of treachery arose, and consent to betrayal passed from one to the many.

Gothic people. Cf. the intervention of Jacques Fontaine in the discussion that follows Hillgarth, "Historiography," 350. For sources of this figure in the panegyrics, see the subsection "Mother and Monster" in the chapter "Literature" above.

31. *genita a se infidelium depasceret membra:* Díaz y Díaz, 91, translates these words using the classical sense of *"depascere,"* i.e. 'to feed upon, to devour': "de engullir los miembros perjuros por ella engendrados." But a later meaning, 'to nourish,' adopted in Powers, 23, is the only one that fits the logic of the passage: the *altrix* can only nourish, not devour her charge (at this point, at any rate, when the rebellion is in its earliest stages). Cf. Niermeyer, *Mediae latinitatis lexicon minus,* s.v.

32. Julian himself was the son of converted Jews; cf. the *Mozarabic Chronicle of 754,* 38 (ed. López Pereira, 56): "Julianus episcopus, ex traduce Judeorum ut flores rosarum de inter vepres spinarum . . . qui etiam a parentibus Xpianis genitus splendide in omni prudentia Toleto manet edoctus. . ." The *perfidia* ascribed to Gallia (cf. "altrix perfidiae" [*Hist.* 5] and "perfidiae signum" [ibid.]) was attributed to Jews in the theological literature of the age; cf. Blumenkranz, "Perfidia."

33. *generatione viperea:* Cf. Matthew 3.7, and 12.34, "progenies viperarum," Matthew 23.33, "serpentes genimina viperarum," and also Deuteronomy 32.5, "generatio prava atque perversa," and Deuteronomy 32.20, "generatio enimque perversa et infideles filii." The adjective *"vipereus,"* much used by Vergil and Ovid, does not occur in the Vulgate. The image of a woman giving birth to snakes is made explicit in *Insultatio* 8, "filii autem tui, qui ex te viperina nativitate sunt proditi" (addressed to a personified Gallia). It has some affinity with the image in Claudian, *In Rufinum* 1, 93–96 (ed. Platnauer, vol. 1, 32), of the fury Megaera as nurse to the evil Rufinus: the baby moves like a serpent and is licked by the reptiles that are part of his *altrix's* body: "parvus reptavit in isto / saepe sinu teneroque per ardua colla volutus / ubera quaesivit fletu linguisque trisulcis / mollis lambentes finxerunt membra cerastae . . ."

(6) The fame of his crime proclaims Hildericus[34] to have been the leader of the rebellion. He, who ruled the city of Nîmes[35] with the title of count, took up not only the name but also the reputation and the works of treason, adopting as accomplices of his wickedness Gumildus,[36] the detestable bishop of the see of Maguelone,[37] and the abbot Ranimirus.[38] This leader in crime, as he kindled the fires of his disloyalty in various men, attempted to draw the bishop of the city of Nîmes, Aregius,[39] a man of holy life, to the disgrace of betrayal. But when he saw him reject his advice with saintly mouth and a loyal heart, he handed him, deprived of rank and see and loaded down with the weight of chains, over the Frankish border into the hands of the Franks, to be jeered at. Thereafter, in place of the deposed prelate he sets abbot Ranimirus, an accomplice of his crimes, as bishop. At his election none of the established procedures is observed; the consent of the king or the metropolitan is not awaited.[40] The summit of arrogance has been reached, and in violation of the traditional prohibitions he is ordained by only two foreign bishops.[41] The bold enterprise once carried out, this poisonous breed of three men—namely Hilderi-

34. Ildericus (or Hildericus): *Prosopografía* no. 84.

35. See Fevrier, "Nîmes," and Dupont, *Les cités de la Narbonnaise première,* 166–167 and 228–231.

36. Gumildus: *Prosopografía* no. 555; see also note 178 below.

37. See Fevrier, "Maguelone," and Dupont, *Les cités de la Narbonnaise première,* 233.

38. Ranimirus: *Prosopografía* no. 560.

39. Aregius: *Prosopografía* no. 559.

40. See Toledo IV canon 19 (Vives, 199): "Sed nec ille deinceps sacerdos erit, quem nec clerus, nec populus propriae civitatis elegit, vel auctoritas metropolitani vel provincialium sacerdotum assensio exquisivit." *"Sacerdos"* is used here with reference to bishops.

41. *ab externae gentis duobus tantum episcopis ordinatur:* Cf. Toledo IV canon 19 (Vives, 199–200): ". . . cum omnium clericorum vel civium voluntate ab universis conprovincialibus episcopis aut certe a tribus in sacerdotio die dominica consecrabitur . . ." Levison, 505 note 6, observes that the "externae gentis episcopi" must have come from the Frankish realms.

cus, Gumildus, and Ranimirus—set boundaries to their conspiracy; from the place that bears the name Montcamel to Nîmes they divide the land of Gallia and appropriate it for their plot, by which measure disloyalty is fully dissociated from fidelity. An army is assembled and they exterminate the inhabitants, deplete the fruit of their toil, and ravage the entire province of Gallia.

(7) Notice of this came swiftly to the king, and soon he sent out to the confines of Gallia an army led by the commander Paul[42] and intended to wipe out the very name of the rebels. Paul, advancing at a slow pace[43] with the troops, broke the impulse of the army by intercalating delays. He himself abstained from combat, did not direct the first onslaughts on the enemy, and by these means diverted the spirits of the warriors from the enthusiasm with which they had longed to fight. Thus Paul, taking up the attitude of Saul,[44] would not surge forward loyally and indeed tried to act against loyalty. Drawn by the desire to reign, he was suddenly stripped of all faith. He violates the love he had vowed to the most pious king,[45]

42. *per manum Pauli ducis:* Lucas of Tuy, who incorporated a version of the *Historia* with many additions of his own into his thirteenth-century *Chronicon mundi,* adds here (PL 96, col. 768) "qui erat de Graecorum nobili natione." García Moreno, *Prosopografía,* 65 (no. III), argues that Lucas's words merely repeat—and displace—a rumor circulated about King Ervig in the late-ninth-century *Chronicle of Alfonso III,* and that they have no basis in fact.

43. *tepenti cursu:* This means literally 'at a lukewarm pace.' Cf. with vocabulary of combustion and high temperature discussed above in the chapter "Literature," at the end of "Words and Images," and with note 12 above and note 50 below.

44. *Sicque Paulus in Sauli mente conversus:* Cf. Acts 13.9, "Saulus autem, qui et Paulus . . ." As Saul before his conversion, Saint Paul had been a merciless persecutor of Christians and involved in the stoning of Saint Stephen (Acts 7.57–59).

45. *promissam religiosi principis maculat caritatem:* The phrase refers to the oath of loyalty sworn by the *primates* and the people to the new king. Cf. Toledo IV canon 75 (Vives, 217): "fidem sacramento promissam regibus suis observare contemnant" and "si violetur a gentibus regum suorum promissa fides." *Iudicium*

forgets his duty to the country, and, as someone has said, he secretly joins and openly abets a usurpation swiftly brought to ripeness.[46]
He proceeds by hidden measures, so that the royal rank he aspires
to may be seen before it is known, having attached as associates
to himself and to his wickedness Ranosindus,[47] military head of
the province of Tarraco, and Hildigisus, who held the rank of
gardingus.[48] Wishing to satisfy his evil ambitions with incredible
celerity, he collects people from everywhere and falsely announces
that he is going to fight the rebels. He sets a day and proposes a
place where they may enter Gallia to make war. Argebadus, bishop

---

6 refers to this same oath as a set of "conditiones, ubi spontanea promissione
in electioni gloriosi domni nostri Wambani regis consenserunt." It is unclear
whether the formal oath of the nobility took place at the election itself or later, at the unction, as an expression of their consent. Wamba's delay of the unction would suggest that it was taken at this later point; cf. Orlandis, *La vida en
España*, 87–89, and Teillet, *Des Goths*, 522–524. On faithlessness as a stain, cf. *Iudicium* 2, "induit se [Paulus] periurii maculam."

The phrase "religiosus princeps" is used 13 times in the HWR, always with
reference to Wamba. Teillet, *Des Goths*, 504–506 and 605–607, discusses its ideological value, emphasizing its imperial origin. The formula also occurs in the
Ordo qvando rex cvm exercitv ad prelivm egreditvr (ed. Férotin, col. 150): "esto presenti
religioso principi nostro . . ."

46. *tyrannidem celeriter maturatam secrete invadit et publice armat:* Cf. Orosius 7, 40,
6 (ed. Arnaud-Lindet, vol. 3, 119): "Nam tyrannidem nemo nisi celeriter maturatam secrete inuadit et publice armat, cuius summa est adsumpto diademate ac
purpura uideri antequam sciri . . ." The context is the defense of the Pyrenees
before the usurper Constantine in 408 by Didymus and Verinianus, Spanish rel-
atives of the emperor Theodosius. On Julian's use of Orosius, see Hillgarth,
"The *Historiae* of Orosius in the Early Middle Ages," 166–167. Straub, *Zum
Herrscherideal* 22–25, discusses the lasting importance of Orosius's formula for
the representation of usurpers.

47. Ranosindus: *Prosopografía* no. 117. See also note 52 below.

48. Hildigisus: *Prosopografía* no. 79; cf. King, *Law and Society*, 58 note 1. The
gardingi were officials in the king's immediate entourage, equal to the *leudes* and *fideles* but with a special military responsibility for the safety of the king and his
servants. See Diesner, "König Wamba," 56–59, who suggests that their specific
obligation was to provide a band of mounted, or at least highly trained, soldiers
at the king's request.

of the see of Narbonne,[49] a man of holy life and distinguished by his anxiety to protect the people, on finding out the truth from the most accurate report of certain men, attempted to block the road to the city before the usurper. But this project too did not remain hidden from Paul. Before the prelate could carry out his plan, Paul suddenly entered Narbonne at great speed[50] and with an army, frustrated promptly the plans made against him, and had the city gates closed by an appointed garrison of armed men. When the surrounding multitude of troops was assembled, Paul himself, the viper-like leader of treason, stood at the center with some of his associates and started by rebuking the bishop for having tried to close off the way to the city before him.

(8) After this, about to make public his secret plot, corrupting the loyalty of the people with divers fraudulent reasonings and firing the emotions of various men to make them proffer insults against the aforementioned King Wamba, Paul swears first, before all others, that he cannot have him as his king, or remain in his service. Rather, he says, "choose a head of government[51] from among yourselves, to whom the crowd will yield in agreement and who may seem fit to rule over us." Thereupon, one of the plotters, an accomplice of his evil schemes, Ranosindus, chooses Paul to be his king; he will have Paul and no other as the future ruler of this people.[52] When Paul perceived this swift coming to fruition

---

49. Argebadus: *Prosopografía* no. 529.

50. *praepropero cursu:* The phrase is intended to contrast with *"tepenti cursu"* (*Hist.* 7). See above note 43.

51. *caput regiminis:* These words echo "vipereum caput perfidiae," used of Paul immediately above (*Hist.* 7). Cf. also "his . . . criminis caput" (ibid.). They are part of an extensive system of metaphors using the body—and especially the relation between the head (*caput, apex,* or *vertix*) and the limbs (*membra*)—as a model for political authority and social subordination. See above in the chapter "Literature" the discussion "Words and Images," and Teillet, *Des Goths,* 510–511, who traces the motif to a theme of imperial ideology: the emperor as head.

52. *unus ex coniuratis, maligni ipsius consilii socius, Ranosindus:* It is unclear why

of his designs, he promptly supplied the consent of his own will, and compelled all men to swear oaths to him. After this, he appropriated sovereignty and with criminal boldness drew to himself by works of treason that band of conspirators that he had not subdued by the use of arms: for he associated Hildericus, Gumildus, and Ranimirus effortlessly to his treacherous projects. Why say more? The entire land of Gallia suddenly plots with the arms of sedition, and even part of the province of Tarraco tries on the arrogance of rebellion.[53] All of Gallia became in a short while a gathering of traitors, a den of disloyalty, an assembly of the damned. So when Paul decided to increase the number of his accomplices in wickedness, he announced and promised gifts and drew whole multitudes of Franks and Basques to fight in his sup-

---

Orlandis, *La España visigótica*, 258, states as a given that this Ranosindus cannot be the previously mentioned *dux* of the Tarraconensis (*Hist.* 7 and *Prosopografía* no. 117), but must be the brother of the bishop of Agde, listed in *Iudicium* 3 among the rebel leaders captured by Wamba's men in that city (*Prosopografía* no. 118).

Julian of Toledo may be suggesting here that Paul's election was rigged and that this intervention was solicited by the usurper beforehand, which is perhaps why Ranosindus is described as "ipsius consilii socius"; cf. Claude, *Adel, Kirche und Königtum*, 160. The passage, in that case, would be meant to contrast with Wamba's divinely inspired election; cf. *Hist.* 2 and note 17 above. Teillet, *Des Goths*, 592, concurs: "Le nom de Paul est lancé non par une foule unanime plus ou moins inspirée par Dieu, comme c'est le cas pour Wamba, mais par une seule voix, celle d'un complice."

53. *cuturnum rebellionis adtemptat:* Cf. "superbiae fastus cuturno sese adtollerat" (*Hist.* 28) and "verborum ille cothurnus" (*Ins.* 4). The expression, part of a vocabulary of overweening pride that also includes *"fastigium," "fastus,"* and *"supercilium,"* occurs in conciliar language both before and after Julian: cf. Narbonne (589) canon 10 (Vives, 148): "quod si sub cothurno superbiae neglexerit implere . . ." and Toledo XVI (693), in Egica's *tomus* (Vives, 487): "Et quia plerique perfidorum cothurno superbiae dediti . . ." Teillet, *Des Goths*, 542, analyzes the imagery of elevation conferred by power as it appears in Visigothic texts.

Use of this image in council acts may derive from Tertullian's denunciation of the buskin among other props of dramatic art: cf. *De spectaculis* 23 (ed. Glover, 286): "Sic et tragoedos cothurnis extulit, quia 'nemo potest adicere cubitum unum ad staturam suam': mendacem facere vult Christum."

port,[54] and remained in Gallia with a great gathering of troops, awaiting the coming of the happy time when he would be able to make war against Spain and to claim recognition of the royal dignity that he had already seized.

(9) At that time, then, when these events were taking place in Gallia, the most pious King Wamba was bringing war to the fierce tribes of the Basques in order to subdue them, and found himself in the region of Cantabria.[55] When the report of what was happening in Gallia found its way to the ruler's hearing, he soon made known to the leading men of the court that they must decide whether they would make their way from there directly to Gallia to fight or whether they would return to their own territories, collect forces from every region, and set out with a vast army on such a far-removed campaign. The king himself, seeing many bewildered by this quandary, addresses them all together as follows: "Warriors, you have heard that evil has arisen, and you know with what defenses the originator of this rebellion has armed himself. It is therefore necessary to anticipate the enemy, so that he may be overtaken by war before he can grow more powerful in this conflagration. Let it be a disgrace to us not to meet such foes in order to make war, or to revisit our homes before the enemy is destroyed. It must seem

54. On the participation of Franks, Gallo-Romans, and Basques in the rebellion, see Rouche, *L'Aquitaine,* 102.

55. Basques and Cantabrians had been at war with the Visigoths from the time of Leovigild; see Besga Marroquín, *La situación política de los pueblos del norte,* 44–46, and Vigil and Barbero, "Sobre los orígenes sociales de la Reconquista." A rebellion led by the Gothic nobleman Froia in the early years of Reccesvind's rule (circa 653) had been supported by the Basques: cf. Thompson, *Goths in Spain,* 199–200, and *Prosopografía* no. 62. On the question of whether Cantabria was a region or a city, see Fear ed. *Lives of the Visigothic Fathers,* 39 note 107, and Collins, "The Basques in Aquitaine and Navarre," esp. 8–9. John of Biclaro, *Chronica* 574, 2 (ed. Mommsen, 213), appears to regard it as a region: "His diebus Leovegildus rex Cantabria ingressus provinciae pervasores interficit . . ."

shameful to us that he who could not subdue our rebels by means of arms should dare to fight against warriors of such fame, and that he who could not capture the wretched hide of a single man to bring peace to his country should dare to present himself as an enemy to the nation, as if judging us effeminate and soft in every way, and thus unable to withstand his usurpation by any arms, any strength, or any planning. What forces does this doomed man command, if he attacks us fighting with Frankish troops? Their prowess is very well known to us, and in no way to be dreaded. Therefore let it be infamy to you for these troops to fear their shield-wall, since you know their courage to have been always inferior to ours. If, however, he attempts to justify his usurpation with the conspiracy of the men of Gallia, it would be disgraceful for this nation to yield to a remote corner of the earth, and for men who hold a vast kingdom to be disturbed by the agitation of those whom they constantly protect by means of a garrison. Whether they are men of Gallia or Franks, let them, if it pleases them, defend the crime of such a conspiracy; we, however, must vindicate with avenging arms our reputation for glory. Indeed, we will not be fighting with women but with men, even though it remains notorious that the Franks have never been able to withstand the Goths,[56] and that without us the Galli have never achieved any notable prowess. And if you hold against me the lack of provisions and vehicles, it will be more glorious for us to achieve victory in need, having done without all these things, than to lead a well-planned war in abundance. He is always more illustrious who achieves fame by his powers of

---

56. On Franks vs. Goths see Teillet, *Des Goths*, 628–630, who stresses how rarely Julian uses the name *"Gothi,"* which he tends to replace with *"Spani,"* especially towards the end of the *Historia* and in the *Insultatio.* Claude, "Gentile und territoriale Staatsideen," 33–34, argues that the characterization of these various groups in the HWR is territorial, and never national or tribal. This practice would be in line with the fact that Visigothic *Hispania* (or *Spania*) is the only early medieval state named after its territory.

endurance rather than by fullness of supplies. Rally now to the standard of victory![57] Scatter abroad the name of the traitors! When the spirit is fired there must be no delay in advancing. Once wrath goads our hearts against the enemy, no pause must detain us. Rather, if it is possible to undertake this journey without breaking our headlong pace, the strongholds of our enemies will be overthrown much more easily. For, as a wise man said, wrath, while active, is powerful; deferred, it grows weak.[58] We should not, therefore, send back the warrior whom an energetic attack will make victorious in combat. We should not give up the direct path. Let us first, therefore, bring destruction to the Basques, and then hasten to extinguish the very name of the traitors."

(10) At these words, the spirits of all take fire and they long to do as they are commanded. He soon enters the Basque territories with his entire army, and there for seven days in every direction ravaging and carnage in the open fields and burning down of strongholds and houses were inflicted with such energy that the Basques themselves, putting aside the ferocity of their spirits, gave hostages and begged, less by entreaties than by means of gifts, to be granted life and offered peace. Thence, once hostages had been given and tributes paid, peace being restored, he takes the straight path and hastens toward Gallia, making his way through the cities of Cala-

57. *"Exurgite iam ad victoriae signum!"* See the *Ordo qvando rex cvm exrcitv ad prelivm egreditvr* (ed. Férotin, col. 152): "et leuat [diaconus] crucem auream, in qua lignum beate Crucis inclusum est, qui cum regem semper in exercitu properat ..." On the ceremony as a whole see McCormick, *Eternal Victory,* 306–311. Cf. note 23 above and also "signum hoc salutis" (*Hist.* 4) for the miraculous vapor and the bee and "perfidiae signum" (*Hist.* 5) for the predisposition of Gallia to treason.

58. The source remains unknown. Lucas of Tuy (PL 96, col. 772) adds: "et illud: nocuit differre paratis," quoting Lucan, *Pharsalia* 1, 280–281 (ed. Bourgery, vol. 1, 14): "Dum trepidant nullo firmatae robore partes, / tolle moras, semper nocuit differre paratis." Curio, the speaker of these words, however, is characterized by Lucan as "audax" and "venali . . . lingua."

horra and Huesca.[59] After that, having chosen generals, he breaks the army into three divisions,[60] so that one will go to Llivia,[61] the capital of Cerdagne, the second will advance by way of Vich[62] to the central Pyrenees, and the third will follow the public road along the coast.[63] The pious ruler himself advanced behind them, preceded by a great crowd of warriors. Because the wicked instincts of some of our people not only sought out plunder, but also made them guilty of the crime of rape as well as the burning of houses, the king punished these misdeeds with such hard penalties that one would have thought he inflicted harsher measures on these men than if they had been fighting against him. This is confirmed by the severed foreskins of the rapists, on whom he imposed this mutilation in punishment.[64] He would say: "Behold, the test of combat is

59. For the itinerary of Wamba's army see Plate 6, which follows the analysis in Pérez Sánchez, *El ejército*, 148–153.

60. The division is reported here with some anticipation: as *Hist.* 11 shows, it was implemented only after the army had taken Barcelona and Gerona. This splitting of the troops into three ("electis ducibus, in tres turmas exercitum dividit") has been interpreted by Teillet, *Des Goths*, 601, and "L'*Historia Wambae*," 419, as a deliberate echo of Judges 9.43 (". . . tulit exercitum suum, et divisit in tres turmas . . ."), and 1 Samuel 11.11 (". . . constituit Saul populum in tres partes . . ."), i.e. Abimelech besieging Sichem and Saul making war on the Ammonites, the analogy being part of Julian's strategy to assimilate Wamba to Old Testament rulers.

61. *Castrum Libiae:* A stronghold of the Visigoths already in the fifth century, Llivia dominates the center of the valley of the Cerdagne. In 475, Sidonius Apollinaris had spent a year under arrest there by order of King Euric: cf. *Epistolae* 8, 3 (ed. Anderson, vol. 2, 406): "dum me tenuit inclusum mora moenium Livianorum."

62. *per Ausonensem civitatem* (Vich/Vicus Ausetanorum): Originally the seat of the Iberian people known as *Ausetani* (cf. Pauly-Wissowa, *Realencyclopädie*, vol. 2, s.v.), Vich lay south of Gerona, which makes this an unlikely stop in the route into Gallia; cf. Pérez Sánchez, *El ejército*, 152.

63. In order to cross the Pyrenees by the Col du Perthus, the second division would have had to follow the Via Domitia, while the third would have advanced along the Via Augusta, skirting the coast. See Vigil and Barbero, "Sobre los orígenes sociales de la Reconquista," 316, and Pérez Sánchez, *El ejército*, 148.

64. This unusual punishment has been connected by McCormick, *Eternal*

already impending, and the soul desires to commit rape? I believe that you are approaching the ordeal of battle: beware, lest you perish in your filth. And I, if I fail to punish these crimes, am already in bonds as I set out. It will come to this for me, that the fair judgment of God will condemn me if, seeing the wickedness of the people, I do not punish it. I must take my example from Eli the priest, noted in holy Scripture, who, not having wanted to rebuke his sons for the vastness of their crimes, heard that they had fallen in battle, and died himself after them, of a broken neck.[65] These are things to be feared by us, therefore if we remain pure of crimes there is no doubt that we will seize victory from the enemy." Leading the army gloriously under this discipline, as we have told, and holding the conduct of the individual warriors to God-given rules,

---

Victory, 312 note 69, with a late addition to the Visigothic lawbook (LV 12, 2 *in fine* [ed. Zeumer, 463]) which makes it a crime to call someone "circumcised" if he is not: "Si quis circumcisum dixerit vel disturpatum, et ille non habuerit, dictor criminis extensus publice CL flagella suscipiat." Wamba's choice of punishment agrees with Julian of Toledo's anti-Judaic sentiments, expressed in *Hist.* 5 and *Ins.* 1–2. It is also possible, especially in light of Wamba's self-justification here, with its explicit reference to 1 Samuel, that this is an allusion to David's bride-payment for Michal, Saul's daughter: cf. 1 Samuel 18.27: "Et [David] percussit ex Philistiim ducentos viros, et attulit eorum praeputia et annumeravit ea regi, ut esset gener eius."

65. 1 Samuel 2.12–14 and 18: Eli rebuked his sons for their sacrilegious behavior (ibid. 2.22–25), but did not restrain them from it. His fatal fall was caused primarily by news that the Philistines had seized the ark of the covenant. For Isidore of Seville, Eli becomes the type of the priest who neglects his duty to correct the people; cf. *Sententiae* 3, 46, 1 (ed. Cazire, 290): "Sic enim Heli sacerdos pro filiorum iniquitate damnatus est, et licet eos delinquentes ammonuit, sed tamen non ut oportebat redarguit." See also his *Quaestiones in Regum* 1, 1, 8 (PL 83, col. 393): "Porro filii Heli, divina sacrificia temerantes, peccabant coram Domino, et deridebant per eos multi sacrificium Dei. Unde et Heli sacerdos pro eorum iniquitate damnatus est, quod eos peccantes minus severa animadversione plectebat." In his *De comprobatione sextae aetatis* 1, 17 (ed. Hillgarth, 163), Julian quotes 1 Samuel 2, 27–31, where God announces to Eli the end of his priesthood and his house, to prove that the priesthood has been taken away from the Jews.

the king saw his plans for warfare and his prospects of victory improve day by day.

(11) Barcelona, of all cities involved in the rebellion, is first brought back into the king's authority, and after it Gerona is taken.[66] The pestilential Paul had addressed a letter to the venerable Amator, bishop of the city, to this effect: "I have heard that King Wamba is preparing to come against us with an army, but do not let your heart be shaken by this; I do not believe it will happen. Nevertheless, whichever of us two your holiness sees arriving there with an army, him you must believe to be your lord, and to him you must remain loyal."[67] This the wretch wrote himself, and unwittingly passed a fair judgment against his own person. And the pious king, wisely interpreting the words of these writings, is said to have asked: "Did not Paul in these things he wrote speak of himself? I believe he was prophesying, even if he did so unknowingly." After this the king, leaving the city of Gerona and giving battle as he went, reached the summit of the Pyrenees. There, after the army had rested for two days, he split it, as has been told, into three divisions on the slopes of the Pyrenees, and so captured and subdued by an extraordinary victory the Pyrenean strongholds known as Collioure, Ultrère, and Llivia, finding in these fortresses many objects of gold and silver that he handed over as booty to his teeming forces. He then sent out his troops before him, and led by two generals they took by storm the bastion named Clausurae.[68] There Ranosindus,

66. Cf. *Iud.* 3, which does not mention the taking of Gerona. The Tarraconensis had joined the rebellion by an initiative of Paul, who made an alliance with Ranosindus, the military head of the province, and with the *gardingus* Hildigisus; see *Hist.* 8.

67. Amator of Gerona: *Prosopografía* no. 619. Levison, 491, suggests that Julian could be quoting from an original letter of Paul, which here would refer to 2 Kings 6.11, "Conturbatumque est cor regis Syriae pro hac re . . ."

68. That Collioure (Caucoliberis) is taken before Clausurae contradicts *Iud.* 3 and suggests that Julian, who had not written the *Iudicium*, failed to revise it thoroughly when he included it in the HWR; cf. Levison, 511 note 4, and Pérez Sánchez, *El ejército*, 152.

Hildigisus, and a flock of other traitors, who had gathered to defend this fortress, were captured, and in this condition, with their hands tied behind their backs, were brought to the king. Witimirus, however, one of the plotters, who was stationed in Cerdane and had entrenched himself there, seeing that our men were about to break in, fled forthwith and was able to reach Paul in Narbonne to bring him news of the great defeat. This report made the usurper very fearful. The pious king, however, having vanquished the armies of these fortresses, came down to the plains after crossing the Pyrenees and waited two days for his army to come together.

(12) When the multitude of troops gathered from various parts had assembled as one army, no delay was made, for he immediately sent out ahead of him[69] a chosen band of warriors led by four generals to storm Narbonne,[70] directing another army to carry out naval warfare there. Indeed, few days had passed since the rebel Paul fled from Narbonne like a slave, having found out with what success the king's party was advancing. Paul, claiming legal authority over the city, hedged it with an abundant garrison of traitors and

69. *ante faciem suam mittit:* This is an expression borrowed from the Vulgate, where it is used particularly of kings; cf. 1 Samuel 22.4, ". . . et reliquit eos ante faciem regis Moab"; 2 Samuel 14.24 and 14.28, ". . . et faciem regis non vidit"; 2 Samuel 14.32, ". . . obsecro ergo ut videam faciem regis," and 24.4, ". . . egressusque est Ioab et principes militum a facie regis"; 1 Kings 12.2, ". . . profugus a facie regis Salomonis . . ." The phrase, used as a formula to convey the ruler's presence, is part of the biblical stylization of royalty in Julian's narrative; cf. Teillet, *Des Goths,* 601 note 118.

70. Narbonne: See Barral i Altet and Fevrier, "Narbonne," 17 (diagram) and 19–20. The Visigoths had besieged the capital of Narbonensis prima as early as 436. Later, sixth-century kings such as Gesaleic and Liuva had ruled from Narbonne (cf. Isidore, *Historia Gothorum* 37 and 48 [ed. Mommsen, 282 and 286]). Sidonius, *carmen* 23, *Ad Consentium* 59–62 (ed. Anderson, vol. 1, 286), describes the city's shattered defenses: "sed per semirutas superbus arces, / ostendens veteris decus duelli, / quassatos geris ictibus molares, / laudandis pretiosior ruinis." It is not known whether the walls of Narbonne in the seventh century or later in the middle ages followed the outline of late imperial fortifications.

gave military powers over it to his general Witimirus.[71] He, mildly exhorted by our forces to hand over the city without shedding of blood, refused absolutely, and after having the gates of the city closed, cursed the pious king's army from the walls.[72] He multiplies maledictions against the ruler himself, and tries to drive away the army by means of threats.[73] The mass of our troops could not suffer this; tempers instantly became heated, and they aimed javelins at the rebels' faces. What use are many words? A savage battle is joined on either side, and the two parties confront each other by exchanging shafts. But when our men grew desperate, not only did they transfix with arrows the rebel soldiers fighting on the walls, but they hurled such showers of rocks into the city that from the clamor of voices and the noise of the stones the city itself would have appeared to be collapsing. From the fifth to the eighth hour of that same day, both sides struggled ferociously. Then the spirits of our warriors were ignited; they could not bear to have victory deferred, so they moved in closer in order to fight at the gates. Assisted by God, they set fire to the gates with victorious hand, leap over the walls, and enter the city as conquerors, compelling the rebels there to submit to them. Witimirus, who made his way to a church with an armed band, shaken by the arrival of our forces, proclaimed from behind the altar of the Blessed Virgin Mary[74] that he

71. Witimirus: *Prosopografía* no. 170.

72. Despite repeated references to city walls, there is no archeological evidence of a late-antique *enceinte* for Narbonne; cf. Barral i Altet and Fevrier, "Narbonne," 20.

73. Invective, threats, and defiant speeches from the walls are also found in *Hist.* 14, where one of the leaders of the rebellion makes a lengthy oration from the walls of Nîmes. Cf. Sallust, *Bellum Iugurthinum* 94, 3 (ed. Rolfe, 340): ". . . non castelli moenibus sese tutabantur, sed pro muro dies noctisque agitare, male dicere Romanis ac Mario vecordiam obiectare, militibus nostris Iugurthae servitium minari, secundis rebus feroces esse." Unlike the people of Narbonne, these Numidians stand before the walls and not on them, and their words are not quoted directly.

74. This reference to a church with an altar of the Virgin coincides with

would defend himself not with the reverence due to the place but by means of his avenging blade, as he held a sword in his right hand and threatened various warriors with death.[75] To contain this swelling of madness on his part, one of our men dropped his weapons, seized a plank, and aimed a powerful blow at him. When he was about to bring the plank down on him with stunning force, Witimirus collapsed trembling and was immediately taken captive, the sword removed from his hand.[76] Soon dragged away disgracefully,[77] he is loaded with chains and punished by flogging, together with the accomplices with whom he had tried to hold the city.

(13) After this, once the city of Narbonne has been conquered and subdued, the itinerary is set on the tracks of Paul, who had removed himself to Nîmes to defend the place.[78] The cities of Béziers and Agde are quickly taken. In the city of Maguelone, how-

---

other testimonies that place a Church of Saint Mary, possibly raised by Bishop Rusticus in 444, "infra muros civitatis Narbone"; cf. Barral i Altet and Fevrier, "Narbonne," 21.

75. Witimirus's act of going into the church and taking his position behind an altar, a clear invocation of the right of sanctuary, is contradicted and nullified by this announcement and by his drawing his sword; cf. LV 9, 3, 2 (ed. Zeumer, 379): "Qui ad ecclesie porticos confugerit et non deposuerit arma, que tenuit, si fuerit occisus, percussor in loco sancto nullam fecit iniuriam nec ullam calumniam pertimescat." See also King, Law and Society, 96–97. Julian himself had written on this subject, apparently two works that have not survived, an "opusculum modicum de vindicatione domus dei, et eorum qui ad eam confugiunt," and a "[liber] responsionum contra eos qui confugientes ad ecclesiam persequuntur" (Felix, Vita 9 and 10 [PL 96, cols. 449–450]).

76. The plank is unusual: its point may be that it does not count as a weapon and that, even though Witimirus has made himself vulnerable, his assailants wish to avoid drawing their weapons in a church. The careful wording of the passage, and especially ". . . ubi tabulam acriter nisus est super eum ingenti ictu percutere, mox in terram tremebundus prosternitur . . ." stresses that even this physical attack, though intended, was not actually carried out.

77. viliter tractus: Cf. Hist. 24, where Paul, dragged out by force from the amphitheater at Nîmes, "viliter contrectatur."

78. On the urban layout of Nîmes and its defenses, see Fevrier, "Nîmes," esp. 55 (diagram) and 57–58.

ever, Gumildus, the local bishop, watching the army that besieged him all around, noticed that the city was surrounded not only by those who had come over land to fight but also by those who had come over water to engage in naval combat; terrified by this form of warfare, he took a shortcut to Nîmes and joined there his associate Paul. Once the Spanish army learned that Gumildus had fled, it soon captured Maguelone by a victory not unlike the previous ones. When our troops move forward in battle order to take the city of Nîmes, a fighting vanguard led by four commanders is first appointed, with selected forces: a division chosen from among them will precede the king by some thirty miles. With a splendid thrust toward Nîmes—where Paul, with the army of Gallia and some Frankish forces, had taken position to fight—they covered the distance marching the whole night at an accelerated pace, avoiding rebel ambushes. Suddenly, as the surging light of dawn shone forth, our troops appeared together, well provided with both weapons and courage. When they are seen from the city, as they are few in number of warriors, the rebels make plans to intercept them with arms in the open fields. However, fearing devious stratagems, they choose to give battle from their walls,[79] within the city, rather than expose themselves to the danger of unforeseeable chances out-side, and to await the arrival of foreign armies sent to assist them. Yet, once the sun shone over the land, our forces join battle. The first phase of the struggle brings the ringing of trumpets and a shower of stones. As soon as the sound of trumpets is heard, our men gather from everywhere with a great roar of their voices and cast stones at the city walls, which missiles, together with javelins and arrows, they aim at those standing on the walls, just as they, re-sisting the onslaught, hurl missiles of all sorts back at our warriors.

---

79. The walls of Nîmes formed an *enceinte* six kms. long, and dated back to the late first century B.C.; cf. Fevrier, "Nîmes," 56–57. On the evolution of Nîmes from a *civitas* into a stronghold *(castrum)*, see Dupont, *Les cités de la Narbon-naise première*, 228.

What shall I say? The fight grows more fierce on either side; the scales of battle lie even for both as they struggle, for indeed they are engaged in an equal contest. Neither our men nor theirs yield in the joined battle. So they fight all day under the double-edged blade of victory.

(14) One of the leaders of the rebellion, seeing the contest become fierce and wishing to insult us from the walls, utters these words: "Why do you remain here fighting vehemently, you who are fated to die? Why do you not go back to your own homes? Is it perhaps that you want to meet the event of death before the decline of your lives?[80] Why don't you rather search for hollows in the rocks where you may hide when the armies of our allies appear? Do believe, therefore, that I pity you, being sure of the outcome of this adventure and the arrival of forces bringing us relief. It is a matter of certainty to me that numerous auxiliary troops are coming to join us. Today is the third day since I came in haste from where they are. Knowing this, in consequence, I await with commiseration the downfall of your wretched prosperity. I will show you your king, for whom you came to fight, in fetters.[81] I will cover him with insults and deride him with invective. It is not in your interest to give battle so fiercely for him, who is perhaps already known to have perished in our men's ambushes. What is worse: when our victory becomes manifest, there shall be no indulgence left for you." By speaking thus, he not only failed to terrify the spirits of our warriors, but caused their passion for fighting to burn all the more angrily. They draw close to the walls, fight more

80. The speaker plays with words, possibly as an expression of self-assurance: "An forte casum mortis ante occasum vitae vestrae excipere vultis?" Cf. further down "miserabilis pompae vestrae occasum contristatus expecto."

81. The speaker anticipates doing to Wamba what Wamba eventually will do to Paul: cf. *Hist.* 27: "Paulus ipse onustus ferro ... consedenti in trono principe exibetur." The humiliation of a defeated usurper was part of a public ritual of Byzantine origin; see McCormick, *Eternal Victory*, 18–19 and 40–41.

savagely than when they started, and take up the joined struggle with renewed ferocity.

(15) When these deeds had been enacted throughout the entire day, night put an end to the battle. In the ardor of that very first day, however, while our men with tireless courage persisted in fighting, they send a message to the king, requesting him to provide auxiliary forces; in this they give thought to their own welfare with no common foresight, in order not to die caught in the wiles of foreign allies of the rebels, or at the hands of those men with whom they were doing battle, once their own strength had been exhausted. And the measure was well taken. For when the king found out that Paul, the leader of the revolt, had joined battle with our men, he allowed no delay in the matter. With extraordinary quickness of command, he appointed some ten thousand selected men under the general Wandemirus to help those who were fighting.[82] Traveling wide awake all that night, they were to complete their headlong journey and by their arrival not only crush the enemy but also bring reassurance more swiftly to the spirits of our men. And as the worn-out garrison of guards were despairing of being able in any way to hold the enemy in the city for long, all of a sudden they saw the auxiliaries sent to them. Immediately sleep vanishes from their eyes, their spirits rejoice and, having received fresh troops, the decision is taken to meet the foe in battle.

(16) Dawn had already risen from the Sun's saffron couch,[83] and the hostile multitude, crowding on the walls, looked out and perceived by the cheerful array of campfires, more numerous than they

82. King, *Law and Society*, 76, discusses this number and concludes that it is probably reliable since, as he puts it, "Julian had better reason to understate than to exaggerate."

83. *Iam soli croceum liquerat Aurora cubile:* Cf. Vergil, *Georgic* 1, 446–447 (ed. Page, 39): "aut ubi pallida surget / Tithoni croceum linquens Aurora cubile . . ." See also Corippus, *In laudem Iustini* 2, 1 (ed. Cameron, 47): "Roscida purpureos Aurora ostenderat ortus, . . ."

had seen the day before, that the number of troops of soldiers had grown. Already Paul, the head of the rebellion, ascends a prominent watchtower to inspect this awful sight.[84] It is told that, as soon as he saw our troops in battle array, his courage wavered and he uttered these words: "I recognize this entire plan of battle as coming from my rival; it is he himself and no other. I recognize him in his strategy." Speaking these words and others like them, he recalls his spirit to courage and goads his men to fight. He says: "Do not be discomposed by dread. Here alone is that famous bravery of the Goths which had boasted, with its usual effrontery, that it would come to defeat us. Here, here is the king, and you must believe his entire army to be present now; there is nothing else left that you should fear.[85] That celebrated courage of theirs existed long ago, as a defense for them and a terror to other nations; now however all prowess in fighting has withered among them; all understanding of combat is lacking. They have no habit of struggle; no experience of warfare is at hand.[86] If together they engage in combat with us, they will soon fly into various hiding-places because their degenerate spirits cannot bear the weight of battle. And indeed, when you begin to fight, you yourselves will prove the truth of what I tell you

84. Berschin, *Biographie und Epochenstil* 2, 204, points out the strongly classical ancestry of this teichoscopy, or scrutiny of the enemy camp from the walls, which can be traced all the way back to *Iliad* 3. Cf. Courcelle, "Une τειχοσκοπια," and Claudian, *In Rufinum* 2, 62–63 (ed. Platnauer, vol. 1, 62), where the villain Rufinus "ex culmine turris / impia vicini cernit spectacula campi."

85. In Nazarius's panegyric of Constantine, 8, 3–4 (*Panégyriques*, vol. 2, 181), the young prince in the course of an early expedition against the Franks does the exact opposite: "Facis uerba, spem illorum agitas et uersas credulitatem, negas te esse praesentem. O uere caeca barbaria quae in illo uultu signa principis non uideris . . ."

86. This passage in Paul's speech displays the heavy use of synonymous phrases characteristic of Visigothic literature; cf. Berschin, *Biographie und Epochenstil* 2, 205–208. Here the phrases are arranged symmetrically to create *parallelismus membrorum*.

here with my words. There is nothing mightier for you to fear, given that you see both the king and his army present in this place." At these words, several of his men objected that a king would not go forth without his standard. He rejoined that the king had come with his banners[87] hidden in order to give his enemies the idea that there was still another army left with which he might yet appear in the future, surrounded by a company even greater than that with which he had arrived just now. "But he creates this illusion and organizes this fraud in order to reduce to panic by a trick those whose courage he is unable to defeat."

(17) He had not finished speaking when, behold, suddenly the trumpets of war ring out from among our troops who, setting about the work of battle, recover the warlike appearance of the previous day. But the enemy, finding their hopes of victory in walls rather than in courage,[88] remain enclosed in the city and hurl shafts down from the walls, taking up once more the renewed struggle against our men. The wish to fight was fervent on either side, but bravery in combat was keener among our soldiers. When they had been fighting with all their might and had wounded their foes inside the city with missiles of various kinds, many of the foreign warriors, sorely hurt and awed by the bravery and persistence of

---

87. *signa bandorum:* A sixteenth-century hand in the margin of ms. 2a (Madrid, Biblioteca nacional 1346; a copy of the codex Ovetensis) notes "son banderas" (Levison, 516 note 1). Here the text refers not to the golden cross handed to the king in the liturgy before his departure (see above note 57) but to the *bandi* given to the standard-bearers later in the course of that ceremony; cf. *Ordo qvando rex cvm exercitv ad prelivm egreditvr* (*Le Liber Ordinum*, ed. Férotin, col. 152): "accedentes unusquisque accipient de post altare a sacerdote bandos suos."

88. *Sed illi plus in muris quam in viribus confidentiam vincendi locantes:* Cf. Pliny, panegyric of Trajan, 49, 1 (ed. Durry, 137): "Ille tamen, quibus sibi parietibus et muris salutem suam tueri uidebatur ..." (a description of Domitian), and Nazarius, panegyric of Constantine, 25, 3 (*Panégyriques,* vol. 2, 185–186): "muris se ab impetu uindicant."

our men, said to Paul: "We do not discern the sluggishness in battle that you attributed to the Goths; we see on their side great bravery and determination to win. Among other things, these wounds we have received prove it;[89] they aim so powerfully at their enemy that the din itself paralyzes him with terror even before the blow ends his life." Paul, aghast at these words, was now torn by the countless spear-points of despair.

(18) But our troops, who fought ever more steadfastly, were unhappy seeing their victory delayed; they rose to a higher pitch of fury and considered themselves defeated in every way unless they were victorious immediately. Burning with yet fiercer rage, until close to the fifth hour of the day they beat against the defenses of the city with continuous thrusts, cast showers of rocks with enormous noise, set fire to the gates, and break through the narrowest breaches of the walls. Then, gloriously entering the city, they open a path for themselves by the sword.[90] Unable to resist the ferocious valor of our warriors, the enemies withdraw to the amphitheater, which is surrounded by a more massive wall and ancient defenses,

---

89. *Haec quae excipimus vulnera docent:* Wounds as evidence of the adversary's courage are an uncommon conceit. In Roman historiography, wounds and scars are usually displayed as proof of their bearers' prowess; cf. Sallust, *Bellum Iugurthinum* 85, 29 (ed. Rolfe, 316): "'Non possum fidei causa imagines neque triumphos aut consulatus maiorum meorum ostentare, at, si res postulet, hastas, vexillum, phaleras, alia militaria dona, praeterea cicatrices, advorso corpore.'" See however Sidonius's panegyric of Maiorianus, 433–435 (ed. Anderson, vol. 1, 98): "nullus non pectore caesus, / quisquis vester erat; nullus non terga foratus, / illorum quisquis. clamant hoc vulnera ..." The phrase is very similar, although the point is made more conventionally than by Julian, who has the speakers' wounds prove the courage of their enemies.

90. *viam sibi ferro aperiunt:* Manitius, *Geschichte* 1, 131 note 2, calls this phrase "echt sallustisch," thinking no doubt of *Bellum Catilinae* 58, 7 (ed. Rolfe, 120), "ferro iter aperiundum est," from Catiline's final speech to his troops. It can also be found in the panegyrics, for instance in the anonymous oration in praise of Constantine of 313, chapter 9, 4 (*Panégyriques*, vol. 2, 131): "nisi uiam tibi caedibus aperuisses."

and shut themselves in.[91] However, when they saw themselves pursued by some of our men, who were engaged in plunder, they cut them off on the spot before they could make their way into their bastion in the amphitheater, and killed them. Indeed, many of our own men from the common people,[92] who went around in search of booty, were struck down by an anticipating blade; not that the enemy, with a display of courage, achieved this against large groups, but they did so rather in the manner of thieves, when they noticed that some of them were approaching the defenses of the amphitheater looking for plunder, and they killed them the more easily because they were divided, so that they did not face even two of them together.[93]

(19) A new rebellion now breaks out among the rebels, and the citizens and inhabitants of the region themselves, having cast the suspicion of treason on some of their own, murder with an avenging sword those upon whom suspicion falls, so that even Paul, seeing one of his men being put to death before him by his partisans, called out with a sorrowful voice that he was his servant, and was nevertheless unable to help the doomed man in any way. Already he himself, indeed, grown pale and terrified, is scorned by his own people and would seem to implore rather than command them. For he was held in suspicion by the natives, as were those others who

91. The Arènes of Nîmes were built very late in the first century AD, on the model of the circus at Arles: cf. Fevrier, "Nîmes," 57. See also Fiches and Py, "Les fouilles de la place des Arènes." On military use of the amphitheater, which in the seventh century becomes the *castrum arenarum*, see Dupont, *Les cités de la Narbonnaise première*, 229.

92. *Plerique tamen et nostrorum e vulgo:* Claude, *Adel, Kirche, und Königtum*, 174, argues that *Gefolgschaften* of slaves played a dominant role in the late Visigothic army, and that those formed by freemen were far less important numerically.

93. Cf. a strikingly similar detail from Gregory of Tours's account of the siege of Gundovald at Comminges, *Historiae* 7, 35 (ed. Krusch and Levison, 357): "Vastabatur in circuitu tota regio; nonnulli autem ab exercitu, quos fortior avaritiae aculeus terebrabat, longius evacantes, peremebantur ab incolis."

had come with him from Spain: he of planning to betray them in order to go free,[94] and the Spaniards[95] of allowing death to be visited upon the natives and then going over to the king's side. Why say more? Inside the city a miserable kind of fighting starts. On either side bands of wretches fall; on either side they are killed, as the very men who fled the swords of our soldiers died by those of their own warriors. The city was filled with a promiscuous pile of dead people, with the corpses of men. Wherever eyes turned, they found either massacred humans or slaughtered animals exposed. Crossroads were heaped with dead bodies, and the rest of the ground was thick with blood. Pitiful death lay openly in houses, and going into the inner rooms of dwellings one found cadavers there. One could see the bodies of men lying on the streets of the city, with a still menacing expression and a savage ferocity, as if standing yet among the troops,[96] but the complexion was ghastly, the skin livid, the horror extreme, the stench unbearable. Some of those who lay there, having received fatal wounds, were putting on the appearance of death to avoid its reality, yet, worn out by their wounds and by the scourge of hunger, not even they escaped extinction except for a single one, who is known to have simulated death and thus gained life.

94. Cf. 1 Samuel.. 29.4: the Philistines, temporarily allied with David, ask themselves concerning him, "Quomodo enim aliter [vir iste] potuerit placare dominum suum, nisi in capitibus nostris?"

95. *Spani:* The mss. use *"Hispania"* but also *"Spania"* and always *"Spani."* This is a "Spanish symptom": see Levison, 499. Julian also writes *"storicus"* and *"spansa fastigia."* On Julian's references to *Spani, Gothi, Galli,* and *Franci* see Teillet, *Des Goths,* 624–632.

96. *Per vias quoque urbis iacere hominum cadavera cerneres, minaci quodam vulto et ferocitate quadam immani, tamquam adhuc in ipsa bellorum acie positi:* Cf. Sallust, *Bellum Catilinae,* 61, 4 (ed. Rolfe, 126): "Catilina vero longe a suis inter hostium cadavera repertus est, paululum etiam spirans ferociamque animi, quam habuerat vivos, in voltu retinens." See Levison, 517 note 3; this is the only Sallustian quotation identified by Levison.

(20) Paul, who had given up the cruelty of usurpers,[97] lamented these events and others like them with deep and heartfelt sighs, for he was unable to stand up to the enemy, or to help his own people in any way. A certain man, a member of his own family, came up to insult him. He said: "What are you doing here? Where are your counselors,[98] who led you to the shame of this disaster? What good did it do you to rise against your people, when now you cannot help yourself or your own men in this massacre?" He insulted him thus not so much for the sake of abuse as moved by feelings of bitterness. Yet, as he was being exhorted by Paul with gentle words to respect his grief and not add to the confusion, he himself fell headlong from the marble steps on which he had stood proffering these insults, and in sight of Paul was surrounded by his comrades and killed. Paul said to them: "Why do you attack him? He is one of my men. Let him not perish." And he begged that the man might be spared, with repeated words of lamentation; however, being himself already held in contempt as if he were fated to die immediately, he could not be listened to. Then, moved by a vast despair, he took off, overwhelmed, the royal garment that he had acquired by a usurper's ambition and not by order of rank,[99] and the admirable and hidden judgment of God disposed that the usurper should renounce royal power on the same date that the pious king had received from the Lord the scepter of government.

97. *Paulus, iam tyrannidis immanitate deposita:* Arbitrary cruelty is a trait shared by usurpers with the more classical (i.e. abusive but not illegitimate) tyrants. See Jerphagnon, "Que le tyran est contre-nature," 44–45. See also Pacatus's sketch of Tarquin the Proud in his panegyric of Theodosius, 20, 4 (*Panégyriques,* vol. 3, 87): "Denique ipsum illum Tarquinium exsecratione postrema hoc damnauere maledictu et hominem libidine praecipitem, auaritia caecum, immanem crudelitate, furore uecordem uocauerunt superbum . . ."

98. *Ubi sunt consiliarii tui . . . ?* Like a king, Paul is assumed to have acted on the advice of counselors.

99. Cf. the panegyric of Constantius Chlorus of 297, chapter 16, 4 (*Panégyriques,* vol. 1, 95): ". . . atque inter hos [iacuit] ipse uexillarius latrocinii, cultu illo quem uiuus uiolauerat sponte deposito . . ."

For this day was the first in the kalends of September (September 1), on which it had long been known that our king assumed royal power. This was therefore the day when—the year's cycle having returned to that point—the fall of the city was reported. On that date the torn royal robe was given up by the usurper and a bloody revenge was taken on the enemy.[100]

(21) The third day following this one had come, and Paul, after the deep sighs of the night, was waiting for death and the end. In the morning he begins to talk to those who had been his associates in this doomed enterprise, so that they might either say a last farewell or, if possible, give him some counsel of salvation. Then Argebadus, bishop of the church of Narbonne, is sent by common decision to the king, to beg for their lives and for the pardon of their offenses. The consecrated hosts were offered to God, and they received the Lord's flesh and blood in holy communion wrapped in the same robes in which they expected not only to suffer the extreme punishment, but to lie unburied, seeing that interment was to be denied them if they were sentenced to death for their crime.[101] Already Argebadus has set forth from among them to beg for forgiveness. And behold: seeing the swift advance of the king with countless troops of warriors at about the fourth milestone from the city, he gets off his horse to run to meet the ruler, crouches in the dust, and implores forgiveness. Coming upon him, the king reined his horse briefly and, being rich in compassion in his en-

100. On this coincidence, clearly an element of the text's providentialist ideology, see Teillet, "L'*Historia Wambae*," 417 and note 11, which gives analogues from Lactantius and Roman panegyrics. Orosius 7, 2 (ed. Arnaud-Lindet, vol. 3, 17–20), compares the histories of Rome and Babylon in terms of numerological clues and coincidences of this type. Teillet argues that the HWR, as a panegyric *historia*, was composed to celebrate the anniversary of Wamba's victory.

101. See Mommsen, *Römisches Strafrecht*, 591 ("Das Staatsverbrechen") on the penalties for high treason: "Versagung des Grabrechts, Verbot der Todtentrauer, Entziehung des ehrenhaftes Gedächtnisses sind mit der Hinrichtung regelmässig verbunden . . ."

trails, he ordered, himself in tears,[102] that the bishop should be raised from the ground. The man, when he stood once again, choked by sobs and weeping, said with a sorrowing voice: "Alas, we sinned against heaven and against you, most sacred ruler. We are not worthy that the effects of your mercy should bear upon us, when we defiled the oath we had sworn to you and have fallen into such an abyss of crime. I implore your kindness to spare us promptly, that no avenging blade may destroy the half-dead survivors of our party, that the sword may not claim more souls than it already has. Command your army to give up bloodshed directly, and citizens to spare other citizens. Very few of us escaped the sword, but for these few a pardon is entreated. Spare therefore those of us who are left, so that even if slaughter has taken the rest, some may remain at least on whom you take pity. For if you do not soon put a halt to the massacre, not even the natives themselves will be left to defend the city."

(22) The pious king was moved to tears at these words and did not prove inexorable, knowing in his innermost heart that everything would be lost to him, however much was said to be lost already, if he did not grant a pardon to the supplicant.[103] The ruler, therefore, replied to the imploring one with the following words: "Hold as certain what I am about to say. Defeated by your

102. Wamba had also wept at his election (*Hist.* 2): tears are a confirmation that the monarch has the capacity for *clementia* and *misericordia* and is not possessed by the characteristic *immanitas* of the usurper.

103. It is important to remember that there were no charges against Argebadus, who had in fact suffered because of his loyalty to Wamba (cf. *Hist.* 7) unless, as Thompson, *Goths in Spain*, 220, suggests, he had eventually joined the rebels. The main reason to suspect that he had joined them is his use of an inclusive first person plural when talking of the rebellion: "reliquias nostrorum semineces," "Heu! peccavimus in caelum et coram te, sacratissime princeps." It is also unclear why he has followed the conspirators to Nîmes.

The passage as a whole appears to hinge on the assumed obligation to honor a supplicant ("precanti," "imprecanti viro").

prayers,[104] I grant you the lives you have begged for. I will not destroy them with the blade of vengeance; today I will shed nobody's blood, nor at any time put out a life, even though the offenses of these men will not go unpunished." The venerable man pleaded at length with him that he should take no revenge by punishment on those whose lives he had granted him. But the king, made once again less merciful by a quickened anger, said: "Do not impose constantly new conditions, when it is enough that I should have granted life to you. Let it suffice that I spare you alone entirely; as to the others, however, I promise nothing." Then, roused by some firing of his spirit, he became angry and went forth at a swifter pace, eager to claim the triumphal celebration of his victory,[105] sending before him a detachment of emissaries to announce that our men were to abstain from combat until the time when the entire force of the army would move ahead with the king to capture the interior of the city.

(23) By an accelerated advance, the king arrived in the city with tremendous ostentation and display of troops. The awe-inspiring standards of war were present. When the sun shone on the shields, the earth itself flashed with a twofold light and the dazzling weapons increased the radiance of the sun more than was usual. What can I say? Who could describe the pomp of the army, the splendor of the weapons, the comeliness of the warriors, the unanimity of their minds? Divine protection was disclosed by the showing of a visible sign. A foreigner there is said to have seen that the devout king's army went forth guarded by an escort of angels, and that the angels themselves displayed the signs of protection as

104. *victus precibus tuis:* The victor can afford to play with this paradox; a likely subtext is 'though not by your plotting.'

105. McCormick, *Eternal Victory,* 302–314, underscores the allusive and incomplete character of Julian's account of the victory celebration, which suggests that the ceremony itself would have been generally familiar.

they flew over the camp of his forces.[106] But we will say little about it and, leaving such matters to silence, follow in proper order the narrative we have begun.

(24) When the king knows the army to be assembled and stationed approximately one stadium from the city, moved by an incredible kindling of his spirit he appoints commanders, sees to the safety of the crowd, divides the troops, telling them how they should fight. Earlier, however, he had placed, as decided long before, a choice group of powerful warriors along the mountains and the coast, where these joined the territory of Francia, so that the main body of the army, prompt and free of care, might follow the plan of battle in greater peace of mind, having nothing to fear from foreign nations. Then he sends out selected commanders, outstanding both in strength and courage, to draw Paul and the other leaders of the revolt from the caves of the amphitheater in which they had hidden, fleeing death. There is no delay in carrying out his commands, and Paul and his fellows are suddenly dragged out from their hiding places in the arena, he being roughly handled[107] as he is brought down from the walls. Then that whole arrogant crowd of men of Gallia and Franks, gathered from both sides to fight against us, is captured and held, with enormous treasures. Once that treacherous mob and its king had been caught and brought together, with the army standing left and right of it, two of our commanders on horseback, with hands outstretched on either side, hold Paul, who is placed between them with his hands entwined in his hair, and bring him forward on foot to be delivered to the ruler.

106. Cf. the priest's *oratio* in the *ordo* for the king's departure on a campaign (ed. Férotin, col. 151): "... ita munitus custodiis angelicis, acta belli ualenter exerceat ..." Teillet, *Des Goths*, 602, discusses the use of Exodus 14.19 as a model (i.e. signs of protection for the Israelites as they leave Egypt). See also Nazarius, panegyric of Constantine, chapter 14, 1 (*Panégyriques*, vol. 2, 177): "In ore denique est omnium Galliarum exercitus uisos qui se diuinitus missos prae se ferebant."

107. *uiliter contrectatur:* cf. above note 77.

(25) Seeing this, the king raises his hands to the skies with tears and says: "I thank you, O Lord, king of all kings, because you brought down the proud man as one wounded, and by the power of your arm destroyed my enemies."[108] These words and other like them the prince uttered, choked with sobs.[109] But when the usurper, raising his eyes, saw the king's face,[110] he instantly cast himself in the dust and ungirt his belt, already swooning and racked by extreme fear, not heeding what might happen to him. It was indeed remarkable to see how from such a lofty height, even if seized unlawfully, he had fallen to such unexpected humiliation and profound disgrace. It was awesome to observe with what ease the change occurred: you saw fallen so suddenly one whom before you had heard exalted, so that the man whom the previous day had found a king now collapsed rapidly into ruin.[111] In this the prophet's saying was wholly fulfilled: "I saw the wicked man exalted and raised above the cedars of Lebanon, and I passed by and behold, he was not, and I sought him, and his place could not be found."[112] What need further words? When Paul himself and others of his faction had been taken and led before the ruler's horse and stood there, he said: "Why did you fall into such a wicked

108. Cf. Psalm 88.11: "Tu humiliasti, sicut vulneratum, superbum; in brachio virtutis tuae dispersisti inimicos tuos."

109. *fletibus interclusus:* see above note 18.

110. *faciem principis vidit:* Teillet, "L'*Historia Wambae*," 419 and note 34, explains "facies principis" as a scriptural translation of "praesentia regis." Cf. Reydellet, *La royauté,* 376–381.

111. Cf. Claudian, *In Rufinum* 1, 21–23 (ed. Platnauer, vol. 1, 28): "iam non ad culmina rerum / iniustos crevisse queror; tolluntur in altum, / ut lapsu graviore ruant."

112. Psalm 36, 35–36: "Vidi impium superexaltatum, et elevatum sicut cedros Libani; Et transivi, et ecce non erat, et quaesivi eum, et non est inventus locus eius." The same lines are quoted in *Epistolae Wisigothicae* 15 (Count Bulgar of Septimania to Bishop Sergius of Narbonne, commenting on the death of King Witteric) (ed. Gundlach, 684). In a previous letter—*Epistolae* 14 to Bishop Agapius (ibid., 682–683)—Bulgar characterizes Witteric as an "impius tyrannus" guilty of "vipereo consilio"; cf. above note 33.

madness, repaying me for good with evil? Yet why should I tarry? Go and be delivered to the guards until a sentence is passed on you in judgment. I will let you live, even though you don't deserve it."[113] Then he shared them out among the army, and assigned them to watchful guards. He commanded that Frankish captives should be treated worthily. For most of them, born of noble parents, had been handed over as hostages; others, however, who were some of them Franks and some of them Saxons, he loaded with tokens of royal liberality and sent back to their homes on the eighteenth day from their capture,[114] saying that the victor should not deal harshly with the vanquished.

(26) On the day before the kalends of September (August 31), war against the city of Nîmes was initiated by our forces. On the day following the kalends of September (September 1) they stormed the city. On the third day, which was the fourth before the nones of September (September 2), the usurper Paul was seized in a celebrated capture. But after this the pious king's spirit becomes eager to rebuild the conquered city; immediately he repairs the breaches in the fortifications, replaces the gates that had been burnt down, gives graves to the unburied, restoring to the natives the plunder taken from them and reimbursing them through the public treasury for any harms suffered. Moved not by the sting of avarice but by divine love, he orders that the mass of treasures they have captured shall be guarded more efficiently, namely so that those objects consecrated to God may be identified readily and returned to

113. Cf. *Iud.* 7, which raises the possibility of capital punishment for the rebels on the basis of a law of Chindasvind against those guilty of high treason, LV 2, 1, 8 (ed. Zeumer, 55): ". . . horum omnium scelerum vel unius ex his quisque reus inventus inretractabilem sententiam mortis excipiat, nec ulla ei de cetero sit vivendi libertas indulta."

114. See Teillet, *Des Goths*, 627: Franks and Saxons are treated as members of foreign nations and hence not guilty of *perfidia* or *infidelitas.* The Galli, by contrast, are considered disloyal subjects of Visigothic Spain.

divine worship. For the most abominable Paul had piled sin upon sin when to usurpation he added sacrilege. As a wise man says: "If he had not sacked the holy churches, there would have been no source from which his treasury might flourish."[115] So it was done, and the many silver vessels stolen from the Lord's treasure, and the golden crown that King Reccared, of sacred memory, had offered[116] to the body of the most blessed Felix[117]—and which Paul dared to place upon his own crazed head—all these things Wamba let be collected and carefully identified, and he resolved most devoutly to restore to each church whatever belonged to it.[118]

(27) The third day after victory had already come for the conquerors, and Paul himself, loaded with irons, was displayed with a few others before the king as he sat on his throne. Then, in the manner of the ancients, Paul, curving his back, offers his neck to the royal feet,[119] and after that he is judged with the others before

115. The identity of this sage remains unknown.

116. On votive crowns see Fontaine, L'art préroman hispanique 1, 242–246, and the *benedictio corone* in the Visigothic *Liber Ordinum* (ed. Férotin, col. 165).

117. This is the martyr Felix of Gerona: cf. Prudentius, *Peristephanon* 4 (on the 18 martyrs of Zaragoza), 29–30 (ed. Lavarenne, vol. 4, 65): "Parua Felicis decus exhibebit / artubus sanctis locuples Gerunda." See also the *passio* of Felix, dated to the mid-seventh century by Fabrega Grau, *Pasionario hispánico*, vol. 1, 144–150, and edited by him (ibid., vol. 2, 320–328). Felix had relics and a church in Narbonne already known to Gregory of Tours; cf. *Gloria martyrum* 91 (ed. Krusch, 99): "Hic vero martyr in Gerunda Hispaniae passus est urbe . . . Huius reliquiae apud Narbonensim basilicam retenentur." For further evidence of Spanish saints' cults in Gallia, see Barral i Altet and Fevrier, "Narbonne," 21, with an indication dated 782 that the cathedral of Narbonne had been dedicated to the Spanish martyrs Justus and Pastor.

118. Wamba, like earlier Clovis with the *vase de Soissons*, is made to play an exemplary role in his relations with clergy and church property. Cf. also Alaric in Isidore's *Historia Gothorum* 16 (ed. Mommsen, 273–274), who had sacred vessels returned to the churches after the sack of Rome because he had heard a virgin call them the property of Saint Peter; the source of this episode is Orosius 7, 39, 3–14 (ed. Arnaud-Lindet, vol. 3, 114–116).

119. See the antiphon in the *ordo* for the king's departure on campaign (ed.

the whole army, and condemned to death by the judgment of all, because they had plotted death for the king.[120] But no sentence of death was applied to them, and they only suffered the punishment of decalvation,[121] as is required.[122] A rumor was spread by some that the Franks would come very soon to rescue the captive. But the king, who was waiting for an opportunity to make war on the Franks, not only on this account, but also wishing to avenge past injuries to his people, held his ground, looking forward every day with an intrepid spirit to their coming and prepared in every way to

Férotin, *Le Liber Ordinum*, col. 152): "IIII. Negabunt te inimici tui, et tu eorum colla calcabis. Ad ultionem." Cf. McCormick, *Eternal Victory*, 310 and 315, on the rite of *calcatio colli* and Teillet, *Des Goths*, 601 and note 119, on its representation in the Psalms and in Samuel and Kings.

120. This is the only reference in the *Historia* to the public trial described in *Iudicium* 5–7.

121. The polemic on whether ousted kings and defeated usurpers were shorn or actually scalped (cf. Hoyoux, *"Reges criniti,"* Kaufmann, "Über das Scheren," Cameron, "How did Merovingian kings wear their hair?") has been limited to Frankish/Merovingian evidence and to the verb *"tundere"* (also *"tondere"*). *"Decalvare"* may be a wholly different matter. Isidore, *Allegoriae* 130, 81 (PL 83, col. 112), states that "Dalila . . . Samson verticem decalvavit . . ." with no suggestion that she scalped him. John of Biclaro, *Chronicon* 590? 3 (ed. Mommsen, 219–220), describes the punishment of the pretender Argemund, who rebelled against Reccared and was "turpiter decalvatus, post haec dextra amputata" and thus displayed to the crowds in Toledo riding an ass, with a clear sense that this treament was dishonoring but not in itself life-threatening. Cf. also the fifth-century *Altercatio ecclesiae et synagogae* (ed. Segui-Hillgarth, 44), 242–243: ". . . quia ob facina et mulieres tuas depilato capite, vel decalvato in asinis saepe vidi damnatas?"

122. [*sententia*] *decalvationis tantum, ut praecipitur:* García López, "La cronología," esp. 123–124, uses the present tense of *"praecipitur"* as evidence that the HWR was written under Ervig, in whose law code decalvation had replaced the gouging of the eyes as a "merciful" alternative to capital punishment: cf. LV 2, 1, 8 (ed. Zeumer, 55): ". . . et si nulla mortis ultione plectatur, aut effosionem perferat oculorum, secundum quod in lege hac hucusque fuerat constitutum, decalvatus tamen C flagella suscipiat . . ." But the usurper Argemund had been decalvated under Reccared already (586–601), so Ervig's law does not appear to introduce a new penalty. See note 121 above.

fight against them. However, when none of the Franks turned up
to do battle, he himself would have resolved to march against them,
had he not been reminded by the mature counsel of his own heart
and of his chief nobles that the broken promise of concord between the two peoples[123] should not give occasion for the spilling
of blood. But while he prepared to make war against them, as has
been told, the fourth day since he captured Paul had passed already,
and he was still awaiting the attack of the enemy nation. Yet no
bold act on the part of the enemy, no incursion, no hostile gathering could be noticed, in as much as the best fortified cities in Francia already lamented, it was said, their own final destruction, and
their citizens, in order to avoid being captured by our troops, had
abandoned the cities and wandered far and wide in unfamiliar
haunts, protecting their lives in well-concealed hiding-places. Now
the devout king stood at a distance from Nîmes, on a plain, with
the army. In that place he pitched camp, and with uncommon
celerity surrounded it with a sturdy wall. As he awaited there the
coming of the enemy, he suddenly heard from an arriving messenger that one of the Frankish commanders, Lupus by name,[124] had
entered in hostile manner the territory of Béziers. At that news,
leaving Nîmes on the fifth day after the capture of Paul and advancing with the army at increasing speed, he strove to prevent the
ambushes of his foe, which had been reported to him. Yet Lupus,
hearing of the king's return at the town named Aspiran, fled in
such terror that the army appeared to lack a general and the general
an army. While in flight, he was unable to wait for his men and they
could not follow him at all; indeed, their hearts were so broken by
fear that they did not scatter along the roads, but ran and tumbled
down the steep mountain paths as if they could see the enemy's

123. *disrupta pactionis inter utramque gentem promissio:* The treaty alluded to here
has not been identified.

124. On the part played by Lupus of Aquitaine see Rouche, *L'Aquitaine*
100–103, and Levison, 486–489.

swords suspended over their heads. By the expedient of flight they were able to save their lives, leaving behind them much prey for our army in this commotion, as much of men who could not keep up with them as of beasts of burden and provisions, of which they had brought a great variety in carts to supply their needs. A select troop of warriors sent out by the king was able to chase them with warlike thrusts, but their escape was so wretched, and they rushed so swiftly to the hiding-places along their border, that they could be said to have left no indication of where they had fled to, where they were hiding or keeping themselves.

(28) The king, once certain that he could not locate Lupus and his men, made an uneventful march to Narbonne and entered the city as a victor. Mitigating with munificence all the losses of the province of Narbona, consumed and devastated, which had been brought upon this land that panted with burning fever by the ravaging and plunder of our armies, he remedies them by decree, provides for them with good counsel, and adjusts the political situation to an admirable peace. He disbands the appointed garrisons, removes all the roots of rebellion, drives away the Jews, gives the cities more compassionate governors through whom the injury of such a crime may be atoned for and the land debauched by so much filth, cleansed in the bath of the king's recent judgment, may be brought back into favor. For when the land of Gallia raised itself to its usual peak of arrogance,[125] it was so racked by merciless plundering and despoiled of wealth and starved of resources, that it may deservedly be thought to have been purged of any rust of corruption it had acquired.[126]

(29) Having exhausted and tamed the men of Gallia, the king, now safe, made his way to Spain, fearing no movements of the Gal-

---

125. *solito superbiae fastus cuturno:* See above note 53.

126. *quidquid rubiginis seu nequitiarum contraxerat:* Cf. Orosius 7, 25, 10 (ed. Arnaud-Lindet, vol. 3, 65): "detrita regii fastus robigine" (Levison, 524 note 3).

li behind him, made anxious by no tricks of the Franks, knowing with certainty that none of his men were meditating war and no foreigners were laying ambushes. With such great courage and firmness of character, he not only did not fear the surrounding barbarian nations,[127] but despised them, so that while still in Gallia, staying in a place called Canaba, he rewarded the entire army with the pleasing news that they had evacuated the region successfully and released them all at once, from that very place. Coming to Elne,[128] he was detained there by a two-day pause. Moving on from that spot, he met with favorable circumstances and entered Spain and came to his capital city again in the sixth month after leaving it. However, it is necessary to describe with what a remarkable procession he entered the royal city, exulting over his enemies, so that just as coming centuries shall acclaim the marvel of his great triumph, in the same way the disgrace of the rebels may not disappear from the memory of future men.[129]

(30) At about the fourth milestone from the royal city, Paul, the chief of the rebellion and other leaders of his conspiracy, with shorn heads,[130] shaved beards, bare feet, and dressed in filthy garments or tunics, are placed on camels.[131] The king of perdition

127. *circumpositas barbarorum gentes:* For Teillet, *Des Goths,* 635–636, this is the ultimate and most extreme gesture in Julian's casting of the Visigothic monarchy as heir of the Roman empire: the surrounding hostile nations, Franks and Basques, become in turn *barbarae gentes.*

128. *Helenam perveniens:* Cf. Fevrier and Barral i Altet, "Elne."

129. According to Rouche, *L'Aquitaine,* 380, the following account of Wamba's victory celebration is contrasted here with a traditional ceremony, "le triomphe derisoire réservé aux rois ou aux tyrans renversés," a ritual inversion that goes back to imperial practice but for which there is evidence only from Merovingian Gaul and Visigothic Spain.

130. *decalvatis capitibus:* See above note 121.

131. *camelorum vehiculis imponuntur:* Some scholars interpret this phrase to mean 'they are placed on carts drawn by camels' (e.g. Berschin, *Biographie und Epochenstil* 2, 204), but cf. McCormick, *Eternal Victory,* 314 note 77. A camel also played a role in the ignominious execution of the Merovingian queen Brunhild,

himself[132] went at the head of the pageant, worthy of all the shame of defeat and crowned with pitch on his flayed scalp.[133] A procession of his ministers advancing in a long line followed the king, all of them sitting on the same sort of conveyances as he and driven forward by the same mockeries, with the people standing on either side as they entered the city. Nor should we believe that this befell them without the consent of the just judgment of God, so that their sitting on these mounts raised above all others[134] should mark

---

of Visigothic extraction, as described in Fredegar, *Chronicon* 4, 42 (ed. Krusch, 142). King Sisebut, in his *Vita Desiderii* 21 (ed. Krusch, 637), provides an account of Brunhild's end and a convincing description of the camel: "Est animal tortuosum, immanem anguis obtinens corpus, habens et naturaliter quosdam anfractus: summitas licet dorsi turgentior atque collectior celsiorem artubus reliquis obtinet locum . . ." The scenes in the *Vita Desiderii* and HWR take place in Gaul, where there is evidence for camels and their use as beasts of burden as early as Gregory of Tours; see Fear, trans. and ed., *Lives of the Visigothic Fathers*, 13 note 48.

132. *Rex ipse perditionis:* According to Teillet, *Des Goths,* 605–606, "rex perditionis" is the antithesis of "religiosus princeps" (see above note 45) on the basis of a standard Visigothic opposition of *"regere"* and *"perdere"* and of a number of scriptural passages that refer to man stirred by Satan as the "filius perditionis."

133. *picea ex coreis laurea coronatus:* No satisfactory translation of these words has been proposed so far: cf. Powers: "crowned with a black garland of leather thongs"; Díaz y Díaz: "coronado con una banda de cuero negra"; and Rouche, *L'Aquitaine,* 380 (translating loosely): "[le prétendant] avait la tête enduite de poix, [et] était coiffé d'une couronne de lauriers." McCormick, *Eternal Victory,* 314, refers to it as " a mock crown." Most extraordinary is the interpretation given by Orlandis, *La España visigótica,* 263: "con una raspa de pescado a modo de diadema, en burlesca memoria de la corona que había pretendido." (He must have read "piscea . . . laurea"!) Livermore, *Origins of Spain and Portugal,* 233, speaks of "a 'laurel wreath' of thorns" for no easily imaginable reason.

A possibility is that "laurea" here is purely rhetorical, used to indicate a grotesque equivalent of the victor's garland; "ex coreis" should perhaps be interpreted with reference to "excoriare" 'to flay,' a verb used often to describe flaying as ignominious punishment.

134. See above note 131. No carts could be this high; the men have to be riding the camels. Symbolic elevation over the watching multitude is also the point in Sisebut's *Vita Desiderii,* 21 (ed. Krusch, 637), which narrates the execution of

the lofty summit of their dishonor and so that those who had aimed at sublime heights beyond human nature through the deviousness of their minds should now expiate the treason of their elevation set high above the rest.[135] Let these events be entrusted to future centuries, for the satisfaction of the righteous and as an example to the wicked, a joy to the faithful and a torment to the disloyal, so that either side on inspection deriving some lesson from them, the one who follows straight paths may escape the danger of falling, and the one who has already fallen may always recognize his plight in their condemnation.

❧ *Here ends the story of Paul*

Brunhild as follows: "In huius centri fastigium [i.e. of the camel's hump] vestibus detecta antefata sustollitur coramque vultibus hostium ignominiose deducitur."

135. *qui ultra humanum morem astu mentis excelsa petierant, excelsiores luerent conscensionis suae iniuriam:* Cf. Julian's vocabulary of arrogant elevation with Isidore's imagery in *Sententiae* 3, 48 (ed. Cazire, 296–299), where he discusses the spiritual dangers of secular power: "sublimari," "sublimitatis gradu," "culmen potestatis," "se tumore cordis extollere." Reydellet, *La royauté,* 574–580, shows that Isidore derives these figures from the works of Gregory the Great.

✤ *Here begins the Humble Historian's*[136] *invective*[137] *against the usurpation of Gallia*

(1) It is right, O Gallia, for the victors to exult over your errors, through which you, wretch,[138] suffered the disaster of such a fall. Where is that freedom of yours with which, while hardly free, you applauded yourself from the summit of your lofty arrogance? Where are the exalted words with which you declared the strength of the Spaniards to be more feeble than your women?[139] Where that swollen pride with which, on account of your vainglory, you refused fellowship with the Spaniards? Where the yawning heights of your mouth, with which you boasted of often uncertain wealth? Where the high-raised necks and thoughts with which your men frequently disdained the rule of their governors?[140] What did you expect

136. *INSULTATIO VILIS STORICI:* McCormick, *Eternal Victory*, 326 note 130, connects "vilis" with "Galliae," i.e. 'the usurpation of wretched Gallia,' as in the explicit of this same section.

137. McCormick, ibid., 326, argues that the *Insultatio* plays pointedly with the "Laus Spaniae" that opens Isidore's *Historia Gothorum* by a simple inversion of its rhetoric, otherwise sharing with it the apostrophe, the personification of a province, and the Spanish patriotism that here triumphs over Gallia. However, all these elements are also present in Claudian's invectives against Rufinus and Eutropius, in which the inversion of praise into slander has been carried out systematically, as it is part of the very definition of invective.

138. *misera:* The *Insultatio* here takes up the *Historia*'s personification of Gallia as a woman; see *Hist.* 5 and note 30 above. Cf. also lines 357–358 of the *Altercatio ecclesiae et synagogae* (ed. Segui-Hillgarth, 50), where Ecclesia addresses her rival as follows: "Audi misera, audi infelicissima, audi mulier parricida . . ."

139. Cf. Wamba's words to his troops in *Hist.* 9: "Neque enim cum feminis, sed cum viris nobis certandum est . . ."

140. Cf. in the anonymous panegyric of Constantine of 310, chapter 11, 4 (*Panégyriques*, vol. 2, 63), the panegyrist's address to the Franks defeated by the emperor: "Vbi nunc est illa ferocia? Vbi semper infida mobilitas?"

would happen when you stabbed at yourself with your own actions, tore at yourself with your own hands, ruined yourself with your own devices, sold yourself out by your own frauds? You were struck by your own works when you added one crime to another, entangled in webs of deceit, sold into whoredom, enslaved to perjury, as you relied more on the friendship of the Jews than on that of the followers of Christ. And so, upholding the law of adultery, you judged whatever you did to be righteous: to wallow among flocks of harlots in the manner of beasts; to assassinate friends in the middle of banquets;[141] to slaughter innocent souls. You pretended to be well-disposed to strangers, but when you gave lodging to any man with his wife and offspring, among draughts of wine you poured out their blood, killing the man, destroying the children, and using the surviving mother to make sport of in your debauch.

(2) Nor indeed, in performing these actions, do you tremble at the dreadfulness of such crimes, but in addition to all this you seek out the company of the Jews, whose infidelity,[142] if you look carefully, you will see has already passed to your children, now that they, who as your offspring used to shine in the quality of Christians, have gone over—it has been proved—to the treachery of the Hebrews; and in fact you always supported their views, when you

141. A narrative tradition associates the Visigoths with regicide in convivial surroundings; cf. Isidore, *Historia Gothorum* 19 (murder of Athaulf) and 58 (murder of Witteric) (ed. Mommsen, 275 and 291), as well as Gregory of Tours's account of the killing of Theudegisel, *Historiae* 3, 30 (ed. Krusch-Levison, 126), in the course of which he refers to the "detestabilis consuetudo" of the Goths of doing away with unpopular rulers, and Fredegar's famous remark in the *Chronicon*, 4, 82 (ed. Krusch, 163), on the "cognetus morbum Gotorum quem de regebus degradandum habebant." The banquet that becomes a massacre is a motif in panegyrics and related literature; cf. Claudian, *De bello Gildonico*, 170–186 (ed. Platnauer, vol. 1, 110–112, and occurs also in Sallust, *Bellum Iugurthinum*, 66, 3 (ed. Rolfe, 278).

142. *quorum infidelitatem:* "Infidelitas" is synonymous with the "perfidia" traditionally ascribed to Jews in theological literature; cf. Blumenkranz, "Perfidia," and note 32 above.

already knew their hearts to have been rejected by God. And how the ill-omened sanctuaries[143] of the Jews could still be venerated by you, in which you so vehemently placed the care of your salvation![144] Acknowledge, wretch, acknowledge that you did so! Let it be enough for you to say that, being in a fever, you lost your memory. But now, the taint of fever removed, acknowledge yourself to be the nurse of scandal, the igniter of evil, the mother of blasphemers, stepmother of treachery, stepdaughter of deceit, timber of brothels, den of betrayal, fountain of perfidy, murderess of souls.

(3) And yet it is not enough that all these evils should have flowed from your breasts, but in addition, so that nothing should be missing from such a disgraceful outrage, having a king, you get yourself another king, by wiles and not by law, deceitfully and not by prowess. Has even one woman ever been found who, having a husband, could desire the society of another without danger to herself? You alone neglect your husband to your peril and, unafraid to betray, bribe for yourself the scepter of betrayal. Who perpetrated the actions just mentioned? In which land did this notorious evil first appear, if not between your breasts? One should therefore admire the womb of your mind, which could become pregnant with such crimes without bursting, but conceived pain so admirably in order that in these our times it might bear such a great abundance of sorrows.[145]

---

143. *infausta sacraria:* 'Sanctuary', 'temple' are the most likely translations for *"sacrarium"* here; cf. Cicero, *In Catilinam* 1, 24 (ed. Lord, 36): "sacrarium scelerum," or, as emended by Haury (ed., 77), "sacrarium sceleratum." On *"infaustus,"* see below note 170.

144. On the Visigothic fear of Jewish proselytism and Judaizing Christians, see LV 12, 2, 15 (Reccesvind) "De interdicto omnibus christianis, ne quisque Iudeum quacumque factione atque favore vindicare vel tuere pertemtet" (ed. Zeumer, 423–424); LV 12, 2, 10 (Reccesvind) "De Iudaizantibus christianis" (ibid., 424); LV 12, 3, 10 (Ervig) "Ne christianus a Iudeo quodcumque muneris contra fidem Christi accipiat" (ibid., 437).

145. These words, together with such phrases as "mother of blasphemers"

(4) And if you should assert that what you yourself begot came from somewhere else, hear whether it was engendered by your advice or that of others; you will not be able to deny that, as to conception, the brood is your own. And if indeed you got it from elsewhere, why did you cherish it and not rather, like a putrid limb, repel it from your boundaries?[146] If, however, you gave birth to it, why did you not eliminate this monstrous offspring before it could grow up? Is it not a virtuous act when righteous women destroy monsters born of them; a criminal act if they destroy healthy offspring and a moral one if they kill misshapen ones?[147] And if you should argue that you could not resist its power, or reject the brood you had conceived, where are then those lofty chambers of your mouth, where the swollen speech, where the exalted emotions, the arrogant gait, the proud elevation of words[148] with which you judged and proclaimed in ringing tones that not only a part of Spain, but all of Spain would be unable to withstand a blow of your fists? Therefore you did not plead for yourself with lawful arguments, for even without weapons you might have persisted in a

---

from *Ins.* 2 take up the motif of giving birth to vipers from *Hist.* 5. See above note 33.

146. This question repeats the strange motif of nourishing a decaying limb from *Hist.* 5. See also *Ins.* 7 and note 31 above.

147. The source of this idea can be found in the ancient practice of abortion and infanticide (cf. Eyben, "Family Planning in Antiquity," 15, note 37), repeatedly condemned by the Visigothic church, as shown by Pérez Prendes, "Neomalthusianismo Hispano-Visigodo," and by the legislation of Chindasvind and Reccesvind as summarized in King, *Law and Society*, 238–239. Julian discussed aborted fetuses and their chance of an afterlife in *Prognosticon* 3, 27 (ed. Hillgarth, 100–101). Gallia is charged with engendering the monster because the rebellion had started among its native nobility before Paul was sent from Toledo to put it down.

148. *verborum ille cothurnus*: Here the *Insultatio* echoes the use of "cothurnus" in the *Historia* in a general, abstract way to mean a high degree of pride or arrogance expressing itself in a particular medium (here through language). See note 53 above. Cf. also Gregory of Tours, *Liber Vitae Patrum* 15, prologue (ed. Krusch, 271): "ob hoc iactantiae coturnosae perflati supercilio."

better-armed faith and endured more loyally the extremity of death among the assaults of traitors. You had freely vowed your loyalty to the pious ruler, offering the promise in the name of God that you would be a foe to his foes and would fight against the enemies of his welfare to the shedding of blood.

(5) Tell, therefore, who among your men fell for the right cause, who among them died to keep his word, which of you showed himself ready to be killed for the truth, who chose to perish for his promise? There was not one of you to whom the soul of his anointed ruler was of greater price, and so, false in your promises, ready to commit perjury, not only do you not quench but you ignite the fire of disloyalty that has arisen within you, and you nourish it not with words only, but with deeds. For these are the triumphant signs of your disposition: that you do not hurt the foe, but kill your fellow, distinguishing yourself by meeting a fellow citizen and not the enemy with fierce combat, as one who always used his strength to slay those men who were his comrades rather than to destroy his adversaries.[149] Since you do not accomplish this by force of arms, but rather by tricks and deceit, your poisons are more to be feared than your weapons; for you have pierced more men with the venom of your bile[150] than with spears.

(6) Nor did we ever see your struggles directed against the enemy on the field, though at home we felt the poison of your breast. We saw, saw indeed your forces ready for the slaughter of citizens, not for the death of foreigners. How can you live befogged with such a thickness of evil[151] that you plan destruction for your libera-

149. Cf. Pseudo-Sallust, *In M. Tullium Ciceronem oratio* 3 (ed. Rolfe, 496): "Immo vero homo levissimus, supplex inimicis, amicis contumeliosus, . . ."

150. *fellis tui antidoto: "Antidotum"* is used here exceptionally to mean poison.

151. *Quomodo tantae crudelitatis nube crassaris:* Cf. Gregory of Tours, *Liber Vitae Patrum* 17, 3 (ed. Krusch, 281), where the devil appears before a saint as "umbra teterrima, statu procera, crassitudine valida." See also Braulio of Zaragoza, *Vita S. Emiliani* 33 (ed. Vasquez de Parga, 34): "sanguine est ipsorum crassatus."

tors, revenge against your defenders ? What need had you to challenge those stronger than yourself, to plot the elimination of those of greater power? Yet this you do not do undeservedly, but in order that, possessed by madness, you should not know whom you dare to attack. For the insane often feel stronger when their constitution appears to have reached the point of ultimate collapse; they act not moved by vital force, but already pining with the malady of death.[152] You, therefore, if after madness you have recovered your memory, would do well to remember what words you used to cry out in your fever, and who they were whom you, ignorantly, judged worthy of contempt.

(7) For, behold, the army of the Spaniards,[153] after those most violent fevers in which you lost your senses, came swiftly to meet you, nor all of it, but reduced to its most limited numbers,[154] and everywhere it overthrew your forces, compelled your neck to bend down, bruised your swollen mouth, and demonstrated more effectively what you could and what you could not do by means of its swords than you did by your speeches. What, therefore, wretched one, shall you say to the victors as you lie defeated so miserably under the conquerors' blade? Behold! The army of the Spaniards, with its rightful ruler, overcame you bravely, wore you down with plundering, placed you in servitude. Yet I do not want you to complain

152. The usurper driven mad by God, Providence, or by the emperor's good fortune is a topos of late-antique panegyrics: cf. Pacatus's panegyric of Theodosius, 30, 2–4 (*Panégyriques*, vol. 3, 96–97); 38, 1 (ibid., 104); 42, 2 (ibid., 108–109).

153. *Spanorum exercitus:* Cf. "exercitus Hispaniae" (*Hist.* 13). Teillet, *Des Goths,* 622–623 and 633–635, argues that Julian makes this army the medieval heir and continuator of the Roman (imperial) army and that what had been in the work of Isidore of Seville the "exercitus Gothorum" is here subordinated to a "religiosus princeps" who is now the king of Spain.

154. According to Pérez Sánchez, *El ejército,* 157, these lines imply that Wamba's army had been recruited only from the regions adjoining the rebellion. That is not what the text says, and the king's address to his troops at the beginning of the campaign (*Hist.* 9) suggests strongly that many of them were far from home.

that he was unmerciful to you for long, you who are covered with his readily-granted favors. When you justly deserved a well-earned slavery, he—like a sane head taking pity on a sickly limb,[155] giving to you, who were reduced to servitude, a pledge of freedom and erasing with a compassionate hand the old marks of your treason—he chose you as a partner in his high worthiness, even before you, by penance, had washed clean the stains you had incurred, so that, because by perverse temerity you lost the dignity of freedom, you will receive a glorious honor.

(8) Yet is it any wonder that he should confer such favors upon you, though you do not merit them, when earlier he always proved your ally in all dangers and, when you were about to be attacked, preferred to risk defeat himself? There is indeed an extraordinary regularity on either side: as much meanness in you as there was kindness in the Spaniards. They bring you peace and you give them deceit; they plan your defense, you their destruction. They would always come riding with an armed force to set you free; you encourage the swords of foreign peoples to bring about their overthrow. They determine that the enemy is to be kept away from you either by force or by cunning; you, making use of both, confront the army of the Spaniards either with tricks of your own or with the strength of others. They always sought to defend you, even with danger to themselves; you, on the other hand, not without bringing about the disaster of your own defeat, raise fortifications against them. When by chance they did not hasten here in arms, they would buy your freedom for a price; you attempted to pay for their

---

155. *ut vere sanum caput languenti membro compatiens:* The image expresses the organological conception of society characteristic of Visigothic political philosophy; cf. LV 2, 1, 4 (Reccesvind) (ed. Zeumer, 47), where it receives its most elaborate development: "Nam si arcem molestia ocupaverit capitis, non potuerit in artus dirivationes dare salutis, quas in se consumserit iugis causa langoris. Ordinanda ergo sunt primo negotia principum . . ." See King, *Law and Society,* 25–26 and 32.

destruction with gifts, since you could not bring it about by arms.[156] When did they either rejoice in your suffering or take pleasure in the deaths of your people? Rather, indeed, if the report of messengers proclaimed you to be besieged by enemies or broken down by the violence of armies, the forces of the Spaniards immediately came out armed to defend you and, disregarding their own danger, clashed with your enemies in battle. Nor did they complain, with so much land between you and them,[157] that they had endured heavy labors, as long as you could have peace. Indeed! It is obvious by now how far the feeling of compassion reached among the Spaniards, and to what degree the storm of treachery raged within you. For you have found the Spaniards, whom you held in contempt, to be your conquerors and your commiserators; your own children, however, born of you like serpents, what did they bring you except hunger, misery, and the sword? May my insults to you thus far be useful, and perhaps what is proclaimed with a strong lashing will offer improvement to your health, so that this harshness of words may be the cause of your self-correction rather than an inducement to despair.

(9) It remains now that you should outdo yourself in tearful wailing, to the same degree that you are altered by pallor and disfigured by emaciation,[158] in order that, guided always by this awareness of your misery, you may blush so over your former betrayals that diseased matter will not break out again from under your scars, nor an ulcer develop in the healed wound,[159] nor the diseased lung

156. This point-by-point comparison is the inverted *synkrisis* of panegyric that characterizes invective; cf. Levy, "Claudian's *In Rufinum*," 63–64.

157. *tot interiacentibus terris:* Cf. the first sentence of *Iud.* 3 and note 171 below.

158. *quanto sis pallore detrita, quanta macie decolorata:* Cf. Orosius 6, 12, 2 (ed. Arnaud-Lindet, vol. 2, 199): "Constitui nunc ante oculos uelim exsanguem defectamque Galliam ... quanta macie quantoque pallore sit ..." (Levison, 529 note 3).

159. The metaphor on the need to avoid a purely superficial healing can be

emit swollen and arrogant breath; instead, everything having been brought back to a state of health, may it be useful that I taunted you and may you be easily persuaded by my reasonings, so that in the future your restored strength may support memory, and memory, itself returned to health, may suppress in you all the impulses of an arrogant heart. And if, led by evil instincts as you are used to being, you reject all those who employ invective and argument, I will finally speak to taunt you with those verses with which a wise man is said to have insulted death.[160] I will therefore say:

> If you will not yield to tears or listen to songs,
> Let these words I speak be as a sword to you.
> May he damn your sting and conquer your infernal depths
> Who vanquished the world by dying on the cross.

✣ *Here ends the imprecation against the wretched Province of Gallia*

---

found in Claudian, *In Eutropium* 2, 13–15 (ed. Platnauer, vol. 1, 184): "ulcera possessis alte suffussa medullis / non leviore manu, ferro sanantur et igni, / ne noceat frustra mox eruptura cicatrix." Julian uses it again later to open the *praefatio*, addressed to Ervig, of his *De comprobatione sextae aetatis* (ed. Hillgarth, 145): "Peritorum mos est iste medicorum, ubilibet uulnus serpit in corpore, ferro uulneris materiam praeuenire, et purulentas primum radicitus amputare putredines, antequam sanas ulcus noxium inficiat partes."

160. The author is unknown.

❧*Judgement Pronounced against the treachery of usurpers*[161]

(1) The crimes of traitors, once discovered, must be punished the more severely because they appear to have been perpetrated by unlawful means.[162] Let those therefore bear the mark of their own undoing who were guilty of breaking their oath of loyalty. Let those whom the kindness of the ruler made ungrateful hand down the name of traitors to their descendants.[163] Let those who planned the destruction of their own people be counted· among the armies of the treacherous, so that they may bear for a posterity of centuries the titles of their infamy, they who became destroyers of their fatherland. May those whom the ruler, out of compassion, al-

---

161. The *Iudicium* is generally thought to be older than the *Historia* and to have been composed immediately after the events it describes, probably in Gallia Narbonensis itself, as an official account of the judgment of Paul and his fellows. Levison, 491, argues that Julian could not have been the author of the *Iudicium* chiefly because there is no evidence that he accompanied the expedition or witnessed the campaign and the trial. One voice in disagreement is that of Sánchez-Albornoz, "El aula regia," 11–13, who believes the trial to have taken place in Toledo and considers Julian a "testigo presencial de los hechos" (ibid., 12), an opinion that has found no followers. Teillet, *Des Goths*, 603–604, sees in the *Iudicium* the narrative basis of the *Historia* and shows how the diplomatic, in no way obviously Christian terminology of the former is stylized into something resembling a *vita* in the latter. García López, "La cronología," 127–129, agrees with Teillet as to the formal relations between the texts, but would ascribe both to Julian.

162. A mysterious statement, which probably means that not only the aim (treason) is criminal, but also the means, i.e. the breaking of a solemn oath.

163. This in spite of the principle in Visigothic law that guilt expires with the criminal: cf. LV 6, 1, 8 (ed. Zeumer, 256): ". . . ille solus iudicetur culpabilis, qui culpanda conmittit, et crimen cum illo, qui fecit, moriatur." See also King, *Law and Society*, 86–87.

lows to live, not escape the gouging of their eyes,[164] who by weakening the glory of their country incurred the charge of betrayal. For, behold, ill-fated treason displayed itself openly, and by joining with bloody embraces the company of criminals moved citizens to scandal, the common people to its own ruin, natives to the destruction of their country, and not only the native-born but also alien nations to the murder of the ruler. The earth, ravaged by their destructions, is witness to what we say; the sky is a witness too, under which the banner of victory[165] was granted to us by God. He broke the bond of his voluntary oath and took on the obligation of a new one who, violating his own spontaneous promise of loyalty, rejected our God-chosen king and threatened him as well as his own country with immediate ruin.[166] For, by a new sort of perjury, he beguiled not only his own soul, but also those of many peoples, so that in them the prophet's words were accomplished, who says: "their princes fall into the snare by the wrath of God, and they shall be scorned over the whole earth,"[167] as well as those which Isaiah speaks about the transgressions of such men, saying: "for evil

164. This penalty corresponds to LV 2, 1, 8 (Chindasvind) (ed. Zeumer, 55): "si fortasse pietatis intuitu a principe fuerit illi vita concessa, non aliter quam effossis oculis relinquantur ad vitam." The reference to decalvation in *Hist.* 27 implies a later legislation, that of Ervig, Wamba's successor, which is why García López, "La cronología," would date the *Historia* no earlier than 681, the year in which Ervig took power and issued his code. This, however, leaves us with no conceivable aim for Julian's composition of the *Historia* at that late date. On blinding as an alternative to capital punishment in early medieval law, see Bührer-Thierry, "'Just Anger' or 'Vengeful Anger'?"

165. *triumphale vexillum:* The phrase can be read as a pure figure of speech for the fact of victory, but also as a reference to the golden reliquary-cross described in *Hist.* 9 as a "victoriae signum." See above note 57.

166. *maturatam ... perniciem exiberet:* Cf. *Hist.* 7 (quoting Orosius): "tyrannidem celeriter maturatam"; *Hist.* 15: "maturatum iter"; *Hist.* 27: "maturato ... consilio"; *Ins.* 7: "maturate tibi occurrit."

167. *Cadent in retia principes eorum a furore irae Dei, et erit subsanatio eorum in omnem terram:* cf. Hosea 7.16: "Cadent in gladio principes eorum, a furore linguae suae. Ista subsanatio eorum in terra Aegypti."

men are found among my people, lying like fowlers, setting slings and snares to catch men. Like a snare full of birds, thus is their house full of deceit."[168]

(2) Let what has been said suffice. For when our most serene lord, King Wamba, sent out the most evil Paul to punish Gallia, so that by a timely strategy he might bring back to the loyalty due to his glory some men who had fallen away from it, suddenly, turning the mission assigned to him into its opposite, not only did he not confront the rebels and remain true to his oath, but instead by himself rebelling made many of his men disloyal. Hence, turning into a usurper against the aforementioned ruler, his people, and his fatherland, he first stripped himself of the loyalty he had sworn and, beginning to weave his web, he took on the stain of perjury. He then hurls curses at the glorious prince and bears witness to all manner of slander and invective against him.[169] After that, and it is a monstrous thing to tell, he took on the kingship against the will of God and compelled the people to swear oaths to him in this criminal election, according to which they would act against their given words and bring either destruction or dispossession upon the ruler, keeping the following form in particular in this series of wicked oaths: that he dared call our lord King Wamba an ill-starred king. For this word, in his interpretation, means 'unfortunate.'[170]

168. The passage is actually Jeremiah 5.26–27: "Quia inventi sunt in populo meo impii insidiantes quasi aucupes, laqueos ponentes et pedicas ad capiendos viros. Sicut decipula plena avibus, sic domus eorum plenae dolo; ideo magnificati sunt et ditati." For a reaction to a comparable error attributing scriptural quotations, presumably from memory, see Braulio of Zaragoza, *epistola* 21 (to Pope Honorius) (ed. Riesco Terrero, 110), where Braulio takes evident pleasure in correcting the pontiff, who had compared the Spanish clergy to "canes muti non ualentes latrare" in the belief that he was citing Ezekiel.

169. For legislation against those who curse or insult the ruler, see Toledo V canon 5 (Vives, 229), "De his qui principes maledicere praesumunt" and LV 2, 1, 9 (Reccesvind) (ed. Zeumer, 57–58), "De non criminando principe nec maledicendo illi."

170. *Felicitas*, especially in late antiquity, was understood as an innate and

Then, having risen to the summit of power by usurpation and bringing the entire province of Gallia and part of the Tarraconensis under the turbulent authority of his rule, he had special fortifications built for every city and appointed his own garrisons in them.

(3) We were forced to take up arms by the criminal boldness of these actions, and to attack the treachery of these malefactors in spite of the many lands that lie between us.[171] Therefore, in order to quench immediately the treason of these conspirators, we came to fight in the provinces of Tarraco and Gallia and, the hand of the Lord being with us,[172] when we reached these cities and strongholds we fortunately captured these same cohorts and garrisons of the cities and fortresses. For, first coming with the army to Barcelona, we seized Euredus, Pompedius, Guntefridus, the deacon Hunulfus, and Neufredus, and liberated the city.[173] Moving from

---

divine quality of emperors, its most tangible manifestation being the public peace and prosperity enjoyed by the empire under their rule. The idea expressed here—that it is treason to deny Wamba's *felicitas*—shows how thoroughly the Visigothic kings had absorbed imperial titles and attributes. There is a possible connection with the explicit that closes the *Iudicium* and the HWR, "EXPLICIT FELICITER." Cf. also "infausta perfidia" in *Iud.* 1, and note 143 above.

171. *et tot interiacentibus terris:* This phrase, which echoes Orosius 2, 11, 5 (ed. Arnaud-Lindet, vol. 1, 107): "tantis spatiis maris terraeque interiacentibus" and Braulio of Zaragoza, *epistola* 21 (to Pope Honorius) (ed. Riesco Terrero, 108): "tot interiacentibus terris tantisque interiectis marinis spatiis," occurs also in *Ins.* 8 (see above note 157), which suggests that the *Iudicium*, whatever its original form may have been, was edited and revised by Julian of Toledo for inclusion in the HWR.

172. *divina nobiscum comitante manu:* The *ordo* for when the king rides out on a campaign (ed. Férotin, cols. 149–153) refers twice to the "manus Dei": "ut manus tue protectione munitus" (col. 151) and "Accipe de manu Domini pro galea iudicium certum" (col. 152). McCormick, *Eternal Victory*, 305, lists other Visigothic references to the "dextera Dei," "dextera Domini," etc.

173. The *Iudicium*, characteristically, contains more information on the rebellion in the Tarraconensis than is preserved in the *Historia*, particularly the names of participants. Orlandis, *La España visigótica*, 260–261, argues that resistance to

there to Clausurae, with our army deployed over the summits of the Pyrenees, we entered the fortress and caught its defenders, namely Ranosindus, Hildegisus, Helias, Carmenus, Maureconis, Wandemirus, Dagarus, Cixanis, and Liubilanis.[174] In this manner, moving forward with warlike thrusts division by division, we arrested in the fortress of Collioure[175] Leufredus and Guidrigildus, together with their wives. Advancing in the same formation, we took the stronghold of Llivia, which is the capital of the region of Cerdagne and which the bishops Iacintus and Arangisclus, joined in perfidy, ruled by the laws of the traitor Paul. But since that same Iacintus was unable to defend the bastion of Llivia, he too, God granting, could not escape from our forces. When the faithless Paul learned—by the escape of those Franks he had assigned to the defense of Clausurae—of the capture of all these men and of our invasion of Gallia, abandoning immediately the city of Narbonne, he took refuge in flight, leaving behind himself as defenders of that city the pseudo-bishop Ranimirus, Witimirus, Argemundus, and the *primicerius* Gultricianis.[176] Ranimirus, having seen the army, fled before the city could be conquered but, soon arrested in the Biterrois, he did not elude our forces. Once we had captured the aforementioned laymen Witimirus and Argemundus and the *primicerius* Gultricianis, who defended Narbonne and fought fiercely against us, we brought the city of Agde under the authority of our glori-

---

Wamba was weak in the Tarraconensis and that the rebels of that province concentrated their efforts in the mountain passes of the Pyrenees.

174. About this and other lists of rebels, Thompson, *Goths in Spain*, 226, observes that on the basis of the linguistic origin of their names alone (which by this date could be insufficient evidence), the rebellion involved an overwhelming proportion of Goths and might be described as a revolt of Gothic nobility against the new ruler.

175. *Hist.* 11 places the taking of Clausurae after the capture of Collioure, which contradicts the *Iudicium* here and is inherently implausible. Cf. Thompson, *Goths in Spain*, 218.

176. A *primicerius* was the first in rank among the clergy of an episcopal see.

ous lord, seizing within it the bishop Wilesindus, Arangisclus, and Ranosindus, the brother of Bishop Wilesindus.

(4) After this, with heaven's judgment in our favor, we came to reduce the city of Maguelone; when Bishop Gumildus saw before him two armies at once, one by land and the other by sea, he immediately abandoned the city and, taking flight, joined the perfidious Paul at Nîmes.[177] As soon as we had captured that city of Maguelone and its defenders with much glory, we made our way to Nîmes to fight the traitor Paul and his satellites. Paul, supported not only by the boldness of his accomplices but also by the assistance of the Franks, had positioned himself there to give battle. In that place, after joining combat most vehemently and persisting in the temerity of his treason, Paul was defeated, captured, and seized when at last the city had been stormed with the assistance of heavenly judgment and our own weapons. It is necessary to commemorate here his accomplices, whom we endured with suffering when they fought against us in that city and who to the very end clung most resolutely to his treachery, until at last they were caught together with the most evil one; they were:[178] Bishop Gumildus, Frugisclus, Floderius, Wistrimirus, Ranemundus, Andosindus, Adulfus, Maximus, Ioannes, among the clergy, and Avarnus, Aquilinus, Odofredus, Iberius, Ioannes, Mosamius, Amingus, Wazimar, Cuniericus, Trasiericus, Trasemirus, Bera, Ebrulfus, Recaulfus, Cottila, Gul-

177. The motivation of Gumildus's flight from Maguelone is identical to that given in *Hist.* 13.

178. *Eius etiam socios commemorari necesse est, quos et expugnantes contra nos in eadem civitate dure pertulimus, et qui tamdiu eius perfidiae instantissime adhaeserunt, quamdiu cum ipso nefandissimo caperentur, id est: Gumildus episcopus, Frugisclus, Flodarius* ... : Díaz y Díaz, 113, translates: "Necesario es recordar a sus compinches, contra quienes heroicamente combatimos en el asalto a esa ciudad, y que resueltamente se adhirieron a su conspiración tanto tiempo, cuanto tardaron en ser capturados junto con el mas bellaco, el obispo Gumildo ..." But "ipso nefandissimo" clearly refers to Paul himself, and "id est" introduces a list of his accomplices. Nothing in particular points to Gumildus as outstandingly villainous.

dramirus, Liuba, Ranila, and Ildericellus, leaving aside the multitude of common soldiers and of Franks who were taken in great numbers in that city.

(5) When, after all of us had been summoned and brought together—that is to say, all the elders of the palace, all the *gardingi*, and all those in the palatine service, in the presence of the entire army—the most wicked Paul appeared in view of our glorious lord in order to be judged,[179] together with his aforementioned followers, our lord, referring to the late conspiracy, addressed him saying: "I exhort you in the name of Almighty God that in this gathering of my brethren you may plead against me in judgment if either I hurt you in anything, or nourished in you any reason for resentment, moved by which you undertook this usurpation and tried to take over the government of the kingdom."[180]

(6) Presently the most evil Paul testified with a clear voice, saying that "by God, I never felt myself hurt by your glory, nor did I ever suffer any evil from you, but you only ordered good things to be done for me, which I in no way deserved. I acted driven by an impulse of the Devil." His associates listed above were asked the same question and all replied in these same terms. Then the oaths were brought forth in which by a voluntary promise the most evil Paul himself and his associates, together with the rest of us, had

179. This highly public character of the trial, in which Wamba confronts Paul as a plaintiff at court, is present only in the *Iudicium*. The *Historia* dwells instead on the spectacle of punishment and humiliation that had been customary among the Visigoths already in the kingdom of Toulouse; cf. McCormick, *Eternal Victory*, 303. The trial itself is barely mentioned in *Hist.* 27; see above note 120.

180. Wamba's question suggests a contractual theory of allegiance that is undocumented in Visigothic law and political philosophy. García Moreno, *Historia*, 320, argues that it might be no more than a gesture of humility on the part of the victorious king, especially credible if the *Iudicium* is attributed to Julian himself, who would have placed his hero in the most becoming light. But Wamba performs no gestures of humility after his "refus du pouvoir" in *Hist.* 2.

consented in the election of our glorious lord, King Wamba, and sworn, taking the divine power as surety, that they would keep unbroken faith to him and to the land, which they also confirmed with the signature of their hands. These oaths having been opened and read, the signatures of their hands on these very promises are displayed for them to see, to the confusion of their treachery.[181] And after these, other oaths, which the same forsworn Paul had made the people swear to him, are read, in which the following sort of impiety and treason was practiced: that all his accomplices swore to this Paul that they would be loyal to him and would all fight together with him against our glorious lord, King Wamba, for whose overthrow or destruction they would give battle to the point of shedding blood, as also against those who should wish to defend our lord. In these oaths they called our glorious lord King Wamba "the ill-starred king," as already said, and many other detestable names which can be found written in the same oaths.

(7) These texts having been examined and read through, the sentence of the Council of Toledo, canon 75[182] was quoted, in the passage which says: "Whoever of us, and of all the peoples of Spain in the future, either by conspiracy or partisanship should desecrate the oath of his loyalty, which he has sworn for the welfare of the land and people of the Goths as well as for the preservation of the king's well-being . . ."[183] And after that the sentence of the law in Book 2, title 1, chapter 6 was referred to, where it reads:

181. On signatures in Visigothic charters, see Zeumer, "Zum westgothischen Urkundenwesen," 15ff. King, *Law and Society*, 104 and note 7, stresses the distinctively Visigothic character of the legal practice of *contropatio*, the expert examination of writing and signatures.

182. *era LXXV:* This is the number of a canon in Toledo IV, and not a Spanish era (cf. DuCange s.v. and Zeumer, *Leges Visigothorum*, 516). The canon in question was given in 633, which would be Spanish era 671 (cf. Levison, 534 note 3).

183. *pro . . . conservatione regiae salutis:* Díaz y Díaz, 114, translates these words as "en pro de la incolumnidad de las prerogativas regias." Vives, 219, proposes, more convincingly, "en favor . . . de la conservación de la vida real."

"Whoever, from the time of King Chintila of revered memory to—God granting—the second year of our reign, henceforth and in future, . . ." etc.[184] Taught by the precept of these holy rulings, we could no longer hesitate or fear to chastise in their bodies and properties with temporal punishment according to this sentence of the law those whom the fathers had already damned in spirit with the eternal condemnation of such a terrible judgment. Therefore, following a disposition of the public law, we all passed a unanimous sentence that this same traitor Paul with his aforementioned associates should be condemned to a most shameful death, in the same way that those who have planned the overthrow of their country and the murder of their ruler are known to be sentenced to eternal damnation. And if by any chance their lives were to be granted to them by the king, they should not be allowed to live except with their eyes gouged out.[185] We decreed also that all the possessions of Paul and his associates should remain in the power of our glorious lord,[186] so that his royal clemency may have undisputed authority to command or to do with them whatever it may choose, and so that the name of these plotters may disappear entirely from the earth and future centuries may shrink from imitating their wretched example, which bears such titles of honor.

❧ It Ends Happily

184. The reference here is to Reccesvind's law-code, specifically to a law going back to Chindasvind: "De his qui contra principem vel gentem aut patriam refugi sive insulentes existunt." See LV 2, 1, 8 (ed. Zeumer, 54); cf. Zeumer, "Geschichte der westgothischen Gesetzgebung II," 57ff.

185. As before (*Iud.* 1), blinding is mentioned as an alternative to death; see above note 164.

186. Under Ervig, the rebels were rehabilitated by Toledo XII (681) (see Vives, 383) and their expropriated possessions were restored to them at Toledo XIII (Vives, 412). The expropriation contemplated here and evidently carried out is not mentioned in the *Historia.*

Works Cited

Primary Sources

Alter, Robert. *The David Story: A Translation with Commentary of 1 and 2 Samuel.* New York: Norton, 1999.

Altercatio ecclesiae et synagogae. In C. Segui and J. N. Hillgarth, *La "Altercatio" y la basílica paleocristiana de Son Bou de Menorca.* Palma de Mallorca: Sociedad arqueológica Iuliana, 1953.

Ammianus Marcellinus. *Römische Geschichte.* Ed. and trans. Wolfgang Seyfarth. 4 vols. Berlin: Akademie, 1968–1975.

Biblia vulgata. Ed. Alberto Colunga and Lorenzo Turrado. Madrid: Biblioteca de autores cristianos, 1965.

Braulio of Zaragoza. *Vita S. Emiliani. Edición crítica.* Ed. Luis Vásquez de Parga. Madrid: Consejo superior de investigaciones científicas, 1943. English translation: "The Life of St. Aemilian the Confessor," in A. T. Fear, ed. and trans., *Lives of the Visigothic Fathers.* Liverpool: Liverpool University Press, 1997.

―――. *Epistolario de San Braulio.* Ed. Luis Riesco Terrero. Seville: Universidad de Sevilla, 1975.

Cassiodorus. *Cassiodori-Epiphanii Historia ecclesiastica tripartita.* Ed. Walther Jacob and Rudolph Hanslik. CSEL 71. Vienna: Hoelder - Pichler- Tempsky, 1952.

Chronicle of Alfonso III in *Crónicas asturianas,* ed. Juan Gil Fernandez. Oviedo: Universidad de Oviedo, 1985.

Cicero. *Orationes in Catilinam.* Ed. and trans. Louis F. Lord. Loeb Classical Library. Cambridge, Massachusetts, and London: Harvard University Press, 1953; ed. Auguste Haury. Paris: Presses Universitaires de France, 1969.

―――. *De divinatione.* Ed. W. Ax. Stuttgart: Teubner, 1965.

Claudian, ed. and trans. Maurice Platnauer. Loeb Classical Library. 2 vols. Cambridge, Massachusetts, and London: Harvard University Press, 1922.

La colección canónica hispana. Ed. Gonzalo Martínez Díez and Felix Rodríguez. 5

vols. Madrid: Consejo superior de investigaciones científicas, 1966–1992.

Concilios visigóticos e hispano-romanos. Ed. José Vives. Barcelona and Madrid: Consejo superior de investigaciones científicas, 1963.

Corippus. *In laudem Iustini Augusti minoris.* Ed. and trans. Averil Cameron. London: Athlone, 1976.

Ennodius. *Panegyricvs dictvs clementissimo regi Theodorico* in *Ennodi opera.* Ed. Friedrich Vogel. MGH AA 7. Berlin: Weidmann, 1885.

Epistolae Wisigoticae. Ed. Wilhelm Gundlach in *Epistolae Merowingici et Karolini aevi.* MGH Epist 3. Berlin: Weidmann, 1892.

Eugenius II of Toledo. *Carmina* in *Evgenii Toletani episcopi carmina et epistvlae,* ed. Friedrich Vollmer. MGH AA 14. Berlin: Weidmann, 1905.

———. *Dracontiana.* Ibid.

Felix of Toledo. *S. Juliani Toletani episcopi vita seu elogium.* PL 96.

Fredegar. *Chronicarum quae dicuntur Fredegarii scholastici libri iv.* Ed. Bruno Krusch. MGH SSRM 2. Hanover: Hahn, 1888.

Fructuosus of Braga, letter to Reccesvind: in *Epistolae Wisigoticae.*

Gallic Chronicle of 452. Richard Burgess, "The Gallic Chronicle of 452: A New Critical Edition with a Brief Introduction." In Ralph W. Mathisen and Danuta Shanzer, eds., *Society and Culture in Late Antique Gaul: Revisiting the Sources* (Aldershot: Ashgate, 2001), 52–83.

Gregory of Tours. *Gregorii episcopi Turonensis libri historiarum x.* Ed. Bruno Krusch and Wilhelm Levison. MGH SSRM 1.1. Hanover: Hahn, 1951.

———. *Liber de gloria martyrum,* in *Gregorii episcopi Turonensis miracula et opera minora,* ed. Bruno Krusch. MGH SSRM 1.2. Hanover: Hahn, 1885.

———. *Liber vitae patrum.* Ibid.

Idalius of Barcelona. *Epistulae Idalii Barcinonensis episcopi ad Iulianum Toletanae sedis episcopum,* in *Sancti Iuliani Toletanae sedis episcopi opera,* ed. J. N. Hillgarth. Vol. 1. CCSL 115. Turnhout: Brepols, 1976.

Ildefonsus of Toledo. *De viris illustribus.* Ed. Carmen Codoñer Merino. Salamanca: Universidad de Salamanca, 1972.

Inscripciones cristianas de la España romana y visigoda. Ed. José Vives. Barcelona: Consejo superior de investigaciones científicas, 1969.

Institutionum Disciplinae, in Paul Pascal, "The 'Institutionum Disciplinae' of Isidore of Seville," *Traditio* 13 (1957), 425–431; also in Jacques Fontaine, "Quelques observations sur les 'Institutionum Disciplinae' pseudo-Isidoriennes," *La Ciudad de Dios* 181; *Homenaje al P. Ángel Custodio Vega* (1968), 617–655; rpt. in Jacques Fontaine, *Tradition et actualité chez Isidore de Séville.* London: Variorum, 1988.

Isidore of Seville. *Allegoriae quaedam scripturae sacrae,* PL 83.

————. *Etymologiarum sive originum libri xx.* Ed. W. M. Lindsay. 2 vols. Oxford: Oxford University Press, 1911.

————. *Historia Gothorvm Wandalorvm Sveborvm,* in *Chronica minora saec. iv. v. vi. vii,* ed. Theodor Mommsen. Vol. 2. MGH AA 11.2 Berlin: Weidmann, 1894.

————. *Quaestiones in vetus testamentum—in regum primum.* PL 83.

————. *Sententiae.* Ed. Pierre Cazier. CCSL 111. Turnhout: Brepols, 1998.

John of Biclaro. *Iohannis abbatis Biclarensis chronica A. DLXVII–DXC,* in *Chronica minora saec. iv. v. vi. vii,* ed. Theodor Mommsen. Vol. 2. MGH AA 11.2. Berlin: Weidmann, 1894.

Jordanes. *Getica,* in *Jordanis Romana et Getica,* ed. Theodor Mommsen. MGH AA 5.1. Berlin: Weidmann, 1882.

Josephus. *The Jewish War.* Ed. and trans. H. St. J. Thackeray. 3 vols. Loeb Classical Library. Cambridge, Massachusetts, and London: Harvard University Press, 1927. English translation: Josephus, *The Jewish War,* trans. G. A. Williamson. Harmondsworth: Penguin, 1970.

Julian of Toledo. *Historia Wambae regis,* in *Passiones vitaeque sanctorum aevi Merovingici,* ed. Wilhelm Levison. MGH SSRM 5. Hanover: Hahn, 1910; rpt. with revised notes and source references in *Sancti Iuliani Toletanae sedis episcopi opera,* ed. J. N. Hillgarth. Vol. 1 CCSL 115. Turnhout: Brepols, 1976. English translation: Sister Theresa Joseph Powers, "A Translation of Julian of Toledo's *Historia Wambae regis* with Introduction and Notes," M.A. dissertation, Catholic University of America. Washington D.C., 1941. Spanish translation: Pedro Rafael Díaz y Díaz, "Julián de Toledo, 'Historia del Rey Wamba' (Traducción y Notas)," *Florentia Iliberritana* 1 (1990), 89–114.

————. *Antikeimenon libri duo,* PL 96.

————. *Apologeticum de tribus capitulis* in *Sancti Iuliani Toletanae sedis episcopi opera,* ed. J. N. Hillgarth. Vol. 1. CCSL 115. Turnhout: Brepols, 1976.

————. *Ars Iuliani Toletani episcopi.* Ed. Maria A. H. Maestre Yenes. Toledo: Instituto provincial de investigaciones y estudios toledanos, 1973.

————. *Prognosticon futuri saeculi* in *Sancti Iuliani Toletanae sedis episcopi opera.* Ed. J. N. Hillgarth. CCSL 115. Turnhout: Brepols, 1976.

————. *De comprobatione sextae aetatis.* Ibid.

Laterculus regum Visigothorum legum corpori praemissus, in *Chronica minora saec. iv. v. vi. vii,* ed. Theodor Mommsen. Vol. 3. MGH AA 13.3. Berlin: Weidmann, 1898.

Leges Visigothorum. Ed. Karl Zeumer. MGH LNG. 1.1. Hanover: Hahn, 1902.

Le Liber Ordinum en usage dans l'église wisigothique et mozarabe d'Espagne du cinquième au onzième siècle. Ed. Marius Férotin. Monumenta ecclesiae liturgica 5. Paris: Firmin - Didot, 1904.

Lucan. *La guerre civile (Pharsale).* Ed. A. Bourgery and Max Ponchont. 2 vols. Paris: Les Belles Lettres, 1926–1929.

Lucas of Tuy, the interpolated text of Julian of Toledo's *HistoriaWambae regis* in Lucas's *Chronicon mundi,* PL 96.

Mamertinus. *Gratiarvm actio de consvlatv svo Ivliano imp.,* in *Panégyriques latins,* vol. 3.

Mozarabic chronicle, *Crónica mozárabe de 754.* Ed. José Eduardo López Pereira. Zaragoza: Anubar, 1980.

Nazarius. *Panegyricvs Constantino Avgvsto dictvs,* in *Panégyriques latins,* vol. 2.

Ordo qvando rex cvm exercitv ad prelivm egreditvr, in *Le Liber Ordinum.*

Orosius, *Histoires (Contre les Païens),* ed. Marie-Pierre Arnaud-Lindet. 3 vols. Paris: Les Belles Lettres, 1990–1991.

Pacatus. *Panegyricvs Theodosio Avgvsto dictvs,* in *Panégyriques latins,* vol. 3; English translation: *Panegyric to the Emperor Theodosius,* trans. and ed. C. E. V. Nixon. Liverpool: Liverpool University Press, 1987.

Panégyriques latins. Ed. Edouard Galletier. 3 vols. Paris: Les Belles Lettres, 1949–1955.

Passio Felicis Gerundensis, in *Pasionario hispánico,* ed. Ángel Fabrega Grau. Vol. 2. Monumenta Hispaniae sacra 6. Madrid and Barcelona: Consejo superior de investigaciones científicas, 1955.

Plautus. *The Captivi.* Ed. W. M. Lindsay. London: Methuen, 1900.

Pliny the Younger. *Panegyric of Trajan* in *Pline le Jeune, Lettres (livre X), Panégyrique de Trajan,* ed. Marcel Durry. Paris: Les Belles Lettres, 1964.

Procopius. *History of the Wars.* Ed. and trans. H. B. Dewing. 5 vols. Loeb Classical Library. Cambridge, Massachusetts, and London: Harvard University Press, 1914–1928.

Prudentius. *Peristephanon liber (Le livre des couronnes).* Ed. and trans. M. Lavarenne. Paris: Les Belles Lettres, 1951.

Pseudo-Sallust. *In M. Tullium Ciceronem oratio,* in Sallust, ed. and trans. J. C. Rolfe. Loeb Classical Library. Cambridge, Massachusetts, and London: Harvard University Press, 1921.

Rufinus. *Historia ecclesiastica.* Ed. Theodor Mommsen, in *Eusebius Werke,* ed. Eduard Schwarz, Vol. 2. Leipzig: Hinrichs, 1908.

Sallust, ed. J. C. Rolfe. Loeb Classical Library. Cambridge, Massachusetts, and London: Harvard University Press, 1921.

Seneca. *De clementia.* Ed. François Préchac. Paris: Les Belles Lettres, 1967.

———. *De ira.* Ed. A. Bourgery. Paris: Les Belles Lettres, 1922.

Sidonius Apollinaris. *Poems and Letters.* Ed. and trans. W. B. Anderson. 2 vols. Loeb Classical Library. Cambridge, Massachusetts, and London: Harvard University Press, 1963–1965.

Sisebut. *Vita vel passio Sancti Desiderii a Sisebuto rege composita.* In *Passiones vitaeque sanctorum aevi Merovingici et antiquiorum aliquot,* ed. Bruno Krusch. MGH SSRM 3. Hanover: Hahn, 1896. English translation: "Life and martyrdom of Saint Desiderius," in A. T. Fear, trans. and ed., *Lives of the Visigothic Fathers.* Liverpool: Liverpool University Press, 1997.

Taio of Zaragoza. *Sententiarum libri quinque.* PL 80.

Tacitus. *Historiarum liber.* Ed. C. D. Fisher. Oxford: Oxford University Press, 1911.

Tertullian. *De spectaculis.* Ed. and trans. T. R. Glover. Loeb Classical Library. Cambridge, Massachusetts, and London: Harvard University Press, 1931.

Valerius of Bierzo, autobiographical writings in: Sister Consuelo Maria Aherne, *Valerius of Bierzo: An Ascetic of the Late Visigothic Period.* Dissertation, Catholic University of America; Washington, D.C., 1949.

Vergil. *Aeneid.* Ed. T. E. Page. 2 vols. London and New York: Macmillan, 1900.

——. *Bucolics and Georgics.* Ed. T. E. Page. London and New York: Macmillan, 1898.

Victor of Vita. *Historia persecutionis Africanae provinciae sub Geiserico et Hunirico regibus Wandalorum.* Ed. Karl Halm. MGH AA 3.1. Berlin: Weidmann, 1879.

Secondary Literature

Abadal i de Vinyals, Ramon d'. "A propos du legs visigothique en Espagne." *Caratteri del secolo vii in Occidente 2. Settimane* 5 (1958), 541–585.

Adam, Traute. *Clementia principis. Der Einfluß hellenistischer Fürstenspiegel auf den Versuch einer rechtlichen Fundierung des Principats durch Seneca.* Stuttgart: Klett, 1970.

Adams, Jeremy du Quesnay. "Toledo's Visigothic Metamorphosis." *People and Communities in the Western World,* ed. Gene Brucker, vol. 1 (Homewood, Illinois: The Dorsey Press, 1979), 115–162.

——. "The Eighth Council of Toledo (653): Precursor of Medieval Parliaments?" *Religion, Culture, and Society in the Early Middle Ages: Studies in Honor of Richard Sullivan,* ed. Thomas F. X. Noble and John J. Contreni (Kalamazoo, Michigan: Medieval Institute Publications, 1987), 41–54.

Althoff, Gerd. "Demonstration und Inszenierung. Spielregeln der Kommunikation in mittelalterlicher Öffentlichkeit." *Frühmittelalterliche Studien* 27 (1993), 27–50.

Ausenda, Giorgio, P.C. Díez et alii, "Current Issues and Future Directions in the Study of the Visigoths," *The Visigoths from the Migration Period to the Seventh Century: An Ethnographic Perspective*, ed. Peter Heather (San Marino [R.S.M.]: Boydell, 1999), 499–527.

Bachrach, Bernard S. *The Anatomy of a Little War: A Diplomatic and Military History of the Gundovald Affair (568–586).* Boulder: Westview, 1994.

Barbero de Aguilera, Abilio. "El pensamiento político visigodo y las primeras unciones regias en la Europa medieval." *Hispania* 30 (1970), 245–326; rpt. in Abilio Barbero de Aguilera, *La sociedad visigoda y su entorno histórico* (Madrid: Siglo veintiuno, 1992), 37–77.

———. *See also under* Vigil, M.

Barral i Altet, Xavier, and Paul-Albert Fevrier. "Narbonne," in Paul-Albert Fevrier and Xavier Barral i Altet, *Topographie chrétienne des cités de la Gaule VII. Province ecclésiastique de Narbonne (Narbonensis prima)* (Paris: De Boccard, 1989), 15–23.

———. *See also under* Fevrier, Paul-Albert

Beckwith, John. *Early Christian and Byzantine Art.* 2d ed. Harmondsworth: Penguin, 1979.

Beeson, Charles H. "Isidore's *Institutionum Disciplinae* and Pliny the Younger." *Classical Philology* 8 (1913), 93–98.

Béranger, Jean. "Tyrannus. Notes sur la notion de tyrannie chez les Romains, particulièrement à l'époque de César et de Cicéron." *Revue des études latines* 13 (1935), 85–94.

———. "Le refus du pouvoir (Recherches sur l'aspect idéologique du principat)." *Museum Helveticum* 5 (1948), 178–196.

Berschin, Walter. *Biographie und Epochenstil im lateinischen Mittelalter. 2 Merowingische Biographie, Italien, Spanien und die Inseln im frühen Mittelalter.* Stuttgart: Hiersemann, 1988.

Besga Marroquin, Armando. *Consideraciones sobre la situación política de los pueblos del norte de España durante la época visigoda del reino de Toledo.* Bilbao: Universidad de Deusto, 1983.

Beumann, Helmut. "Zur Entwicklung transpersonaler Staatsvorstellungen." In *Das Königtum. Seine geistigen und rechtlichen Grundlagen*, ed. T. Mayer (Lindau and Konstanz: Thorbecke, 1956), 185–224.

Blaise, Albert. *Lexicon latinitatis medii aevi, praesertim ad res ecclesiasticas investigandas pertinens.* Turnhout: Brepols, 1975.

Blumenkranz, B. "Perfidia." *Archivum latinitatis medii aevi* 22 (1952), 157–170.

Brunhölzl, Franz. *Geschichte der lateinischen Literatur des Mittelalters. 1 Von Cassiodor bis zum Ausklang der karolingischen Erneuerung.* Munich: Fink, 1975.

Bührer-Thierry, Geneviève. "'Just Anger' or 'Vengeful Anger'? The Punishment of Blinding in the Early Medieval West." *Anger's Past: The Social Uses of an Emotion in the Middle Ages*, ed. Barbara H. Rosenwein (Ithaca and London: Cornell University Press, 1998), 75–91.

Cameron, Alan. *Claudian: Poetry and Propaganda at the Court of Honorius.* Oxford: Oxford University Press, 1970.

Cameron, Averil. "How did the Merovingian Kings Wear Their Hair?" *Revue belge de philologie et d'histoire* 43 (1965), 1203–1216.

Castellvi, Georges. "Clausurae (Les Cluses, Pyrénées-Orientales): forteresses - frontière du Bas Empire romain," Aline Rousselle ed. *Frontières terrestres, frontières célestes dans l'antiquité* (Paris: De Boccard, 1995), 81–104.

Charlesworth, M. P. "Imperial Deportment: Two Texts and Some Questions." *Journal of Roman Studies* 37 (1947), 34–38.

Claude, Dietrich. *Adel, Kirche und Königtum im Westgotenreich.* Sigmaringen: Thorbecke, 1971.

———. "Gentile und territoriale Staatsideen im Westgotenreich." *Frühmittelalterliche Studien* 6 (1972), 1–38.

———. "The Oath of Allegiance and the Oath of the King in the Visigothic Kingdom." *Classical Folia* 30 (1976), 3–26.

———. "Freedmen in the Visigothic Kingdom." In *Visigothic Spain: New Approaches*, ed. Edward James (Oxford: Oxford University Press, 1980), 159–188.

———. "Remarks about Relations between Visigoths and Hispano-Romans in the Seventh Century." In *Strategies of Distinction: The Construction of Ethnic Communities, 300–800*, ed. Walter Pohl and Helmut Reimitz (Leiden: Brill, 1998), 117–130.

Collins, Roger. "Julian of Toledo and the Royal Succession in Late Seventh-Century Spain." In *Early Medieval Kingship*, ed. P. H. Sawyer and I. N. Wood (Leeds: University of Leeds, 1977), 30–49.

———. "The Basques in Aquitaine and Navarre: Problems of Frontier Government." In *War and Society in the Middle Ages: Studies in Honour of J. D. Prestwich*, ed. J. Gillingham and J. C. Holt (Cambridge: Boydell, 1984), 3–17; rpt. in Roger Collins, *Law, Culture and Regionalism in Early Medieval Spain.* Aldershot: Variorum, 1992.

———. "The 'Autobiographical' Works of Valerius of Bierzo: Their Structure and Purpose." *Los Visigodos: Historia y civilización. Antigüedad y critianismo* 3 (Murcia: Universidad de Murcia, 1986), 425–442; rpt. in Roger Collins, *Law, Culture and Regionalism in Early Medieval Spain.* Aldershot: Variorum, 1992.

———. "Literacy and the Laity in Early Medieval Spain." In *The Uses of Lit-

eracy in Early Medieval Europe, ed. Rosamond McKitterick (Cambridge: Cambridge University Press, 1990), 109–133; rpt. in Roger Collins, *Law, Culture and Regionalism in Early Medieval Spain*. Aldershot: Variorum, 1992.

————. "King Leovigild and the Conversion of the Visigoths." In *El Concilio III de Toledo: XIV centenario, 589–1989* (Toledo: Arzobispado de Toledo, 1991), 1–12; rpt. in Roger Collins, *Law, Culture and Regionalism in Early Medieval Spain*. Aldershot: Variorum, 1992.

————. "Julian of Toledo and the Education of Kings in Late Seventh-Century Spain." In Roger Collins, *Law, Culture and Regionalism in Early Medieval Spain*. Aldershot: Variorum, 1992.

————. *Law, Culture and Regionalism in Early Medieval Spain*. Aldershot: Variorum, 1992.

————. *Early Medieval Spain: Unity in Diversity, 400–1000*. 2d ed. New York: St. Martin, 1995.

Courcelle, Pierre, "Une 'τειχοσκοπία' chez Grégoire de Tours." *Mélanges Marcel Durry. Revue des études latines* 47 bis (1970), 209–213.

————. "Le jeune Augustin, second Catilina." *Revue des études anciennes* 73 (1971), 141–150.

de Jong, Mayke. "Adding Insult to Injury: Julian of Toledo and His *Historia Wambae*." In *The Visigoths from the Migration Period to the Seventh Century: An Ethnographic Perspective*, ed. Peter Heather (San Marino [R.S.M.]: Boydell, 1999), 373–402.

Demougeot, Émilienne. "La Septimanie dans le royaume wisigothique, de la fin du Ve siècle à la fin du VIIe siècle." *Actes des IXe journées d'archéologie mérovingienne: Gaule mérovingienne et monde méditerranéen* (Lattes, 1988), 17–39; rpt. in Émilienne Demougeot, *L'empire romain et les barbares d'Occident (IVe–VIIe siècle). Scripta varia*. Paris: Publications de la Sorbonne, 1988.

Díaz y Díaz, Manuel C. "La cultura de la España visigótica del siglo VII." *Caratteri del secolo VII in Occidente* 2, *Settimane* 5 (1958), 813–844.

————. "El Latín de España en el siglo VII: Lengua y escritura según los textos documentales." In *Le septième siècle: changements et continuités*, ed. Jacques Fontaine and J. N. Hillgarth (London: The Warburg Institute, 1992), 25–40.

Diesner, Hans-Joachim. "König Wamba und der westgotische Frühfeudalismus." *Jahrbuch der österreichischen Byzantinistik* 18 (1969), 7–35.

————. "Politik und Ideologie im Westgotenreich von Toledo: Chindasvind," *Sitzungsberichte der sächsischen Akademie der Wissenschaften zu Leipzig. Philologisch-historische Klasse* 121.2 (1979), 3–35.

Díez, P. C. *See under* Ausenda, Giorgio

Du Cange, Ch. Du Fresne dom. *Glossarium mediae et infimae latinitatis.* 10 vols. Paris: Librairie des sciences et des arts, 1937–1938.

Dupont, André. *Les cités de la Narbonnaise première depuis les invasions germaniques jusqu'à l'apparition du consulat.* Nîmes: Chastanier, 1942.

Elbern, Stephan. *Usurpationen im spätrömischen Reich.* Bonn: Habelt, 1984.

Ewig, Eugen. "Zum christlichen Königsgedanken im Frühmittelalter." In *Das Königtum. Seine geistigen und rechtlichen Grundlagen,* ed. T. Mayer (Lindau and Konstanz: Thorbecke, 1956), 7–73.

——. "Résidence et capitale dans le haut Moyen Age." *Revue historique* 230 (1963), 25–72.

Eyben, E. "Family Planning in Graeco-Roman Antiquity." *Ancient Society* 11/12 (1980/1981), 5–82.

Fabrega Grau, Ángel. *Pasionario hispánico (siglos VII–XI).* 2 vols. Madrid and Barcelona: Consejo superior de investigaciones científicas, 1953–1955.

Feige, Peter. "Zum Primat der Erzbischöfe von Toledo über Spanien. Das Argument seines westgothischen Ursprungs im Toledaner Primatsbuch von 1253." *Fälschungen im Mittelalter. Internationaler Kongreß der Monumenta Germaniae Historica. München 16–19 September 1986. 1 Kongreßdaten und Festvorträge: Literatur und Fälschung* (Hanover: Hahn, 1988), 675–714.

Fevrier, Paul-Albert, and Xavier Barral i Altet. "Elne," in Paul-Albert Fevrier and Xavier Barral i Altet, *Topographie chrétienne des cités de la Gaule VII. Province ecclésiastique de Narbonne (Narbonensis prima)* (Paris: De Boccard, 1989), 39–43.

Fevrier, Paul-Albert. "Maguelone." Ibid., 51–52.

——. "Nîmes." Ibid., 53–60.

—— and Xavier Barral i Altet. *Topographie chrétienne des cités de la Gaule VII. Province ecclésiastique de Narbonne (Narbonensis prima).* Paris: De Boccard, 1989.

Fiches, J. L., and M. Py. "Les fouilles de la place des Arènes, aux abords de l'enceinte romaine de Nîmes." *École antique de Nîmes, bulletin annuel* 19 (1981), 117–140.

Flaig, Egon. "Für eine Konzeptionalisierung der Usurpation im spätrömischen Reich." In *Usurpationen in der Spätantike,* ed. François Paschoud and Joachim Szidat (Stuttgart: Steiner, 1997), 16–34.

Fontaine, Jacques. "Die westgotische lateinische Literatur. Probleme und Perspektiven." *Antike und Abendland* 12 (1966), 64–87.

——. "Quelques observations sur les 'Institutionum Disciplinae' pseudo-Isidoriennes." In *La Ciudad de Dios* 181. *Homenaje al P. Ángel Custodio Vega* (1968), 617–653; rpt in Jacques Fontaine, *Tradition et actualité chez Isidore de Séville,* London: Variorum, 1988.

——. *L'art préroman hispanique* 1. La Pierre-qui-Vire (Yonne): Zodiaque, 1973.

―――. "L'affaire Priscillien ou l'ère des nouveaux Catilina. Observations sur le 'sallustianisme' de Sulpice Sévère." In *Classica et Iberica: A Festschrift in Honor of the Reverend Joseph M. F. Marique, S.J.*, ed. P. T. Brannan, S.J. (Worcester, Massachusetts: Institute of Early Christian Iberian Studies, 1975), 355–392; rpt. in Jacques Fontaine, *Culture et spiritualité en Espagne du IVe au VIIe siècle*. London: Variorum, 1986.

―――. "Un cliché de la spiritualité antique tardive: *stetit immobilis*." In *Romanitas-Christianitas. Untersuchungen zur Geschichte und Literatur der römischen Kaiserzeit, Johannes Straub zum 70. Geburtstag am 18 Oktober 1982 gewidmet*, ed. Gerhard Wirth et alii (Berlin and New York: de Gruyter, 1982), 528–552.

―――. *Isidore de Séville et la culture classique dans l'Espagne wisigothique*. 2d rev. ed. 3 vols. Paris: Études augustiniennes, 1983.

Fornara, Charles William. *The Nature of History in Ancient Greece and Rome*. Berkeley and Los Angeles: University of California Press, 1983.

Fouracre, Paul, and Richard Gerberding. *Late Merovingian France: History and Hagiography, 640–720*. Manchester: Manchester University Press, 1996.

García Gallo, Alfonso. "El testamento de San Martin de Dumio." *Anuario de historia del derecho español* 26 (1956), 369–385.

García López, Yolanda. "La cronología de la 'Historia Wambae.'" *Anuario de estudios medievales* 23 (1993), 121–139.

García Moreno, L. A. *Prosopografía del reino visigodo de Toledo*. Salamanca: Universidad de Salamanca, 1974.

García Moreno, L. A., and Juan José Sayas Abengochea. *Romanismo y germanismo. El despertar de los pueblos hispánicos* (vol. 2 of *Historia de España*, ed. Manuel Tuñón de Lara). Barcelona: Labor, 1982.

―――. *Historia de España visigoda*. Madrid: Cátedra, 1989.

Gerberding, Richard. *See under* Fouracre, Paul.

Giancotti, Francesco. *Strutture delle monografie di Sallustio e di Tacito*. Messina and Florence: D'Anna, 1971.

Goffart, Walter. "Byzantine Policy in the West under Tiberius II and Maurice: The Pretenders Hermenegild and Gundovald (579–585)." *Traditio* 13 (1957), 73–118.

―――. "Rome, Constantinople and the Barbarians." *American Historical Review* 86 (1981), 275–306; rpt. in Walter Goffart, *Rome's Fall and After* (London and Ronceverte: Hambledon, 1989), 1–32.

Goulon, Alain. "Quelques aspects du symbolisme de l'abeille et du miel à l'époque patristique." In *De Tertullien aux mozarabes. Mélanges offerts à Jacques Fontaine à l'occasion de son 70e anniversaire*, ed. Louis Holtz and Jean-Claude Fredouille. Vol. 1. (Paris: Institut d'études augustiniennes, 1992), 525–535.

Harries, Jill. "Not the Theodosian Code: Euric's Law and Late Fifth-Century Gaul." In Ralph W. Mathisen and Danuta Shanzer, eds., *Society and Culture in Late Antique Gaul: Revisiting the Sources* (Aldershot: Ashgate, 2001), 39–51.

Heather, Peter, ed. *The Visigoths from the Migration Period to the Seventh Century: An Ethnographic Perspective.* San Marino (R.S.M.): Boydell, 1999.

Hillgarth, J. N. "Historiography in Visigothic Spain." *La storiografia altomedievale* 1 Settimane 17 (1970), 261–311 and 345–352.

———. "Las fuentes de San Julián de Toledo." *Anales toledanos* 3. *Estudios sobre la España visigoda* (1971), 97–118.

———. Review of Suzanne Teillet, *Des Goths à la nation gothique. Journal of Ecclesiastical History* 39 (1988), 578–581.

———. "The *Historiae* of Orosius in the Early Middle Ages." In *De Tertullien aux mozarabes. Mélanges offerts à Jacques Fontaine à l'occasion de son 70e anniversaire,* ed. Louis Holtz and Jean-Claude Fredouille. Vol. 2 (Paris: Institut d'études augustiniennes, 1992), 157–170.

Hoyoux, J. "*Reges criniti,* chevelures, tonsures et scalps chez les Mérovingiens." *Revue belge de philologie et d'histoire* 26 (1948), 479–508.

James, Edward. "Septimania and Its Frontier: An Archaeological Approach." In *Visigothic Spain: New Approaches,* ed. Edward James (Oxford: Oxford University Press, 1980), 223–241.

———. ed. *Visigothic Spain: New Approaches.* Oxford: Oxford University Press, 1980.

Jerphagnon, Lucien. "Que le tyran est contre-nature. Sur quelques clichés de l'historiographie romaine." *Cahiers de philosophie politique et juridique* 6 (1984), 41–50.

Kaufmann, Ekkehard. "Über das Scheren abgesetzter Merowingerkönige." *Zeitschrift der Savigny-Stiftung für Rechtsgeschichte* 72 (1955), 177–185.

King, P. D. *Law and Society in the Visigothic Kingdom.* Cambridge: Cambridge University Press, 1972.

———. "King Chindasvind and the First Territorial Law-Code of the Visigothic Kingdom." In *Visigothic Spain: New Approaches,* ed. Edward James (Oxford: Oxford University Press, 1980), 131–157.

Klauser, Th. "Akklamation." *Reallexikon für Antike und Christentum,* vol. 1 (Stuttgart: Hiersemann, 1950), cols. 216–233.

Koep, L. (with H. Gossen and Th. Schneider). "Biene." *Reallexikon für Antike und Christentum,* vol. 2 (Stuttgart: Hiersemann, 1954), cols. 274–282.

Latham, R. E. *Dictionary of Medieval Latin from British Sources.* Oxford, 1975.

Lear, Floyd Seyward. "Contractual Allegiance vs. Deferential Allegiance in

Visigothic Law." *Illinois Law Review* 34 (1940), 557–566; rpt. with minor corrections in Floyd Seyward Lear, *Treason in Roman and Germanic Law: Collected Papers* (Austin, Texas: University of Texas Press, 1965), 123–135.

———. "The Public Law of the Visigothic Code." *Speculum* 26 (1951), 1–23; rpt. in Floyd Seyward Lear, *Treason in Roman and Germanic Law: Collected Papers* (Austin, Texas: University of Texas Press, 1965), 136–164.

———. *Treason in Roman and Germanic Law: Collected Papers.* Austin, Texas: University of Texas Press, 1965.

Levene, D. S. "Sallust's *Jugurtha:* An 'Historical Fragment.'" *Journal of Roman Studies* 82 (1992), 53–70.

Levy, Harry L. "Claudian's *In Rufinum* and the Rhetorical Ψόγος." *Transactions of the American Philological Association* 77 (1946), 57–65.

———. "Themes of Encomium and Invective in Claudian." *Transactions of the American Philological Association* 89 (1958), 336–347.

Liebeschuetz, Wolf. "Citizen Status and Law in the Roman Empire and the Visigothic Kingdom." In *Strategies of Distinction: The Construction of Ethnic Communities, 300–800,* ed. Walter Pohl and Helmut Reimitz (Leiden: Brill, 1998), 131–152.

Linehan, Peter. *History and the Historians of Medieval Spain.* Oxford: Oxford University Press, 1993.

Livermore, H. V. *The Origins of Spain and Portugal.* London: Allen and Unwin, 1971.

Long, Jacqueline. *Claudian's In Eutropium: Or, How, When, and Why to Slander a Eunuch.* Chapel Hill and London: University of North Carolina Press, 1996.

MacCormack, Sabine. "Change and Continuity in Late Antiquity: The Ceremony of *Adventus.*" *Historia* 21 (1972), 721–752.

———. "Latin Prose Panegyrics." In *Empire and Aftermath: Silver Latin II,* ed. T. A. Dorey (London and Boston: Routledge, 1975), 143–205.

Magnin, E. *L'église wisigothique au VIIe siècle.* Vol. 1. Paris: Picard, 1912.

Manitius, Max. *Geschichte der lateinischen Literatur des Mittelalters. Erster Band. Von Justinian bis zur Mitte des zehnten Jahrhunderts.* Munich: Beck, 1911; rpt. 1974.

Martin, Jochen. "Zum Selbstverständnis, zur Repräsentation und Macht des Kaisers in der Spätantike." *Saeculum* 35 (1984), 115–131.

———. "Das Kaisertum in der Spätantike." In *Usurpationen in der Spätantike,* ed. François Paschoud and Joachim Szidat (Stuttgart: Steiner, 1997), 47–62.

Martínez Díez, Gonzalo. *La colección canónica hispana I. Estudio.* Madrid: Consejo superior de investigaciones científicas, 1966.

Martínez Pizarro, Joaquín. *A Rhetoric of the Scene: Dramatic Narrative in the Early Middle Ages.* Toronto: University of Toronto Press, 1989.

———. "Images of Church and State: From Sulpicius Severus to Notker Balbulus." *Journal of Medieval Latin* 4 (1994), 25–38.

Matthews, John. *Western Aristocracies and Imperial Court, AD 364–425.* Oxford: Oxford University Press, 1975.

McCarthy, Joseph M. "The Pastoral Practice of the Sacraments of Cleansing in the Legislation of the Visigothic Church." *Classical Folia* 24 (1970), 177–186.

McCormick, Michael. *Eternal Victory: Triumphal Rulership in Late Antiquity, Byzantium, and the Early Medieval West.* Cambridge: Cambridge University Press, 1986.

Miles, George C. *The Coinage of the Visigoths of Spain, Leovigild to Achila II.* New York: American Numismatic Society, 1952.

Miranda Calvo, José. "San Julián, cronista de guerra." *Anales Toledanos* 3. *Estudios sobre la España visigoda* (1971), 159–170.

Mittellateinisches Wörterbuch bis zum ausgehenden 13. Jahrhundert. Ed. Bayerische Akademie der Wissenschaften and Deutsche Akademie der Wissenschaften zu Berlin. Munich: Beck, 1967–.

Mommsen, Theodor. *Römisches Strafrecht.* Leipzig: Duncker and Humblot, 1899.

Müller, Eva. "Die Anfänge der Königssalbung im Mittelalter und ihre historisch-politischen Auswirkungen." *Historisches Jahrbuch* 58 (1938), 317–360.

Murphy, Francis X. "Julian of Toledo and the Condemnation of Monothelitism in Spain." In *Mélanges Joseph de Ghellinck, S.J.* 1. *Antiquité* (Gembloux: Duculot, 1951), 361–373.

———. "Julian of Toledo and the Fall of the Visigothic Kingdom in Spain." *Speculum* 27 (1952), 1–27.

Navascués, Joaquín María de. *La dedicación de San Juan de Baños.* Palencia: Diputación provincial, 1961.

Neri, Valerio. "L'Usurpatore come tiranno nel lessico politico della tarda antichità." In *Usurpationen in der Spätantike*, ed. François Paschoud and Joachim Szidat (Stuttgart: Steiner, 1997), 71–98.

Niermeyer, J. F. *Mediae latinitatis lexicon minus.* Leiden: Brill, 1997.

Nixon, C. E. V., and Barbara Saylor Rodgers. *In Praise of Later Roman Emperors: The Panegyrici Latini: Introduction, Translation, and Historical Commentary.* Berkeley: University of California Press, 1994.

Orlandis, José. "En torno a la noción visigoda de tiranía." *Anuario de historia del derecho español* 29 (1959), 5–43; rpt. in José Orlandis, *Estudios visigóticos III.*

El poder real y la sucesión al trono en la monarquía visigoda (Rome and Madrid: Consejo superior de investigaciones científicas, 1962), 13–42.

———. "La sucesión al trono en la monarquía visigoda." In José Orlandis, *Estudios visigóticos III. El poder real y la sucesión al trono en la monarquía visigoda* (Rome and Madrid: Consejo superior de investigaciones científicas, 1962), 57–102.

———. *Historia de España. La España visigótica.* Madrid: Gredos, 1977.

———. *La vida en España en tiempo de los godos.* Madrid: Rialp, 1991.

Palol, Pedro de. *La basílica de San Juan de Baños.* Palencia: Diputación provincial, 1988.

Paschoud, François, and Joachim Szidat, eds. *Usurpationen in der Spätantike.* Stuttgart: Steiner, 1997.

Paulys Real-Encyclopädie der classischen Altertumswissenschaft, rev. ed. by A. Pauly, G. Wissowa, W. Kroll. 37 vols. Stuttgart: Metzler, 1894–1972.

Pérez-Prendes, José Manuel. "Neomalthusianismo hispano-visigodo." *Anuario de historia económica y social* 1 (1968), 581–584.

Pérez Sánchez, Dionisio. *El ejército en la sociedad visigoda.* Salamanca: Universidad de Salamanca, 1989.

Pohl, Walter, and Helmut Reimitz, eds. *Strategies of Distinction: The Construction of Ethnic Communities, 300–800.* Leiden: Brill, 1998.

Potter, David S. *Literary Texts and the Roman Historian.* London and New York: Routledge, 1999.

Price, Simon. "From Noble Funerals to Divine Cult: The Consecration of Roman Emperors." In *Rituals of Royalty: Power and Ceremonial in Traditional Societies,* ed. David Cannadine and Simon Price (Cambridge: Cambridge University Press, 1987), 56–105.

Reydellet, Marc. *La royauté dans la littérature latine de Sidoine Apollinaire à Isidore de Séville.* Bibliothèque des écoles françaises d'Athènes et de Rome 243. Rome: École française de Rome, 1981.

Reimitz, Helmut. *See under* Pohl, Walter.

Riché, Pierre. "L'éducation à l'époque wisigothique: les 'Institutionum Disciplinae.'" *Anales Toledanos* 3. *Estudios sobre la España visigoda* (1971), 171–180.

Ripoll López, Gisela. "The Arrival of the Visigoths in Hispania." In *Strategies of Distinction: The Construction of Ethnic Communities, 300–800,* ed. Walter Pohl and Helmut Reimitz (Leiden: Brill, 1998), 153–179.

Rivera Recio, J. F. "Los arzobispos de Toledo en el siglo VII." *Anales Toledanos* 3. *Estudios sobre la España visigoda* (1971), 181–217.

Rodgers, Barbara Saylor. *See under* Nixon, C. E. V.

Roth, Norman. *Jews, Visigoths and Muslims in Medieval Spain: Cooperation and Conflict.* Leiden: Brill, 1994.

Rouche, Michel. *L'Aquitaine des wisigoths aux arabes, 418–781. Naissance d'une région.* Paris: Éditions de l'école des hautes études, 1979.

Roueché, Charlotte. "Acclamations in the Later Roman Empire: New Evidence from Aphrodisias." *Journal of Roman Studies* 74 (1984), 181–199.

Saitta, Biaggio. *L'antisemitismo nella Spagna visigotica.* Rome: "L'Erma" di Bretschneider, 1995.

Salway, Benet. "What's in a Name? A Survey of Roman Onomastic Practice from c. 700 B.C. to A.D. 700." *Journal of Roman Studies* 84 (1994), 124–145.

Sánchez-Albornoz, Claudio. "El aula regia y las asambleas políticas de los godos." *Cuadernos de historia de España* 5 (1946), 5–110.

————. "La 'ordinatio principis' en la España goda y postvisigoda." *Cuadernos de historia de España* 35–36 (1962), 5–36.

Schwöbel, Heide. *Synode und König im Westgotenreich. Grundlagen und Formen ihrer Beziehung.* Cologne: Böhlau, 1982.

Sivan, Hagith. "The Invisible Jews of Visigothic Spain." *Revue des Études Juives* 159 (2000), 369–385.

Smalley, Beryl. "Sallust in the Middle Ages." In *Classical Influences in European Culture A.D. 500–1500,* ed. R. R. Bolgar (Cambridge: Cambridge University Press, 1969), 165–175.

Springer, Friedrich-Karl. "Tyrannus. Untersuchungen zur politischen Ideologie der Römer." Diss. Cologne, 1952.

Steidle, Wolf. *Sallusts historische Monographien. Themenwahl und Geschichtsbild.* Wiesbaden: Steiner, 1958.

Stocking, Rachel L. *Bishops, Councils and Consensus in the Visigothic Kingdom, 589–633.* Ann Arbor: University of Michigan Press, 2000.

Straub, Johann. *Zum Herrscherideal in der Spätantike.* Stuttgart: Kohlhammer, 1939.

Stroheker, Karl-Friedrich. "Leowigild." *Die Welt als Geschichte* 5 (1939), 446–485; rpt. in Karl-Friedrich Stroheker, *Germanentum und Spätantike* (Zürich and Stuttgart: Artemis, 1965), 134–191.

————. "Das spanische Westgotenreich und Byzanz." *Bonner Jahrbücher* 163 (1963), 252–274; rpt. in Karl-Friedrich Stroheker, *Germanentum und Spätantike* (Zürich and Stuttgart: Artemis 1965), 207–245.

————. *Germanentum und Spätantike.* Zürich and Stuttgart: Artemis, 1965.

Szidat, Joachim. *See under* Paschoud, François.

Teillet, Suzanne. *Des Goths à la nation gothique. Les origines de l'idée de nation en Occident du Ve au VIIe siècle.* Paris: Les Belles Lettres, 1984.

————. "L'*Historia Wambae* est-elle une oeuvre de circonstance?" In *Los visigodos: Historia y civilización. Antigüedad y cristianismo* 3 (Murcia: Universidad de Murcia, 1986), 415–424.

————. "La déposition de Wamba. Un coup d'état au VIIe siècle." In *De Tertullien aux mozarabes. Mélanges offerts à Jacques Fontaine à l'occasion de son 70e anniversaire*, ed. Louis Holtz and Jean-Claude Fredouille. Vol. 2 (Paris: Institut d'études augustiniennes, 1992), 99–113.

Thompson, E. A. *The Goths in Spain*. Oxford: Oxford University Press, 1969.

Vigil, M., and Abilio Barbero. "Sobre los orígenes sociales de la Reconquista: cántabros y vascones desde fines del imperio romano hasta la invasión musulmana." *Boletín de la Real Academia de la Historia* 156 (1965), 271–337.

Wallace-Hadrill, Andrew. "Civilis princeps: Between Citizen and King." *Journal of Roman Studies* 72 (1982), 32–48.

Weisgerber, F. *Au seuil du Maroc moderne*. Rabat: Les éditions la porte, 1947.

Wengen, Paul à. *Julianus, Erzbichof von Toledo. Sein Leben und seine Wirksamkeit unter den Königen Ervig und Egica*. St. Gallen: Zollikofer, 1891.

Werner, Karl-Ferdinand. "Gott, Herrscher und Historiograph. Der Geschichtschreiber als Interpret des Wirken Gottes in der Welt und Ratgeber der Könige (4. bis 12. Jahrhundert)." In *Devs qvi mvtat tempora. Menschen und Institutionen im Wandel des Mittelalters. Festschrift für Alfons Becker*, ed. Ernst Dieter Hehl et alii (Sigmaringen: Thorbecke, 1987), 1–31.

Wolf, Kenneth Baxter. *Conquerors and Chroniclers of Early Medieval Spain*. Liverpool: Liverpool University Press, 1990.

Wolfram, Herwig. *Intitulatio I. Lateinische Königs- und Fürstentitel bis zum Ende des 8. Jahrhunderts*. Mitteilungen des Instituts für österreichische Geschichtsforschung. Ergänzungsband 21. Graz, Vienna and Cologne: Böhlau, 1967.

Wood, Ian. "The Secret Histories of Gregory of Tours." *Revue belge de philologie et d'histoire* 71 (1993), 253–270.

Zeumer, Karl. "Geschichte der westgothischen Gesetzgebung I." *Neues Archiv der Gesellschaft für ältere deutsche Geschichtskunde* 23 (1898), 421–516.

————. "Geschichte der westgothischen Gesetzgebung II." *Neues Archiv der Gesellschaft für ältere deutsche Geschichtskunde* 24 (1899), 41–122.

————. "Geschichte der westgothischen Gesetzgebung III." Ibid., 573–630.

————. "Zum westgothischen Urkundenwesen." Ibid., 17–38.

————. "Geschichte der westgothischen Gesetzgebung IV." *Neues Archiv der Gesellschaft für ältere deutsche Geschichtskunde* 26 (1901), 93–149.

————. "Die Chronologie der Westgothenkönige des Reiches von Toledo." *Neues Archiv der Gesellschaft für ältere deutsche Geschichtskunde* 27 (1902), 411–444.

Ziegler, Aloysius K. *Church and State in Visigothic Spain*. Washington, D.C.: The Catholic University of America, 1930.

Index